CLASSICAL ARCHITECTURE

for the

TWENTY-FIRST CENTURY

*The Institute of Classical Architecture & Classical America is the organization dedicated
to the classical tradition in architecture and the allied arts in the United States. Inquiries
about the mission and programs of the organization are welcome and should be addressed to:*

The Institute of Classical Architecture and Classical America
www.classicist.org

CLASSICAL ARCHITECTURE

for the

TWENTY-FIRST CENTURY

An Introduction to Design

J. FRANÇOIS GABRIEL

in association with
THE INSTITUTE OF CLASSICAL ARCHITECTURE
AND CLASSICAL AMERICA

W. W. NORTON & COMPANY
NEW YORK – LONDON

Unless credited to another source, all drawings and
photographs are by the author.

Every effort has been made to ensure the accuracy of
the material in this book. The author welcomes notification
of any errors or oversights and will endeavor to include
any corrections in subsequent editions.

For information about permission to reproduce selections
from this book, write to Permissions, W. W. Norton &
Company, Inc., 500 Fifth Avenue, New York, NY 10110

Manufacturing by Quebecor World Kingsport Press
Book design by Abigail Sturges
Production manager: Leeann Graham

Library of Congress Cataloging-in-Publication Data
Gabriel, J. François, 1930-
    Classical architecture for the twenty-first century :
an introduction to design /
    Jean-François Gabriel
        p. cm.
    Includes bibliographical references and index.
    ISBN 0-393-73076-X
        1. Architecture—Composition, proportion, etc. 2.
Classicism in architecture. I. Title: Classical architecture
for the 21st century. II. Title

NA2760.G24 2004
720'.1—dc.22
                                    2004057561

ISBN 0-393-73076-X

W. W. Norton & Company, Inc.,
500 Fifth Avenue, New York, N.Y. 10110
www.wwnorton.com
W. W. Norton & Company Ltd.,
Castle House, 75/76 Wells St., London W1T 3QT

0 9 8 7 6 5 4 3 2 1

*This book is dedicated
with love, respect, and gratitude to*
HENRY HOPE REED,
founder of Classical America

CONTENTS

FOREWORD

by Leon Krier

We understand immediately from the title of this beautiful book that the author is not so much interested in the history of architectural classicism as in tits timeless design technology. For him the subject is not a matter of the past and of archeology but rather of present building and polity.

Ideological objections to contemporary classicism are legion; they still have a hold on the minds of many who are not aware of the fact that their moral objections have collapsed with modernism itself. There remains a misapprehension among those who believe that classicism is out of date and that it is too easy a choice, that the condition of man has become too complex, too turbulent, too contradictory to accommodate ideas of beauty, harmony and scale, of elegance, balance and melody, in short, that the spirit of our time and classicism are irreconcilable.

Why should art and architecture express the tragedy of our time, breathe panic and mourning while all other fields of human production may go about their business unaffected by zeitgeist pathos? The self-evidence and persuasiveness of the author's life-long observations are marvelously aloof from fashionable obscurantism. He unravels his subject matter which, while rich and complex, does not pose insuperable technical or epistemological problems. Its principles are as accessible to lucid and sensitive souls as those of beautiful landscapes, plants, or animals. The exclusion of these universal concepts from many architecture schools continues to do unsurpassed harm to the environment and to ourselves.

Instead, François Gabriel widens our horizon by laying bare the rational structure of classical architecture. He explains what can be understood and appreciated by all. He steers clear of fashionable cults of uncertainty and complexity and ignores sectarian newspeak. For him, the authority of classical architecture needs no mythological mediation; it imposes itself by the evidence of its principles and the self-contained rationality of its nature.

INTRODUCTION

The mission of the architect is to design the best possible building for a given situation. The object of architecture is to shape buildings, and it is with forms in space that architects are concerned.

When Vitruvius defined architecture in three words, *utilitas*, *firmitas*, and *venustas*, he achieved a rare feat, for his definition is both concise and comprehensive. What else indeed can be required of a building if it is functional, solidly built, and beautiful? But, while there can hardly be disagreement regarding the first two attributes, the same cannot be said of the third. For what is beauty in our time? Are we, as a society, in agreement on the definition of beauty? The word has become suspect, and it is rarely used in schools of architecture or in architectural criticism. The expression "good taste" is not popular either. It implies that one person's taste may not be as good as another's, an offensive suggestion to those who believe that members of a democracy are equal by definition. Adding to the dilemma, taste is seen as a matter of individual preference, and the right to freedom of opinion must be observed.

If the idea of beauty cannot be discussed without discomfort, perhaps "harmony" should be considered instead. Harmony is the state in which we prefer to see things around us. In an age that prides itself on good sense, harmony is the result of practicality and efficiency. The conditions of harmony are order, simplicity, coherence, and regularity. In architecture, harmony is achieved when we make certain choices: clarity over unnecessary complication; reference to the human body over abstraction; and order over chaos. Harmony is hostile to contradiction, confusion, ambiguity. When we consider architecture as a social art, we find that harmony is hostile to arbitrary originality and to novelty for novelty's sake.

Harmony among people is the achievement of civilization; it occurs when we treat one another kindly, or at least with respect. Courtesy makes us relax our defenses; a smile brings out a smile in another. Courtesy is also called manners, which can be seen as an element of taste: the sense of what is proper or least likely to offend in a social situation. Good manners and good taste go hand in hand, and they are distinct from individual preferences. Both are defined by the society in which we live. The connection between good sense and good taste is as intimate as that between beauty and harmony.

Until the beginning of the twentieth century, architecture was a social art, and everyone felt involved. It is unfortunate that today many people feel unqualified to judge new buildings and prefer to leave the matter in the hands of "experts." But buildings can be loved or detested, as we all know from our daily lives and our travels. Good buildings are kind toward us, and we are grateful to them. Bad buildings are rude, and they deserve our contempt. Every culture has the architecture it deserves, and architecture is everybody's business.

Good buildings are expensive. They always have been. A study published some years ago showed that a single marble column cost the ancient Greek builders the equivalent of nearly a million dollars (Haselberger, 1985). How did small rural communities justify such expense? They undoubtedly felt deeply committed to build a superior civilization. They believed in a great future for it, and they wanted their institutions to endure. The cost of their buildings did not seem extravagant because they wanted them to last, and last they did.

Although much of the material in this book is taken from history, the content is concerned with the future, not the past. This book is intended as a guide to shape our architectural future in a harmonious, humanistic way. Classical architecture is not a historic style; it has evolved through many phases for more than two millennia. Invented by the Greeks, developed by the Romans, and reinvented in the Renaissance, the classical spread from Italy to France, Great Britain, and North America, becoming the first true international style. After a fifty-year eclipse, we should be grateful that it is now making a comeback.

Promoting classical architecture does not, however, imply a rejection of modern architecture. The contributions of the great architects of the twentieth century cannot be ignored. Frank Lloyd Wright, Le Corbusier, Mies van der Rohe, Louis Kahn, and others have enriched our cultural heritage, and they should be carefully studied, for there is much to learn from their built work. There are masterpieces to emulate, but also disasters to avoid.

In recent decades, architectural excesses have been committed under the rubric of the right to freedom of expression for the artist. We pride ourselves in being rational, but our society tolerates, even encourages, arbitrary forms and meaningless gestures in architecture. Perhaps it is regrettable that we now have the means to build so quickly that there seems to be no time for serious reflection. Many architects are competing for attention, in the belief that the more outrageous the design, the greater the chance to be noticed. Albert Einstein's words to the effect that perfection of means and confusion of goals seem to characterize our time are quite apt.

The "novelty for novelty's sake" approach has spread to aspiring architects. The situation was so bad in the 1980s that I heard one of my students declare that he wanted to learn "how to do something weird" so that he would become famous. That was the moment when, as a teacher, I recognized the need to encourage higher ideals among my students, to raise standards of professional and civic responsibility, and to try to restore some discipline in the design process. From then on, we began each term by taking a close look at the classical orders and learning the rules that govern their use. The students went along with moderate enthusiasm at first, but when I asked them to design a simple classical building, they discovered that the rationale of the classical language actually made things easier for them. For the most part, they adapted quite easily. They no longer felt that they were working in a vacuum where "anything goes" and "taste is a matter of opinion." Responsible and surprisingly handsome designs took shape under their very eyes and, to my delight, they began to enjoy themselves in the studio. Since then, not a term has ended without a crop of architectural designs that the students were proud of.

Mies van der Rohe is rumored to have said that one cannot invent a new architecture every Monday morning. Unfortunately, the profound wisdom of that remark did not quell the widespread illusion that architecture could be reinvented single-handedly by one architect or another. Originality at any cost continues to be a popular goal. Contrast this with the humility that characterized the great classical architects of the past. In a discussion of Michele Sanmicheli's Palazzo Grimani in Venice in *Italian Renaissance Architecture*, the great teacher Georges Gromort remarked that "in seeking simply to copy, he displayed creative genius." Cass Gilbert, an early twentieth-century American architect, gave similar advice: "Aim for beauty. Originality will take care of itself." This says it all. Originality comes naturally to talented artists and architects; it cannot be coaxed into being. To be original has become an obsession, whereas to focus honestly on the task at hand and design the best possible building is sometimes regarded as pedestrian.

The best musicians aim to be good interpreters of music; far from trying to reinvent the musical language everyday, they follow their music line closely. Why is it that an architect cannot be satisfied to be a good interpreter of architecture? Is it not better to copy a good design than to invent a poor one? Indeed, it is because classical architects "copied" one another, emulated one another, and competed with one another that the quality of their architecture reached unequaled heights. It is because architects "all did the same thing" or, more precisely, used the same form-language, that the language itself became so rich, so versatile and eloquent, and that it continues to appeal to us today. The classical celebrates enduring values, not passing fashions.

There is a vast literature on the subject of classical architecture. Many excellent treatises and essays have been written over the centuries. So, why another book? Because there has been a tremendous increase of interest in classical architecture in the last fifteen years. More and more, people want to live and work in traditional buildings, endowed with charm and dignity, and

many practicing architects are re-learning ways to design timeless, people-friendly environments. This book was written in part to help them make the transition. It also addresses itself to beginners who have some drafting ability. Classical architecture is an architecture of logic and good sense where a reason can be given for every decision made by a designer familiar with the language. It is the reasonableness, the rationalism of classical architecture that is its greatest asset, and its power to move us is principally derived from harmony and clarity.

As a student, I was fortunate to receive a solid academic background in classical architecture. In spite of it, numerous aspects of the classical form-language still eluded me. If they have become clearer over the years, it is mainly due to observation of all forms of architecture, personal experience, and reflection. Also, the necessity for a teacher to respond to questions is a powerful motivation to learn the answers; indirectly, students themselves are teachers. I have discovered that it is infinitely more rewarding to teach the correct use of the classical language than to attempt to teach "modernist design" because classical architecture is based on unambiguous rules that can be clearly articulated and are therefore easily transmitted.

Since there is no need to repeat what has been said, and said very well, by previous authors, the focus here is on what is not covered in depth in other books. This book begins with the fundamentals: ten constants that can be observed in the arrangement of classical forms across the centuries with all their subtle adjustments and deserve the name of canons. Their timelessness and universality are illustrated by the profusion of sketches, diagrams, and photographs in these pages.

The second chapter presents the vocabulary, the basic forms used in classical architecture, as well as the precepts that guide the classical architect in putting them together, that is to say, the grammar. While it may appear restrictive at first, the discipline of classical design is liberating: the inherent logic in the way the parts come together facilitates their assemblage.

Originality is simply not an issue in classical architecture, as can be seen in chapter three, which suggests the vast range of possible classical solutions to the most elementary design problems. The art of architecture—any kind of architecture—begins with the definition of rooms. Confronted with the task of designing a truly complete space, the student and the professional designer should not underestimate the complexities of designing a satisfactory spatial unit. This unit, which we call a "room," is very different from the unfinished or "leaking" space of modernist architecture. There are obvious differences but also many similarities between indoor and outdoor rooms. Open to the sky or not, the well-defined space is the foundation of classical architecture. Those who understand that will pay more attention to the means employed, and to what effect, in the design of all pleasing environments.

Design cannot be considered independently from the act of drawing. Nearly always, the better designers are fine draftsmen. This stands to reason, as good design comes with an educated eye, and the best possible way to learn to really see is to learn to draw. To be able to sketch rapidly and accurately what is on your mind is an invaluable skill. Chapter four elaborates on this and introduces other drawing techniques such as watercolor wash, the traditional graphic method of classical architects. Color is not just decorative: it describes building materials. As such, it is an essential aspect of architectural design.

Readers whose goal is to develop their skills are invited to address a sequence of four design problems, beginning with a simple one-room building. Following this comes a pair of twin one-room pavilions, then a room within a room—one of which is an outdoor room—and finally a small complex of interrelated indoor and outdoor rooms.

It is a great joy for architects to discover that, once the classical language is assimilated, fresh designs emerge. Robert Adam, a classical architect currently practicing in London, put it bluntly when he said, "Your fingerprints are on the gun."

Chapter five explores classical interiors, paying particular attention to the most public and the most private rooms, the vestibule and the bedroom, and the ordering of rooms and their shape in large and small buildings alike. In chapters six and seven, there is a detailed analysis of the major issues of facade design, followed by a thorough study of the challenges presented by the three-dimensional composition of buildings.

Chapter eight proposes six design problems, more ambitious than the first four, beginning with a small town house and ending with varied institutional buildings. What all these programs have in common is a specific site, real or imaginary. While restricted sites appear at first to be constraining, they actually make the architect's job easier. There is nothing more difficult than working in a vacuum. When there is nothing but a program and an unlimited amount of land available, you are thrown on your own resources, and the choice between an infinity of apparent possibilities is daunting. Designs solutions proposed by students illustrate each program. In following the guidelines of the first two chapters, the students have given their designs what Geoffrey Scott would have called "at least a measure of distinction."

Whether you wish to try your hand at solving the proposed problems or not, much can be learned from looking closely at the student projects. To derive the most from critical sessions, be sure that you thoroughly understand the program and the precise nature of the site. Formulate questions as well as positive and negative criticisms and write them down for yourself or to share with a friend or colleague with similar interests.

Chapters nine and ten concern themselves with necessary refinements. Chapter nine focuses on often neglected details, such as rustication and bollards, which are capable of greatly enhancing design intentions. Chapter ten goes into detail about edges, which are perhaps the most critical aspect of defining architectural spaces.

A final series of ten design problems is found in chapter eleven. In general, these are larger and more complex than the others. In most cases, site pressures are insignificant, if they exist at all. More freedom is therefore given to the designers, but also greater responsibilities. Architecture is too serious to be arbitrary; a rationale must determine the location of each one of the parts required of a building or a complex of buildings. It is mostly the study of the program requirements that suggests the design strategies that are

briefly discussed. Principles for giving shape to the buildings are found in the first two chapters.

The last chapter presents a selection of recent buildings. The growing number and variety of classical designs promise the most interesting developments in the architecture of the twenty-first century.

My hope is that this book will make a modest contribution in the right direction. What shape will the future of architecture take? No one can tell. Architects cannot alone solve the world's many problems, but they can make significant contributions towards a humanistic, life-enhancing, and harmonious environment in our houses and our cities. It seems to me that this is a useful and worthy task.

CHAPTER 1

TEN TIMELESS CANONS

The real act of discovery is not in finding new lands but in seeing them with new eyes.
—MARCEL PROUST

No matter how talented a designer is, instinct, inspiration, and vision do not suffice. As with other creative endeavors, architects must let reason be their guide, not whim. Canons have been formulated and tested throughout centuries of experiments, and it is from looking at good buildings and thinking about what makes them successful that we can learn to distinguish the good from the inadequate.

Canons are useful guidelines that will help us to evaluate the choices architects have to make. They are nothing more. They do, however, define classical architecture. If they are found together on a piece of architecture or in an ensemble, there cannot be any doubt about its classicism.

These are the canons I propose:

1. bilateral symmetry
2. anthropomorphism
3. clear and simple geometry
4. defined space
5. juxtaposition of discrete forms
6. emphasis on center, corners, and sides
7. limited inventory of parts
8. inherent formal hierarchies
9. tripartite organization: the rule of three
10. regularity

There are undoubtedly others, and the material covered in these ten could be organized in different ways, but I believe that this group can provide the basis for a sound design process.

BILATERAL SYMMETRY

Most classical compositions are symmetrical, that is to say, the left side of the building is a mirror image of the right. Bilateral symmetry is the most obvious and probably the most effective form of visual order. It proclaims permanence and immutability. Symmetry in architecture sends a powerful message because we are attuned to the symmetry of our bodies. Without symmetry, we would experience difficulties maintaining our equilibrium. Symmetry is a sign of health, or at least of normalcy. True, no one is perfectly symmetrical, and we expect to see slight variations between one half and the other, in buildings as well as in people.

The plane that divides a composition is, of course, an abstraction. It is usually referred to as the *axis of symmetry* because it is represented as a line on a plan or an elevation. The unique nature of the axis is recognized in the special dash-dot line used on construction drawings. The axis is the most important line in a design because it structures and organizes the whole. Although it does not have a physical reality and therefore is invisible, the axis is the backbone of a design. It plays a paradoxical role, comparable to that of the conductor of an orchestra; the only silent person on the stage, he is the most important musician there.

Symmetry is a visual necessity, evidence that architectural form makes its own demands. On the interior, the plan of one side of a building need not reflect the other. Variations are often required by functional or site pressures, but they must be concealed by a symmetrical facade. Such an assertion contradicts the modernist dictum of the 1930s that required that the building envelope faithfully reflect the interior. The early Viennese modernist Adolf Loos continued to adhere to the tradition of symmetrical facades, behind which he wanted to be free to organize the volumes as he saw fit. That freedom was clear on the rear elevation, which he felt could be relaxed (figs. 1.1, 1.2). He referred to this design approach as *Raumplan*, or plan of volumes.

Classical architects have found skillful ways to bend or shift axes of symmetry gracefully. "French hôtel" is the name given to a large urban establishment that, in the past, combined the functions of a residence with those of an administrative, financial, and political center for a rich and powerful family. The presence of such a complex was clearly advertised on the street side, often with a monumental porte cochere carrying the coat of arms of the family. This was placed in the middle of a forbidding wall enclosing a forecourt and framed by a pair of identical pavilions or the extremities of wings. Although there were other design solutions, this particular symmetrical design was extremely successful and was the model for many variations over a period of three hundred years. At the Hôtel d'Hallwyl in Paris, the eighteenth-century architect Claude Nicolas Ledoux was faced with a regular but small site (fig. 1.3). Convention required that the house stand between forecourt and garden, and he managed to give both a reasonable size and a

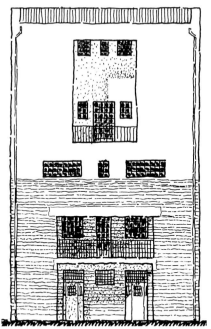

1.1. House for Tristan Tzara, Paris, 1930. Adolf Loos. Street facade.

1.2. House for Tristan Tzara. Rear elevation.

13

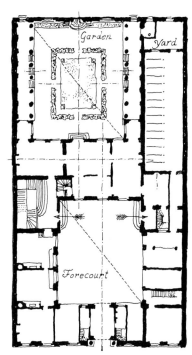

1.3. Hotel d'Hallwyl, Rue Michel-le-Comte, Paris, 1766. Claude Nicolas Ledoux.

1.4. Hotel d'Hallwyl. Street facade.

regular shape. The main difficulty was accommodating service buildings that were twice as large as the house. Ledoux solved the problem by extending the stables—for fifteen horses—along the side of the garden in back. This meant the axis of symmetry that controlled the street facade and the forecourt had to be shifted laterally so that the rear facade would appear symmetrical from the garden as well. Visitors enter the house in the rear corners of the courtyard and reach the center from the sides. They are oblivious to the fact that the axis of symmetry of the entire design is dislocated (fig. 1.4).

Fitting a classical—that is a harmonious and symmetrical—design in a small and wildly irregular site was brilliantly accomplished in the Loire Valley area by the French architect Pierre Patout in the early 1950s. Party walls make up two sides of the triangular site and the third side borders a curving street with a substantial slope. The main axis coincides with the longest possible vista within the site. The two main spaces of the composition are the living room and the small formal garden; they are lined up on the axis, which originates in the hearth inside and terminates at a fountain outside. The cross-axis, bent to make regular spaces possible in other rooms, intersects the main axis in the oval living room. Nearly symmetrical wings frame the formal garden, and the tall roof over the living room gives stability to the composition (figs. 1.5–1.8).

In classical architecture, one expects to find an opening at the center of the main facade. This was true of ancient Greek temples, where front and back had an uneven number of bays framed by an even number of columns. To make this intention perfectly clear, porticos along the sides of the building have a column at the center that precludes a door. In Paestum, for example, the Temple of Ceres (fig. 1.9) has six columns in the front and thirteen on the side. A rare exception is the so-called basilica with nine columns in the front and eighteen on the side (fig. 1.10). It is now believed

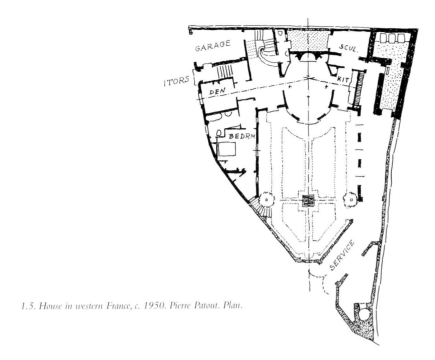

1.5. House in western France, c. 1950. Pierre Patout. Plan.

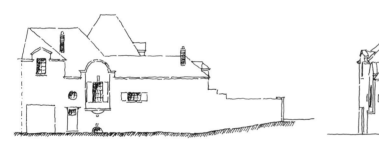

1.6. House in western France. Elevations.

1.7. House in western France. Model showing the garden facade.

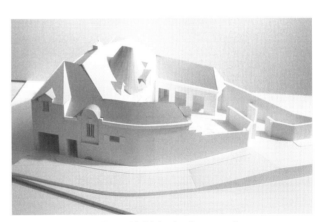

1.8. House in western France. Model showing the street wall.

1.9. Temple of Ceres, Paestum, c. 500 B.C.

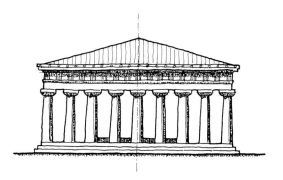

1.10. Basilica, Paestum, c. 500 B.C. Reconstitution by Henri Labrouste.

1.11. Federal house, Fayetteville, New York, c. 1830.

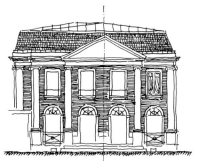

1.12. House in Sceaux, near Paris, date unknown.

that this temple was dedicated to both Zeus and Hera, two deities of nearly equal status, which explains the division right on the main axis.

The preference for a door on center certainly reflects anthropomorphism. Buildings that do not follow the rule are somewhat unsatisfactory, regardless of the other qualities they may possess. Consider a charming house in Fayetteville, New York, with a facade divided in two bays by a central pier (fig. 1.11). Another house at Sceaux, near Paris, boasts classical features, among which is a pediment (fig. 1.12). There are two bays under the pediment, where we would expect to see three. A pediment is essentially a ceremonial embrace, a way to gather elements together to form a unit. In these two houses, that unity is destroyed by a solid piece of masonry in the middle, which splits the composition.

ANTHROPOMORPHISM

Most classical buildings present a front, a back, and two sides to the world, but only the front and the back are symmetrical. If the facade you are looking at is not symmetrical, you are probably looking at a side. There are exceptions to this rule, of course. One of the most notable is Palladio's Villa Rotonda, a design viewed with veneration by most architects (fig. 1.13). There, the two perpendicular axes of symmetry are identical and so are the four facades. In this iconic design, Palladio's main objective was formal perfection, which he achieved through the use of square and circle, centered on a vertical axis. In his opinion, neither site conditions, functional demands, nor any other factor required that one facade be different from the other three.

In large compositions, symmetry is needed to balance lateral or secondary facades, but at the royal palace of Versailles, there simply is no lateral facade. The cross axis is located *outside*, and parallel to, the facade of the central block overlooking the park. The axis stretches out north and south from a large terrace in the middle, soberly defined by a few steps and two large vases marking the corners (fig. 1.14). That axis forms the backbone of two large gardens, the winter garden on the north and the summer garden on the south (fig. 1.15). This strategy unites the building and garden into a single composition.

The "front" of a building is often defined as the side with the main entrance. This makes sense in public buildings, but it is not necessarily the case in residential architecture, where the public front may be more guarded than the private side overlooking the garden. Even in a palace the size of Versailles, the main facade is unquestionably that facing the royal gardens. Although symbolically important and very grand, the city side is more severe. Again anthropomorphism should be our guide to understanding the classical message: In the human body, the face is clearly distinguished by the location of the eyes and other sensors. Similarly in buildings, the front should be where there are more windows, or "wind-eyes" as they used to be called. It is therefore natural to accept the fact that many buildings, public or private, are entered through the back.

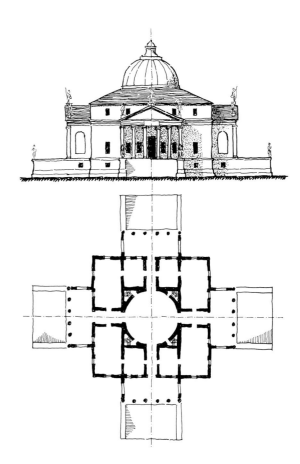

1.13. Villa Rotonda, near Vicenza, 1566. Andrea Palladio. Plan and elevation.

1.14. Royal palace at Versailles, begun 1661. Louis Le Vau and J. H. Mansart. The cross-axis of the vast composition is marked by two large vases at the corners of the west terrace.

1.15. Royal palace at Versailles. Bird's-eye view. The cross-axis stretches from the north garden on the left to the south garden on the right. The vases are marked "V."

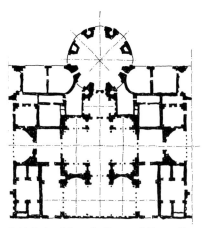

1.16. Baths of Caracalla, Rome, c. 215 A.D. Plan.

1.17. Palazzo Chiericati, Vicenza, 1551–57. Andrea Palladio. Attic base in the courtyard.

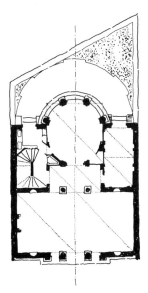

1.18. Town house, Boulogne sur Seine, 1933. Emilio Terry. The main floor is entirely derived from squares.

CLEAR AND SIMPLE GEOMETRY

According to Ledoux, "The circle and the square are the letters of the alphabet designers use in the fabric of their best works." Squares and circles are, with the triangle, the easiest forms to identify; they are the least ambiguous. They are perfect in their regularity. That is why they are the most commonly used forms in classical buildings. In the huge plans of Roman baths, there are rectangular rooms—inevitably derived from the square—some of which terminate in a semicircular niche called an exedra (fig. 1.16). The small circles that punctuate the plan represent columns. At the other extreme of the scale, the profiles of classical moldings are made up of segments of circles alternating with straight lines, either vertical or horizontal. Column shafts are cylindrical and, in the Attic base, which is the most frequently used design, so are the *fillets* that occur three times. In elevation and in section, both shafts and fillets appear on drawings as straight lines. The *torus*, which occurs twice in the base, and the single *scotia* in between, are drawn as segments of circles (fig. 1.17). From the bottom up, the sequence is a torus, a fillet, a scotia, a fillet, another torus, and a third fillet.

Classical openings are based on the square. In a typical door or window, the width of the opening is half the height. Why a double square? Because it is the easiest rectangle to identify; even an untrained eye will see that it is made of two squares, one above the other. Classical architecture favors the vertical over the horizontal because, as the French architect Auguste Perret put it, "A vertical window is a frame for a human being." The ratio 1 : 2 is ubiquitous. A case in point is the enormous door of the Pantheon in Rome. In large public buildings such as the Louvre in Paris, where openings must be proportionate to the size of palatial rooms, the height of windows is often increased to three or four times their width. It is neither practical nor necessary to increase the width of windows.

In contrast to the classical window, the horizontal window advocated by Le Corbusier does not do much to dignify human beings. It is the outcome of the "free facade" ideology, essentially derived from the spanning capabilities of reinforced concrete. Referred to as a "strip window," the horizontal window does not take into consideration the importance of people in the built environment. Nor does it recognize the wall as a substantial element.

Squares and circles fit into one another harmoniously, that is, in an easy, natural way. A circle can either be tangent to the sides of a square or intersect the four corners. An equilateral triangle also fits in a circle, and a circle fits in an equilateral triangle, but the square and the triangle are incompatible. When the square and the circle must be modified, the circle either becomes a hexagon or an octagon, and the square also can turn into an octagon. As restricted as these operations appear, they open up an immense range of formal and spatial configurations. Above all, a classical architect does not want to arbitrarily modify, truncate, warp, or otherwise mutilate a pure shape. Geometric figures must be handled with consideration.

The respect for clear and simple forms and their relationship with one another is expressed by following simple rules. Circles and squares normally do not overlap or jostle one another for supremacy; one could say that they like to live side by side in peace. In plan, an axis of symmetry is the backbone of the composition involving a series of varied spaces, corresponding to a straight sight line through a series of openings, informing the visitor of the spatial sequence ahead.

A small town house built in 1933 by Emilio Terry in Boulogne-sur-Seine is a fine exercise in geometry applied to classical planning (fig. 1.18). The plan is based on a series of squares and double squares related to one another in a straightforward way. The main block of the town house is approximately square in plan. Half is occupied

1.19. Louis XVI Chapel, Boulevard Haussmann, Paris, 1815–26. Pierre Fontaine.

by the drawing room, which is therefore made of two smaller squares. The dining room would almost fit in half the drawing room; its shape is a slightly elongated circle. The little study on the side, also a double square, would fit four times in the living room. Even the small, columniated hallway at the center is in the proportion 1 : 2. The hallway plays an essential part in the monumental *enfilade*, or series of openings on axis, and resolves the circulation efficiently.

Translated into the third dimension, the squares of a plan become cubes, and the circles become cylinders or hemispheres. It is well known that the shapes of Palladio's rooms are combinations of cubes and half-cubes. The shaft of a classical column is a vertical cylinder, and the most common vault in classical architecture is the barrel vault, a half-cylinder. Classical domes usually are half-spheres or approximations. The Louis XVI chapel in Paris, by Pierre Fontaine, also is an elegant exercise in pure geometry (fig. 1.19). It consists essentially of a cubic block surmounted by a hemisphere. There are three projections on the sides and on the back of the main block, all in the shape of a half-cylinder capped by a quarter-sphere. The front facade is distinguished by a single pediment—an isosceles triangle—that is supported by four Doric columns

1.20. Louis XVI Chapel. Interior.

(cylinders). The entablature runs around the entire building, holding the shapes together. The geometric purity of the design creates a serene and powerful effect. The same disciplined simplicity characterizes the interior (fig. 1.20).

DEFINED SPACE

What distinguishes classical architecture from other form-languages is not so much the shape or the size of its rooms but the fact that there are rooms at all. Twentieth-century architects intended to blur the definition of space with their buildings. Frank Lloyd Wright made it one of his main goals to "destroy the box," as he put it, and he was quite good at it. People now realize again that there is something satisfactory in being inside a well-defined space. To limit the formal vocabulary of architects to the two basic shapes of square and circle may appear to restrict their freedom. In fact, rules do not constrain; they liberate as long as they are properly understood and sensibly applied. No one would doubt the expressive power of poetry, yet it is the more exacting rules that distinguish poetry from prose.

Twentieth-century architects have used the terms "free plan" and "open plan" to characterize their designs. This implies that other types of planning must be "restrained" or "closed." But good planning, open or not, must follow some rules. Undisciplined planning is not "free"; it is arbitrary, confusing, capricious, or disorderly.

In classical thinking, the basic spatial unit is called a room, but it is not necessarily found inside a building. The term must be understood broadly as a well-defined portion of space, indoors or outdoors. For such a room to exist, it must be defined by firm boundaries and openings must be few in number and moderate in size. The significance of doors or windows does not increase with their size or number. The fewer the openings, the more important they become; too many openings weaken the sense of enclosure and the clear definition of space.

Classical rooms are regular spaces, also called figural spaces. Regular spaces are sometimes obtained by carving them out of less important spaces around them, called residual or ancillary spaces. The variety of classical rooms is inexhaustible. They may be large or small, simple or complex, polygonal or circular in plan, ornate or plain. They may be capped by flat ceilings, vaults of varied shapes, or domes. The plan of Woodlands in Philadelphia (fig. 1.21) includes squares, circles, rectangles, ovals, and rooms that combine rectangular and circular parts. A cohesive design is achieved with axes of symmetry and the visual device of enfilade.

Because of their size, outdoor rooms can accept a solid object at their center, especially in urban contexts. Obelisks, monumental statues, and fountains are the most commonly used markers. In a park, a pool or a lawn is a restful and welcome surface. A pool has the additional merit of reflecting the sky, and this is enough to create the impression of a vault.

The boundaries of outdoor rooms may take forms other than walls, but they must be clear enough to define a space and strong enough to contain it. The influential eighteenth-century architectural theorist Abbé Laugier suggested that the basic strategy should be similar in an urban or a rural context: outdoor rooms are carved out of the city fabric or out of the forest. In one of the famous views of the ideal city attributed to the school of Piero della Francesca, an urban square is defined by a substantial layering of the ground plane and a two-dimensional pattern, aided by five objects: a fountain in the middle and columns marking the four corners of the space (fig. 1.22). The diminutive fountain does not encroach on the open space and simply acts as a symbolic marker. The columns are very tall and they seem to enclose the space in a virtual cube. The urban fabric consists of a variety of buildings, the most significant of which is a triumphal arch on axis with the outdoor room.

The Pont Alexandre III in Paris is one of the rare bridges designed as an outdoor room (fig. 1.23). About 300 feet long and 75 feet wide, it is

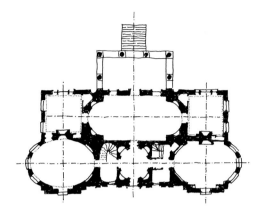

1.21. Woodlands, Philadelphia, completed 1789.

1.22. Ideal City, from a painting of the school of Piero della Francesca, c. 1480.

1.23. Pont Alexandre III, Paris, 1897–1900. L.J Résal, chief engineer. J. H. Mansart's golden dome can be seen in the background.

1.24. Dormer window in a mill in the Anjou region of France.

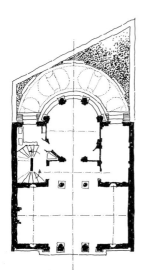

1.25. Town house, Boulogne sur Seine. The main floor plan is coordinated by lines of vision and symmetry.

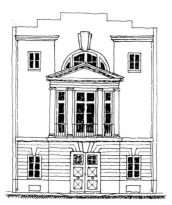

1.26. Town house, Boulogne sur Seine. Street facade.

part of an enfilade of grand urban spaces terminating in the magnificent dome of Jules Hardouin Mansart's Invalides chapel. The bridge was designed by a team of architects and engineers working in collaboration. To allow the eye to embrace the entire perspective over the bridge, the surface is absolutely horizontal, challenging the engineers to create a daringly low arch. The monumental pylons that mark the corners are both structural and emblematic, acting as a grand gateway to the gigantic square in front of the Hôtel des Invalides.

JUXTAPOSITION OF DISCRETE FORMS

In classical architecture, every component is complete in itself. Forms are sharply defined, and so are the spaces between them. Boundaries are clearly outlined and ambiguity and overlap systematically avoided. In a village in western France, a stone dormer on an old mill has a perfect square opening surmounted by a triangular pediment (fig. 1.24). Between them, a third element acts as a mediator; it is a rectangle taking the place of the conventional frieze. The simple moldings delineating the main components are in character with the bold geometry of the overall design.

Every classical space is a complete world. In a classical building, you never have the disconcerting impression of having a foot in one room and the other in another. Knowing exactly where you are contributes to self-awareness. It helps you become aware of who you are at the moment. This does not mean that the transition between spaces is abrupt. The enfilade, for example, is an arrangement that makes clear where you are going and where you are coming from.

Let us turn again to Emilio Terry's design for a town house (fig. 1.25). From the entrance at street level, stairs lead up to a small vestibule at the heart of the *piano nobile*, or principal story, of the house. There the three major rooms are revealed in enfilade along the main axis of symmetry. Secondary axes and counter axes hold the composition together by pointing out symmetrical relationships. The main axis continues past the oval dining room, which opens on the garden-terrace built over the garage and reaches out to the woodland of the Bois de Boulogne.

The street facade (fig. 1.26) is as clearly organized as the plan. The main openings are centered, one on each level and each with a different form, appropriate to its function and to its location. While the main door to the house is suitably plain, the large opening on the piano nobile is given prominence with a small temple front. The third and last of the main openings, on the third level, is a so-called thermal window. Four smaller, rectangular windows mark each corner of the rectangular facade. The rustication, or exaggerated stonework, of the ground floor gives a strong base to the temple front.

The garden facade, more private, is also freer (fig. 1.27). The vertical surface of the wall is maintained and reaffirmed by rectangular windows in the four corners, as in the design of the street facade. But three-dimensional geometry takes over in the middle section, where the oval shape of the dining room projects beyond the plane of the wall. As if to compensate, the upper part of the same wall is recessed to coincide with the inner enclosure of the dining room. In other words, the wall plane is split into two curved surfaces, convex below and concave above. The cylindrical form of the dining room enriches the wall and transforms it completely, but it does not annihilate it.

The juxtaposition of discrete forms in the plan of the house is the guiding principle of the three-dimensional development of the design (figs. 1.28, 1.29). It was particularly striking in the back, which has been completely obscured by renovation. Fortunately, the street facade is intact.

1.27. Town house, Boulogne sur Seine. Garden side, now destroyed.

1.28. Town house, Boulogne sur Seine. Half-model.

1.29. Town house, Boulogne sur Seine. Half-model.

EMPHASIS ON CENTER, CORNERS, AND SIDES

A room defines a portion of space, and that space must be celebrated. The essence of the room is its emptiness. Since space by itself is invisible, it can only receive visual significance from the thoughtful design of the enclosure. In a well-designed room, homogeneity is achieved when opposite walls share the same basic articulation. They reflect one another and they share axes of symmetry. This is how all four walls address themselves to the center of the room. Two paneled walls (figs. 1.30, 1.31) present enough similarities for visual comfort, yet close examination reveals that they were not built at the same time. Both walls are divided in three parts, and the center bays are occupied by significant elements facing one another: a door on one side and a fireplace on the other. Unity and balance are thus achieved.

Although Frank Lloyd Wright always denied any influence on his work, he did agree with the Chinese philosopher Lao-Tse that the reality of a room consists not in its walls but in the space within. The success of Wright's best early rooms lies precisely in the fact that there is no furniture in the middle. Exception was made for the dining table, which plays an important social and ceremonial role and finds its natural place in the center of the room. To make sure no one moved the

1.30, 1.31. Two opposite walls in an eighteenth-century room in western France.

table, Wright had it screwed to the floor. This does not contradict the notion of clearly defined space since the diners, facing one another across the table, form a sort of enclosure. At about the same time, Charles Rennie Mackintosh demonstrated brilliantly the power of chairs with very tall backs to create the impression of a mini-room within a larger one, best seen in his well-known designs for Mrs. Cranston's tea rooms in Glasgow.

To achieve spatial unity, floor and ceiling should also reflect each other, with the difference that the ceiling can and should be three-dimensional above, while the floor must be absolutely flat. Even optical illusions of relief make walking uncomfortable.

While the center of a room should be open, the corners should be solid. It is in their nature to be so, as is easily demonstrated by drawing a rectangle. All that is necessary to create the figure are the four points marking the corners. The lines connecting them are secondary. In a rectangular room as well as in the four-point diagram, the sides can be interpreted as "soft" and the corners as "hard." For this reason, openings naturally belong in the sides, not in the corners.

Although we tend to pay more attention to the decoration of walls and ceilings, especially when we are seated, the articulation of a floor can either help with the coherence of a room or contribute to its disintegration. Consider the popular pattern that architects call the "nine-square diagram" (fig. 1.32). If the size of the four squares in the corners is reduced, the square in the middle grows larger and the four figures along the sides become long and narrow rectangles. The center square dominates by its size and accentuates the primacy of space; the small squares focus on the four corners of the room and add density to them; finally, the long and narrow rectangles along the sides contribute to the framing of the central area. Each of the nine quadrangles makes a special contribution to the shape of the room. This diagram works with almost any rectangular room, providing a wealth

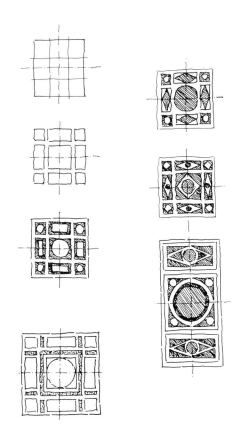

1.32. The nine-square diagram used in floor articulation.

1.33. Floor patterns in circular rooms.

of variations. Once again, care must be taken to avoid overlaps and any impression of depth. The varied shapes of the floor design must be juxtaposed, as in a large mosaic, and they should organize the floor area hierarchically

Floor articulation in circular rooms should be based on the essential geometry of a circle, which consists of concentric circles and straight lines radiating from the center (fig. 1.33). Although circles are not directional, buildings usually are, and perpendicular axes of symmetry may be nec-

1.34. The dome room at Bagatelle, Paris, 1775. François Joseph Bélanger.

1.35. Library at Pitzhanger Manor, Middlesex, 1802. Sir John Soane.

essary to anchor circular rooms and orient them consistently with the overall composition. This is why circular rooms are generally divided in multiples of four: eight, twelve, or sixteen sides.

To confirm the unity of a circular space, the wall should carry a simple, repetitive subdivision such as A-A-A or A-B-A-B. As in rectangular rooms, opposite walls should reflect one another (fig. 1.34). They all frame the same space, and the eye should meet a similar design when looking from one side of the room to the other. Discrepancies in the articulation of opposite walls are confusing and disorienting.

It does not matter much how closely the division of the floor matches that of the walls, since the roles of walls and floors are very different. But it is important—if we are to perceive a clear spatial identity in a room—that the articulation of the floor reflect the articulation of the ceiling. The library at Pitshanger Manor, Sir John Soane's house in Middlesex, demonstrates the level of unity achieved when floor and ceiling carry closely related designs (fig. 1.35).

LIMITED INVENTORY OF PARTS

The vocabulary of the classical language is made of specific, distinct, and easily recognizable elements; that is the main characteristic of any style. While there is a tendency to identify styles with earlier periods of history and to dismiss them as irrelevant to our time, the classical has the potential to express contemporary sensibilities and to satisfy today's needs.

Each element of the classical vocabulary is so sharply defined and has such a strong individuality that it cannot be confused with another. All have specific roles to play in a composition. The column, with its distinctive base and capital, is the most important. There are several variations on the design of columns, each called an *order*, in recognition of their principal use as ordering devices. Often acting as structural supports, columns have other functions in design. They are as often used to express structure as to actually carry loads. Even more often they simply articulate a bay system, *ordonnance* in French, an untranslatable word that means the general formal *parti*, or organization, of a facade. Sometimes columns are used in pairs to frame an opening and emphasize its importance.

Columns can be freestanding, *engaged* (partially buried), in a wall, or flattened against a wall to form pilasters. They are wonderful elements, refined to perfection over centuries by gifted architects who devoted considerable attention to them. It is no wonder that fine columns look as if they had been caressed by lovers' hands! Indeed, columns are a metaphor for human beings. They are endowed with the elegance, the grace, and the dignity we all wish we had. Columns are a subtle combination of geometric and organic forms. The main part, the shaft, is basically a cylinder, but it never is just that. It is subtly modified by a delicate swelling called *entasis*. Even more than base and capital, entasis is the distinctive mark of a classical column. Without it, the shaft would be an abstract form, an impersonal rod, or an inanimate cylinder.

Some writers have attempted to assign a specific and therefore limited personality to each order, the Doric, the Ionic, and the Corinthian, in particular. This approach, carried too far, is probably a mistake. To remain a metaphor, a thing must remain in the realm of generalities. It is where and how the orders are employed, and to what purpose, that they contribute to the character of a design. The most that can be said is that it seemed reasonable for Thomas Jefferson to use the sober Doric order (fig. 1.36) at Monticello, his house in Virginia, and nobody will dispute the selection of the Corinthian (fig. 1.37) for the magnificent Pantheon in Rome. But there are also many successful designs for Doric temples, Ionic residences, and Corinthian garden pavilions. On the other hand, it would be difficult to sanction the Ionic order on a factory or the Corinthian on a prison.

1.36. Doric order at Monticello, Charlottesville, Virginia, 1777–1809. Thomas Jefferson.

1.37. Corinthian order at the Pantheon in Rome.

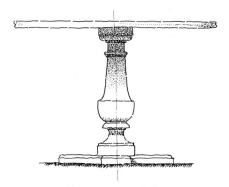

1.38. Stone table, c. 1950. Jean-Charles Moreux.

1.39. The Marino Casino. Dublin, 1759. William Chambers.

A column may be used alone as a monument or a marker in a park or a city, but typically columns are part of a colonnade. Columns may be raised on pedestals, which have three parts as well: a *base*, a *die*, and a *cap*. The complete order includes entablature and pedestal, thus reiterating the "rule of three." Columns may also stand on plain dice, cubic blocks without moldings, which should never be taller than they are wide.

Surprising as it may seem, only two or three more elements, such as balustrades (fig. 1.38) or openings in walls, are needed to complete the basic vocabulary of the classical. Notwithstanding a widespread belief to the contrary, classical elements are flexible and versatile, and they play different roles in different places in buildings. The frame of a door can adopt the profile of an *architrave*, or a chimney may be based on the design of a pedestal. So may a *stylobate*, the base of an entire building, in which case the pedestal is stretched to the required length. Indoors, the much-used *dado,* or wainscot, is an interpretation of the stylobate. And the cornice, a transitional member between wall and ceiling, often is borrowed from the upper part of an entablature.

INHERENT FORMAL HIERARCHIES

In design, hierarchy means the ordering of parts according to their importance. Rooms that are important, whether for functional reasons or representational purposes, belong to the center and to the front of a building. Secondary functions are housed in the wings, i.e., the lateral parts of the building, in the back, or in the basement. This instinctive classification results from the fact that the important organs are found in the center and towards the top of the human body. Observe how the eighteenth-century English architect William Chambers made the central portion of the Marino Casino in Dublin (fig. 1.39) more prominent than the sides, while a running Doric order maintains the unity of a deceptively small building. Begun as a one-room garden building, it ended up as a three-story residence with all the necessary support spaces.

Classical designs also signify status by raising important rooms above the ground plane. This tendency derives from the hierarchy inherent in the metaphorical use of the terms "high" and "low." The expressions "looking up" and "looking down" are not idle. Nor is the term piano nobile. On the north shore of Lake Geneva,

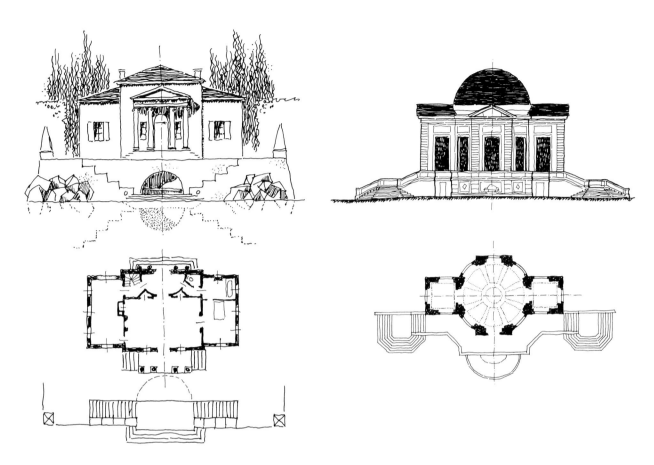

1.40. Bath house, 1922. Emilio Terry.

1.41. Pavillon de l'Aurore, Sceaux, c. 1672. Claude Perrault or Antoine Le Pautre.

Emilio Terry raised a bathhouse upon a massive podium to endow a simple pleasure building with dignity (fig. 1.40).

Another way to enhance important rooms is to give them regular geometric forms. They are then said to be figural spaces. Minor functions are squeezed in the oddly shaped residual spaces found around or between figural spaces. Under Louis XIV, prime minister Colbert ran France from a domed circular room framed by two offices for his aides. Although regular in shape, their size and position indicate their secondary status (fig.1.41).

Classical columns themselves have a built-in hierarchy that suggests a kinship with the organic world. The base of a column is plainer than the capital, and the shaft itself is wider at the bottom than it is at the top. When orders are superposed, the more slender are placed above sturdier ones. Starting at the bottom, the sequence will be Doric, Ionic, and Corinthian. Structural logic is always observed, and the Ionic is never seen under the Doric, or the Corinthian under the Ionic. In spite of these restrictions, a great deal of flexibility is possible. For instance, a second Doric may be placed directly over a

1.42. Design for a palace, attributed to Colen Campbell.

1.43. Eighteenth-century façade, Place Dauphine, Paris, seen from the ground.

Doric, or a Corinthian over a Doric, without the mediation of an Ionic. A single order may also stand by itself on a plain base (fig. 1.42).

Hierarchy requires greater height for the public rooms on the piano nobile. This is the most important story, and it is the climax of a composition, but its location, level with the ground or elevated, is determined by a variety of factors. In most cases, additional stories are found above or below. Their height decreases progressively as they get farther away from the piano nobile. Seen from the ground, the physical reduction of the floor heights will be optically enhanced by perspective (fig. 1.43).

TRIPARTITE ORGANIZATION: THE RULE OF THREE

It is critical for a composition to have three parts: a beginning, a middle, and an end. This rule takes many forms, and it can be seen even in the elementary components of the classical language. A column begins with a base, continues with a shaft, and ends with a capital. It would be unnatural to begin the description of a column at the top. A building is constructed from the ground up; in this sense it can be compared with a growing plant. Louis Kahn, who was profoundly influenced by his Beaux-Arts training, made a strong case for the design process of any building to begin at the ground level and continue upwards.

Many other elements of the classical vocabulary are tripartite: the entablature, with architrave, frieze, and cornice; the pedestal, made of plinth, die and cornice; the balustrade, with a plinth, a row of balusters, and a handrail. Three distinct parts can even be identified in the individual baluster: base, shaft, and capital (fig. 1.44).

Laterally, the rule of three takes another form. As we have seen, symmetry postulates a middle and two sides, as in A-B-A. The Palladian window (fig. 1.45) is a particularly striking example.

Even in very large compositions which can be read as C-B-A-B-C, the A and C parts are usually more important than the B parts, which are often treated as links. In fact, these links may even be voids; if the A and C parts have enough in common to appear formally related, a physical connection is not necessary. In Robert Adam's Pulteney Bridge in Bath (fig. 1.46), two rows of shops facing each other are framed by customs offices at both ends. The middle shop is given a more monumental appearance than the others for no other reason than that the classical canon mandates a dominant center. The prominence of the end pavilions is motivated by a similar demand: the beginning and the end of a formal composition must be emphasized. Links are played down, so that the whole appears to be made of three strong parts connected by hyphens.

At the Couvent des Capucins in Paris (fig. 1.47), designed by Alexandre Théodore Brongniart, the room on the right is given as monumental a facade as the much larger church on the left for the sake of visual balance. The

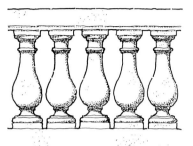

1.44. Eighteenth-century stone balustrade in Georges Gromort's house in Paris.

1.45. Eighteenth-century British adaptation of the Palladian window.

1.46. Pulteney Bridge, Bath, c. 1769. Robert Adam. Longitudinal section.

1.47. Former Couvent des Capucins, Paris, 1783. Alexandre-Théodore Brongniart.

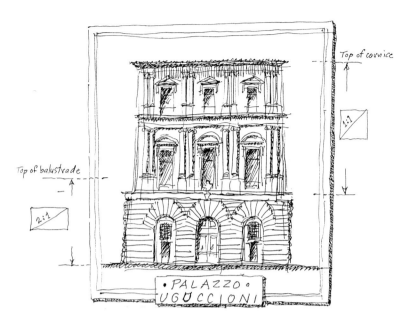

1.48. Palazzo Uguccioni, Florence, c.1550. Attributed to Raphael.

1.49. Hôtel de la Monnaie, Paris, 1775. Jacques-Denis Antoine. One of the end pavilions of the lateral facade.

middle section is essentially a link between church and meeting room; it is a shallow structure that screens the courtyard. Nevertheless, the door in the middle dominates the composition, mainly because of its central location but also because it is much more ornate than the rest of the facade.

In these last two designs, the main door—or what looks like one—is placed right in the middle. The main entrance always is one of the most important elements of a building. Entering a building is, or should be, gaining access to a privileged place, and it should be celebrated. What better way is there than to give the place of honor to the main entrance?

One of the more satisfying classical archetypes is a facade that combines a horizontal division into three parts with a vertical layering of three tiers. The pattern is a vertical nine-square diagram with an opening in each square, as can be seen at Palazzo Uguccioni in Florence (fig. 1.48). Two hundred years later, a similar strategy was used at the Hôtel de la Monnaie in Paris (fig. 1.49). The major difference between the two designs is the presence of superimposed orders on the upper two stories of the palazzo.

The lateral division of a wide facade into three parts has greater presence when the central portion of the building is moved forward or backward. In a design schema that has rarely failed, a colonnade surmounted by a pediment gathers two stories in one gesture (fig. 1.50). This gives prominence to the center portion and makes possible a double reading of the three-tier concept. One reading is that of three clearly expressed stories; in another reading, there is the rusticated base and the entablature with the pediment at the top; between them is a large area encompassing two stories.

The "rule of three" is one of the canons that has made classical architecture so enduring. We sense in it a powerful metaphor for the three main phases of life itself.

REGULARITY

Environmental chaos is disquieting, and regular patterns in architecture are reassuring. What guidelines can help us to generate visual order? First we must realize that not everything in the world can be organized. That said, the elements to be organized should fit in a few categories; if they are too disparate, they will be difficult to sort out. A third principle is that, to be clear to the eye, ordering devices must be simple patterns or grids.

A grid for a plan should be more regular than a grid for a facade. The reason for that is based on experience: there are many more opportunities to see a facade than to visually apprehend the plan of a building or that of an urban area. When the plan fits into a simple grid, the mind grasps it more easily. The mental image we carry with us is like a map, which helps us find our way.

Appropriate plan grids (fig. 1.51) are made from squares [a x a] and rectangles [a x b]. Varied frameworks can be obtained by alternating [a] and [b] in two directions. One result is a plaid pattern, made of three different elements: a small square (a x a), a large square (b x b) and a rectangle (a x b).

Simple grids suitable for elevations (fig. 1.52) are obtained from a single horizontal module [a] or two alternating modules [a and b]. As a rule, vertical divisions can be equal or decrease in height as they move up from the main floor. The height of the ground floor must always be different from the others to acknowledge its unique position. A general design rule extrapolated from this case can be formulated very simply: different things must always *look* different from one another.

One of the earlier buildings endowed with extreme regularity was the Palazzo Strozzi (fig. 1.53), erected in Florence by Cosimo il Vecchio for his two sons at the very beginning of the Renaissance. Perfectly symmetrical in plan, sec-

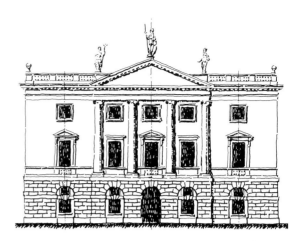

1.50. *Project for the Bank of England, c. 1732. Theodore Jacobsen.*

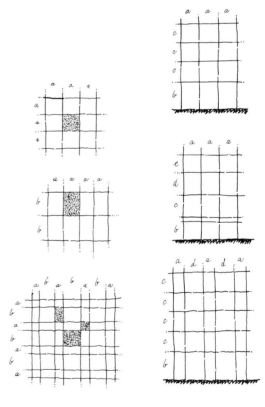

1.51. *Simple grids used to organize plans.*

1.52. *Simple grids used to organize facades.*

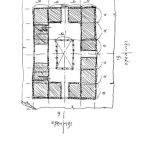

1.53. Palazzo Strozzi,
Florence, 1489–1547.
Benedetto di Maiano and Il
Cronaca.

1.54. Court of honor, Hôtel des Invalides, Paris, 1671–76. Libéral Bruant.

tion, and elevation, the building exudes enormous power and serenity. Imagine the impression it must have made in the turbulent 1500s.

Visual unity cannot be achieved without a great deal of repetition in large architectural compositions. The court of honor at Hôtel des Invalides (fig. 1.54) measures 300 by 200 feet and is surrounded by two tiers of open galleries on all sides. Thousands could and still can watch parades and ceremonies from there in relative comfort. The austerity of the design is due less to its regularity than to the military nature of the program.

Regularity of a less severe character can be experienced in coordinated street designs such as those in Bath, London, and Paris, among other cities. Subtle variations repeated at regular intervals introduce rhythm and reduce the fatigue induced by monotony. In many cases, the ground floor is formed by arches flexible enough to accommodate one or two stories and to satisfy a variety of needs: shops, vehicular and pedestrian entrances without altering the unity of the wall (figs. 1.55, 1.56).

The regularity sought in classical architecture places strong demands on the architect, who must balance requirements of function, structure, and visual harmony. Sometimes the visual imperatives for symmetry and regularity require that a door or a window be placed on a facade where it is not needed. The conflict is then resolved by the addition of what is called, erroneously, a "false opening." A better term would be "metaphorical opening." On an ancillary building at the chateau in Cheverny, a blind arch is included to visually organize the elevation of a pavilion (fig. 1.57). Similarly, in a design for a stable (fig.1.58), the only necessary opening is surrounded by as many as eight non-functional openings. A two-dimensional representation of an animated and balanced facade seemed more satisfying than a blank wall with a single opening, whose asymmetrical position would have been disturbing.

1.55. Place Dauphine.
Reconstitution of the facade.

1.56. Eighteenth-century facade,
Rue de Condé, Paris.

1.57. Outbuildings at Cheverny, probably
built in the seventeenth century.

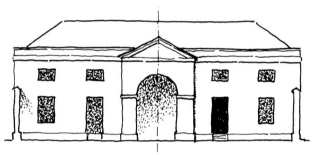

1.58. The only functional opening in this design is the door to the right of the
central arch.

Another solution to the conflict between function and the need for regularity is to make an opening as unobtrusive as possible. "Invisible doors" are nowhere more common than in Florence, where, as an example, a door disguised as a pier is adjacent to another disguised as rusticated stone (fig. 1.59).

Blind windows and invisible doors are part of a larger issue, that of trompe-l'oeil, which early modernists regarded as an ethical issue. In spite of its name, trompe-l'oeil rarely fools the eye. Its purpose is not to create illusions but to induce a mood through allusions.

This discussion illustrates the strategies with which classical architecture ensures visual order. In the final analysis, regularity is one of the more effective ways to achieve peace and balance. It is essentially a rhythmical repetition of one or more elements, and its most common form is the arcade or the colonnade, which can assume any character, grand or modest, simple or complex, severe or friendly.

1.59. Town house in Florence with doors disguised as masonry, invisible when closed.

CHAPTER 2

THE LANGUAGE OF CLASSICAL ARCHITECTURE: FIFTEEN THINGS TO KNOW

It is common sense to use a time-tested body of knowledge to cope with present-day exigencies.
—DEMETRI PORPHYRIOS

A lifetime of experiment, observation, and reflection is not too long to master the subtleties, the refinements, and the wealth of the classical language. At the same time, a perfect knowledge of the theory alone does not guarantee good design. The aspiring classical architect should try to design as early as possible. It should be encouraging to know that good results can be achieved in a short time with a limited body of knowledge. This chapter presents the basic classical elements and the rules that control their use, so that the reader can learn to design small and simple classical buildings or portions of larger ones. Even at an early stage of the learning process, it should be possible to satisfy the expectations of a capable classical architect.

The diagrams of classical elements that follow are accurate, but they are only diagrams, intended to focus on the essentials. Do not conclude that classical architecture is crude. The geometric and proportional relationships between the parts are simple, but they are rigorous. They must be well understood to be useful. Only fundamentals are presented here. More sophisticated studies are presented in treatises, which include detailed comparative plates of the orders. By all means look at them: not only are they informative, but they also are things of beauty.

THE MODULE

There is no question that classical architecture begins and ends with the orders. Even when the orders are not visible, they are always implied. The orders must be understood and learned first because they embody the very essence of classical architecture. They can be studied sequentially, beginning with the simpler ones, the Tuscan and the Doric, then proceeding to the more complex ones, the elegant Ionic, the exuberant Corinthian, and finally the ambiguous Composite. Or it may be easier to study them concurrently. What the orders have in common is simple enough, and the differences between them reveal their distinct personalities.

The largest component of a column is the shaft, situated between the base and the capital. It is almost, but not quite, a cylindrical form. Although the proportions of the shaft have been subjected to subtle adjustments by experienced architects, an ideal ratio between the height of the shaft and its diameter has been adopted for each order. This is not an arbitrary proportion; it has been arrived at through trial and error by some of the greatest architects over centuries of experiments.

One of the reasons for a different ratio for each order is to give architects a choice. At one end of the range is the sober Tuscan and its sturdy proportions, and at the other is the refined Corinthian with its slender shaft.

The height of classical columns can vary from 10 to 200 feet. Since classical aesthetics depend largely on orderliness, it became necessary to devise a system to coordinate all the parts of a building. A basic unit was chosen for this system, independently of actual measurements, which might be metric or based on feet and inches. The unit is called the *module*, and it is always equal to half the diameter of the shaft where it is widest. This occurs at one third of its height from the bottom; the shaft is always narrower at the top, which gives the impression of a gentle bulging, or swelling, called entasis. The module coordinates the entire classical vocabulary in a self-referential system that is used at any scale.

By consensus, the height of a Tuscan shaft is equal to 14 modules, or seven times its diameter. The height of a Doric shaft is 16 modules, or eight times the diameter. The height of the Ionic is 18 modules, or nine times the diameter. The height of a Corinthian or Composite shaft is 20 modules, or ten times the diameter.

ENTASIS

Although subtle, entasis is critical. Only the lower third of the shaft is a true cylinder; the upper two thirds taper upward in an almost imperceptible curve reducing the diameter to 5/6 of its largest dimension. In the Ionic, Corinthian, and Composite, tapering occurs in the lower third as well, but downwards, and to a less pronounced extent. In all cases, the shaft is wider at the bottom than at the top.

Why entasis? Why such a refinement? As a metaphor for the human form, a classical column must have something of the organic in it. Without entasis, a shaft could not be said truly to have a beginning, a middle and an end. Entasis is a formal acknowledgment by the shaft of the base

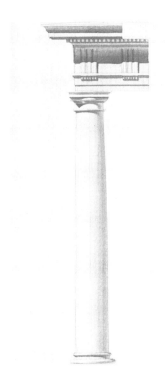

2.1. Corner column in the Doric order. Student exercise at the Ecole des Beaux-Arts, 1950s.

2.2. Columns without entasis on a newer building in Boston.

and the capital and of the load-bearing role of the column. Although essential, entasis must be barely visible (fig. 2.1). Excessive entasis looks worse than none (fig. 2.2). Precise methods for drawing the entasis are included in most treatises.

2.3. Fluted Ionic columns at Rosehill Mansion, Geneva, New York, c. 1835. Architect unknown.

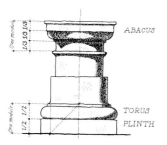

2.4. Tuscan order: base and capital.

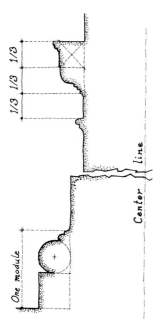

2.5. Roman doric order: base and capital shown in profile; compare with fig. 2.4.

BASE AND CAPITAL

Columns are either structural or suggestive of structural support. It is not enough for a structure to be reliable; it must also look reassuring. The base and the capital are the beginning and the end of the column, and their main function is to negotiate a harmonious transition between the vertical shaft and the horizontal elements above and below.

Bases are wider than they are high, as if they were half-crushed under the weight of the shaft. Whatever their design, they measure one module in height. Capitals also are one module in height, with the exception of the Corinthian and the Composite, which look like an efflorescence and express upward thrust. This is consistent with the more slender proportions of the shaft, which suggests a stem. Elongation is further reinforced by the vertical lines of fluting (fig. 2.3), more common in the Corinthian than in the other orders, and never found in the Tuscan.

Base and capital also negotiate the transition between the geometry of the plan, most often based on a rectangular grid, and the section of the shaft, which is a circle. To reconcile these geometries, square elements are found at the top and bottom of the complete column. The base begins with the square *plinth*, and the capital ends with another square, the *abacus*. The parts between plinth and abacus are all circular in section.

On the Tuscan order, the base is divided into two parts of nearly equal height, the plinth and the *torus*, which is circular in plan. The capital, more elaborate than the base, is made of three parts of equal height (fig. 2.4).

The Tuscan order is a Roman derivation of the original Doric invented by the Greeks, with which no base was used at all, as can be seen at the Parthenon, for example. The base of the Roman Tuscan may be omitted to emphasize strength and simplicity. The Roman Doric order is very similar to the Roman Tuscan. The base and capital are shown in figure 2.5.

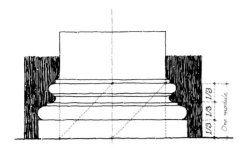

2.6. Attic base.

2.7. Attic base adapted for use as a pedestal for a bust.

There are only two essential designs for the bases of all the orders: the Doric base and the Attic base, which can be used with both the Ionic and Corinthian orders and is often substituted for the more complex and varied bases specifically designed for them. The Attic design has the advantages of clarity and simplicity (fig. 2.6). There is something so satisfying in the rhythmic alternation of curved and straight lines in its profile that the Attic base has been adapted for other purposes. With some changes in the proportions but none in the basic design, it has, for instance, become a nearly perfect pedestal for small busts or heads displayed indoors (fig. 2.7).

Although the Ionic and Corinthian capitals are exceptionally rich and beautiful, their formal structure is so simple that it can be captured in diagrams. While both orders mark the transition from the vertical to the horizontal with a flourish, the Ionic emphasizes the horizontal. The height of the Ionic capital (fig. 2.8) is one module, not including the elegant spiral volutes, and the overall width is almost three modules. The distance between the "eyes" of the volutes is two modules, and the ratio between the width of a volute and the distance between a pair is 3 : 5.

The main thrust of the Corinthian is vertical, which makes it appear taller than it is wide. The Corinthian capital is three modules wide at the top, and its height is determined by drawing lines at a 45-degree angle from the top to the shaft (fig. 2.9).

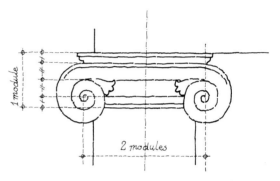

2.8. An approximate method for drawing the Ionic capital.

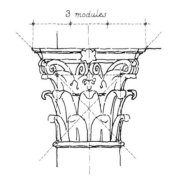

2.9. Diagram of a Corinthian capital.

2.10. Ionic entablature at the Château de Bénouville, Normandy, 1768–77. Claude Nicolas Ledoux.

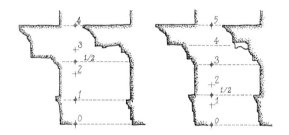

2.11. Profiles of different entablatures and their proportional subdivisions. From left to right, Tuscan, Doric, Ionic, and Corinthian.

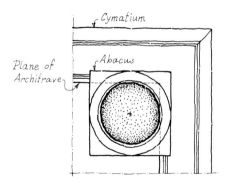

2.12. Horizontal section through a Tuscan column, looking up: shaft and architrave are perfectly aligned.

ENTABLATURE

The entablature (fig. 2.10) completes an order and is designed especially for it. Its height is always equal to a quarter of the column height. In spite of its major role and its considerable mass, the entablature is often overlooked by inexperienced designers.

Like the column, the entablature is composed of three parts, the architrave, the frieze, and the cornice. The architrave acts as a lintel, sitting directly on the capitals and spanning the intervals between them, and its structural function is expressed by horizontal striations. The uppermost element of the entablature is the cornice, which caps the order and projects forward to protect it. The third element, the frieze, is inserted between the architrave and the cornice. It is probably there that transverse beams rested on the lintels of early buildings. Since the frieze is a "soft" element between two "hard" ones, it is sometimes omitted, with the result that the entablature becomes slimmer. The frieze may also be made more assertive by having it bulge out (in which case it is called a *pulvinated* frieze) or by having it carry rich ornamentation.

Compare the profiles of the entablatures (fig. 2.11), which determine the character of each order. Moving from Tuscan to Corinthian, the height of the architrave increases as the height of the cornice decreases. There is a graphic method to obtain the relative height of the elements. Divide the entablature of the Tuscan and Doric into four parts; one part becomes the architrave while the rest is divided equally between the frieze and the cornice. For the Ionic and the Corinthian, divide the entablature in five parts; the cornice will take two parts. The frieze and the architrave will divide the rest equally between them.

Columns are always rigorously aligned with the face of the frieze and architrave. In other words, if this plane were expanded, it would be tangent to the upper part of the columns (fig. 2.12).

An entablature is always supported at a corner; it must never be cantilevered. This is an absolute rule. An entablature may move forward and backward, but it must always be accompanied by an element on which it sits squarely, whether it be a column, a pilaster or even a wall. At the Chiesa Nuova in Rome (fig. 2.13), the entablature moves forward from the wall to the top of pilasters and then back again to the wall. An entablature directly supported by a wall must project slightly outward so that a shadow line indicates where the wall ends and the entablature begins.

The design of corners gives classical architects the opportunity for a wide range of inventive solutions—all within the rules. Looking up and down a corner of the palace at Versailles (fig. 2.14), the diversity of solutions is such that the eye is always challenged but never confused.

Corners should be seen as "solid" in contrast to "soft" facades. In masonry buildings, corners must give an impression of strength while the facades, which are penetrated by many openings, will be more inviting. Modern architects have often done the reverse in order to dematerialize corners. In many of his buildings, however, Mies van der Rohe used steel and glass in a classical way (fig. 2.15). It should not be forgotten that the most admired architects of the twentieth century were very much aware of the classical language and classical design solutions.

The cornice (fig. 2.16) is the part of the entablature that most requires close attention. The cornice projects from the vertical plane of the frieze and architrave and is therefore highly visible. Like the column and the entablature, the cornice is divided in three parts. The middle part, or *corona*, is a bare, vertical surface exposed to full light. When the sun is out, it casts a significant shadow. The *sima* above and the *bedmold* below the corona are both angled and are more or less in the shade. In the Ionic,

2.13. Chiesa Nuova, Rome, begun in 1575 after a design of Giovanni Battista Soria. An entablature moves back and forth with its support.

2.14. Royal palace at Versailles, begun 1661. Louis Le Vau and J. H. Mansart. A corner emphasized through iteration.

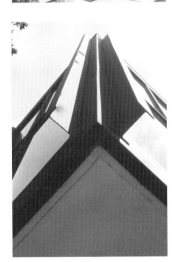

2.15. A corner of the Museum of Fine Arts, Houston, 1954 and 1974. Mies van der Rohe.

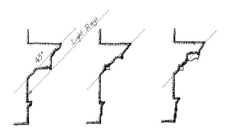

2.16. *From left to right, the profiles of the Doric, Ionic, and Corinthian cornices.*

2.17. *Determining the projection of the cornice from the wall. From left to right, the profiles of the Tuscan, Ionic, and Corinthian entablatures, shown in cross section.*

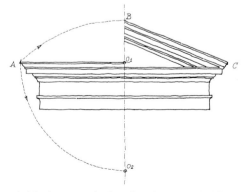

2.18. *Processing plant at the Royal Saltworks, Arc-et-Senans, France, 1775–79. Claude Nicholas Ledoux. Used here without columns, a pediment glorifies the center of a facade.*

2.19. *Method for determining the slope of a pediment. On the left side, the entablature used as a starting point; on the right, the pediment generated from the entablature.*

the projecting edge divides the cornice in half. The dividing line is lower in the Doric and higher in the Corinthian, making the latter more delicate and giving the former a heavier, stronger aspect.

The projection of the cornice is determined by a 45-degree angle from the top of the frieze (fig. 2.17). R. A. Cordingley, in his introduction to Normand's *Parallel of the Orders of Architecture*, suggests a projection of 3/4 of the module for the Tuscan, Ionic, and Corinthian, but architects tend to prefer a graphic method over a mathematical formula.

The designers of canonical classical forms paid great attention to profiles, that is, the forms in space seen in elevation or in section. Unfortunately, the full effect of these forms is not conveyed by line drawings. Perspective drawings are more successful, but they are not accurate; dimensions cannot be taken from them. A more effective method is to use a light source and draw the resulting shading. This technique was used empirically until the eighteenth-century geometer Gaspard Monge invented a scientific method to draw shading. His method allows a trained eye to derive accurate and complete information and an untrained eye to perceive the third dimension. Without shading, planes and curved surfaces would appear equally flat in a picture.

Monge proposed the angle of the diagonal of a cube, or 36 degrees, 16 minutes, which is seen at 45 degrees in plan as well as in elevation. This convention confirms the significance of the heavy shadow cast by the Tuscan cornice, compared with that of the Ionic or the Corinthian cornice.

PEDIMENT

A pediment interrupts the entablature to emphasize a special place, usually at the center of a facade (fig. 2.18). The triangular shape reinforces the vertical thrust already suggested by the columns or piers underneath. Since the dynamic effect is powerful, the pediment should be used with moderation and only where appropriate.

The slope of a pediment can be determined with a simple geometric operation (fig. 2.19). Place the point of a compass on 0_1, where the axis intersects the top line of the cornice. Trace a curve from A, at the extremity of the cornice, to 0_2 on the axis. Place the compass on 0_2 and trace a curve from A to B. This determines the apex of the pediment. The slope of the pediment is obtained by joining B to A or C.

The profile of the existing cornice is not affected by the introduction of a pediment, but the sima is now sloping to form the top member of the pediment. In the process, the fillet underneath is duplicated so that it retains its horizontal position while its clone follows the sima in its new sloping position. The meeting point of the two fillets is the hinge between the horizontal cornice and the new cornice of the pediment (fig. 2.20). Along with the sima and the fillet, the corona and the bedmold underneath are duplicated so that there are now two cornices. But in the end, the sima belongs with the pediment, not with the horizontal cornice (fig. 2.21).

The relationship between pediment and entablature is described here in such detail because it is a remarkably ingenious design solution. Since the correct relationship between pediment and entablature is constant for all the orders, it is important to understand it well. The slope of a pediment should never be increased. It can and should be reduced when the width of a facade would require a pediment of great height, since its mass would appear to crush the building underneath (fig. 2.22). A variant is the curved, or segmental, pediment (fig. 2.19). Instead of joining A to B with a straight line, use the curve shown as a dotted line between the same two points (fig. 2.23).

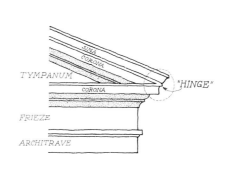
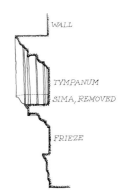

2.20. Cornice and pediment articulated around a hinge point. The stippled area identifies the original bedmold and its clone.

2.21. Cross section of an entablature carrying a pediment. The sima has been eliminated from the horizontal cornice to form the cap of the pediment.

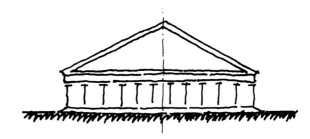

2.22. A pediment that is too large will overwhelm a building by its excessive mass.

2.23. The Brick Market, Newport, Rhode Island, 1761–72. Peter Harrison. Curved and straight (triangular) pediments alternate here.

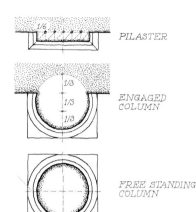

PILASTER

ENGAGED
COLUMN

FREE STANDING
COLUMN

2.24. The three column variations: freestanding, engaged in the wall, or pilaster applied to the wall.

2.25. St. Peter's Square, Rome, begun 1656. Bernini used 280 columns, each 50 feet high, to unify a huge and complex urban space. The architect combined Doric columns with an Ionic entablature.

2.26. Colonnaded galleries of the Palazzo della Ragione, Vicenza, begun in 1549. Andrea Palladio.

VARIATIONS ON THE COLUMN

Of the three forms the column might assume, the freestanding one is the most familiar. The other two are the engaged column and the pilaster. With an engaged column (fig. 2.24), the proportion of exposed to hidden is important. Revealing only half of the column gives an impression of uncertainty, as if the column could not decide whether to be part of the wall or not. When two thirds are exposed, the column nearly appears to be whole, which is more satisfying. The wall in which the column is engaged should be thicker than the column to avoid the impression that the load is carried by the column rather than the wall.

With a pilaster, the profiles of shaft, base, and capital remain the same, but the horizontal curves are replaced with straight lines so that all horizontal cross sections will be rectangular. The normal ratio between the width of the pilaster and its depth is 1 : 6. This is all that is needed since a pilaster is a mere suggestion of a column. For the same reason, entasis is unnecessary and the width remains constant from top to bottom.

Columns, freestanding, engaged, or in the form of pilasters, may be used together as long as they are of the same order, have the same height, and are rigorously aligned. Their common purpose is to ensure regularity and unity in a building, or a portion of a building. It would defeat that purpose to alter a colonnade beyond these restrictions (fig. 2.25).

Combining two sets of columns of different heights in the same composition presents a number of difficulties that have been successfully overcome in the past. Two famous examples are Michelangelo's twin palaces on the Campidoglio in Rome, and Palladio's Palazzo della Ragione, also known as the Basilica, in Vicenza (fig. 2.26). The latter is the more classical of the two. When two sets of columns alternate, the height of one set should not be half of the other. The best rela-

2.27. A corner of the entry building at the Royal Saltworks. In the Doric order, the spacing of columns is determined by mutules, triglyphs, and metopes or by denticles.

2.28. Touro Synagogue, Newport, Rhode Island, c. 1763. Peter Harrison. An Ionic porch showing the relationship of Ionic capitals and modillions. The modified Ionic capitals are of the "Scamozzi" type. Note how the rear columns are engaged in the back wall.

tionship is two to three, which suggests a closer kinship between the two sets.

COLONNADES

To say that a colonnade is a row of columns is true, but it is an incomplete description, for colonnades come in many forms. Double, triple, or quadruple rows of columns produce very different effects. Columns may be paired off; they may alternate with piers or be placed in front of walls; columns may be joined by arches as *arcuated* colonnades or by lintels as *trabeated* colonnades; arches can also alternate with lintels. As noted earlier, the purpose of a colonnade is to regularize and dignify a wall, a building, or an outdoor room. That is why a colonnade must consist of identical columns of constant height or, at the most, of two sizes, and the intervals between them must obey clear rules.

How far should the columns be from one another in a colonnade? Architects and scholars have been arguing for centuries over the ideal spacing, and they have often disagreed.

Intercolumniation is the formal term for the subject. What is certain is that columns may not be so close that their capitals interfere with one another. As for the maximum distance, a square bay is most likely to be structurally unsound, and it will look precarious. A ratio of 1: 2 (the equivalent of two superposed squares) looks reassuring. So does a narrower bay. Paired columns alternating with wider bays introduce variety in a colonnade without making a disorderly impression.

Other restrictions make the discussion of ideal proportions somewhat irrelevant. In the Doric order, the spacing of columns is contingent upon brackets, called *mutules*, situated under the corona. Mutules match the *triglyphs*, which alternate with *metopes* in the frieze (fig. 2.27). Triglyphs and mutules are one module wide and metopes are $1^{1}/_{2}$ module square. Since triglyphs are centered on columns, the options are limited to $2^{1}/_{2}$, 5, or $7^{1}/_{2}$ modules. With the Ionic and the Corinthian, spacing depends on the *modillions*, another type of bracket, also centered on columns (fig. 2.28). The Ionic order does enjoy more flexibility when the elements that regulate

2.29. The double colonnade at the Grand Trianon, Versailles, 1687–90. Robert de Cotte for J. H. Mansart.

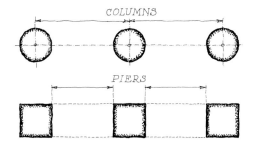

2.30. Measurement of bay widths when points of support are columns or piers.

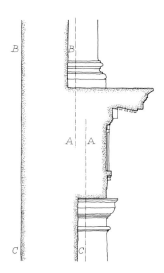

2.31. Two tiers of engaged columns. The base of an upper order must be in the same fictitious vertical plane as the entablature underneath. This precludes the column axes from being aligned (A-A.) As a consequence, the wall must be thicker in the lower tier (C-C) than in the upper one (B-B).

the spacing of columns are not modillions but *denticles*, little cubes found under the corona.

In order to sustain the regularity of the colonnade, the spacing of columns must be either constant, as in A-A-A, or consist of two different alternating widths, as in A-B-A-B. The colonnade designed at the suggestion of Le Nôtre for the Grand Trianon in Versailles is an example of the latter (fig. 2.29). Any further subdivision would result in confusion and unsettle the observer.

Measurements between columns are taken from axis to axis because the curved surface of the columns combined with entasis makes any other measurement meaningless. Only where piers are used instead of columns do the intervals between structural supports have a definite form that can be accurately measured (fig. 2.30).

SUPERPOSING THE ORDERS

The rules controlling the vertical relationship of columns are simple. There are a few cases where the same order is used in a two-tier design but superposition usually involves different orders. The sequence, sensibly enough, always places a heavier order under a more slender one.

As noted, it is essential that the front plane of an entablature, i.e., the plane of architrave and frieze, be perfectly aligned with the upper part of the shaft (fig. 2.31). This rule also applies to the base of an upper order and the entablature of the order underneath. Since a base is wider than a shaft, the entablatures of superposed orders cannot be in the same plane, and the order on top will recede substantially from the one underneath. If this occurs two or three times, the wall against which the orders are applied will be considerably thicker at the base than at the top. But that is logical since more material is required at the base to support the compounded weight of the building.

The rule of decreasing section was also applied by Mies van der Rohe in some of his high-rise buildings, even though there are other ways to

2.32. Apartment building, Nun's Island, near Montreal, 1969. Mies van der Rohe. The section of the steel supports is reduced above the third regular story and again above the eighth story.

2.33. The central bay of the chateau at Anet, west of Paris, 1455–1555. Philibert Delorme. Re-erected at the Ecole des Beaux-Arts, Paris, 1804. An elegant sequence of superposed Doric, Ionic, and Corinthian twin columns. Although receding towards the wall, the axes of superposed columns remain in the same vertical plane perpendicular to the wall.

solve the problem of compounded weight in steel or concrete structures (fig. 2.32). Mies may have done this for visual effect, in homage to the classical tradition that he knew well.

Another important issue is the relative height of superposed columns. Should their height be equal, shorter, or taller? J. N. L. Durand, in his *Leçons d'Architecture*, stipulates that, if the columns are the same order, those in the upper tier must be shorter. If the columns are different orders, they may be the same height. But his main concern is with the diameters: the maximum diameter of an upper column must be equal to or less than the minimum diameter of the column below (fig. 2.33).

2.34. The triumphal arch at the Tuileries Gardens, formerly the gate to the Royal Palace, Paris, 1806–8. Charles Percier and Pierre Fontaine.

PEDESTAL

Pedestals are placed under columns to increase their vertical reach without increasing their bulk. They may be considered an integral part of the order (fig. 2.34). The height of the pedestal is one-third of that of a column, regardless of the order (fig. 2.35). The width of the die is deter-

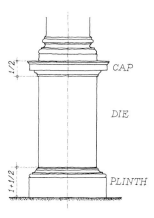

2.35. A pedestal supporting a column.

2.36. *Villa Rotonda, near Vicenza, 1566. Andrea Palladio. One of eight simplified pedestals, each supporting a statue. What appears to be a pedestal stretches out to form the base of the entire building. The design of the attic story resembles that of a pedestal; it can be glimpsed above the entablature.*

2.37. *Design variations on the pedestal motif at the Tuileries, Paris.*

mined by the base of the column; its height may be reduced but not increased. The cap is a simplified cornice, one half module in height; the plinth is a module and a half in height.

A pedestal may be expanded laterally when it is placed under twin columns (fig. 2.33). As noted earlier, a pedestal becomes a *stylobate* when stretched out to serve as the base of an entire building and a *dado* when defining an interior wall. Another application of the extended pedestal is the *attic*, a plain upper story that terminates a building above an entablature. Palladio used the pedestal motif as a base for the entire building in his design for the Villa Rotonda (fig. 2.36), and again for the upper story of the main block.

The shape of a pedestal can be given to many elements—chimneys, for example. Freestanding pedestals can animate gardens, and they are often used to define outdoor spaces (fig. 2.37).

BALUSTRADES AND PARAPETS

Balustrades are familiar because of their distinctive balusters, but a *parapet* is a solid form of balustrade, and its design is very similar. A parapet is, in fact, a stretched out pedestal. Parapets are used in place of a very long balustrade (fig. 2.38). This may be on a ridge in a garden, where it would be extravagant to line up hundreds of balusters with so many other elements competing for visual interest. In either form, the frame is made of a die and a cap stretched between consecutive pedestals, which retain their block-like shape. Balusters are inserted between the die and the cap, and the latter forms the handrail.

The width of the balusters and the space between them should be approximately equal. Increasing the distance between balusters inevitably results in an unpleasant, weak appearance. A row of more than twelve balusters looks relentless; to relieve the monotony, residual dice are inserted at regular intervals (fig. 2.39). These do not affect the continuity of the handrail, and no ornaments should be placed on them. Sometimes half-balusters are placed against dice and pedestals at each end of a row. A long stretch of parapet should be broken up with pedestals at regular intervals. To emphasize a rhythmic effect, ornaments such as urns, vases, or even statues can be placed on the pedestals.

Balustrades are ornamental design elements that should only be used on buildings or in their vicinity. Their practical use is to prevent falls, but they are also used on inaccessible roofs to soften the transition between the solid mass of the building and the sky above.

The baluster, an invention of the Renaissance, is an interesting motif because it is seen at close range and can be touched with the hand. Although there are many slight variations, there are constants (figs. 2.40, 2.41). The height of a baluster is three times the width, measured at its greatest, in a, b, and c. This dimension also controls the thickness of the residual die. The width of the baluster is reduced by half in three places, d, e, and f, where the baluster is at its most narrow.

The handrail is about a foot wide, or a third of the balustrade's height on the upside (g). It is logical to increase the height of a balustrade on the downside (h), but no specific ratio can be given because it depends on the circumstance.

We have seen that the width of a baluster varies between one and two. If we divide these extremes in two and four parts respectively, six parts give us the depth of both die and handrail. Eight parts give us the maximum depth of the pedestal at the level of plinth and cap.

When a balustrade is used between columns on pedestals, the height of the pedestals must conform to that of the balustrade, even if that violates the rule that prescribes a height of one third of a column for the pedestal (fig. 2.42).

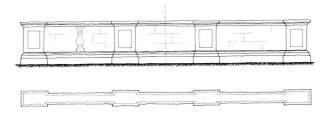

2.38. Plan and elevation of a parapet. Cap and plinth are stretched from one pedestal to the next. A thin wall replaces balusters.

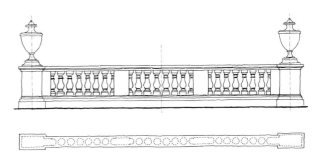

2.39. Plan and elevation of a balustrade. Residual dice are interspersed at regular intervals for visual relief and stability.

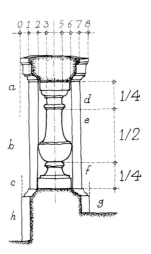

2.40. Cross section of a balustrade, showing a typical baluster.

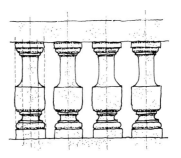

2.41. Seventeenth-century balustrade at the chateau of Bussy-Rabutin in Burgundy. The horizontal cross section of the balusters is square from top to bottom.

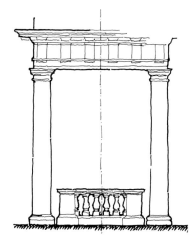

2.42. If a balustrade is necessary in a colonnade, the height of the pedestals is determined by the height of the balustrade.

2.43. A balustrade should nearly fill the space between columns, but it must not touch them.

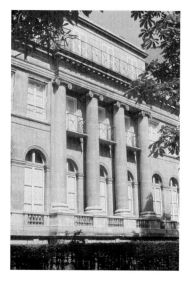

2.44. Town house, Avenue Gabriel, Paris, 1780. Lemoine de Couzon. Unobtrusive metal guardrails are appropriate on the three balconies added at the second story at a later date. Metal brackets also support the thin stone slabs.

Since columns are the preeminent classical element, they should stand in proud isolation. If pedestals cannot be used in a colonnade where a balustrade is necessary, there must be no actual contact between the two elements. Each section of balustrade must be complete in itself between columns; in other words, it must begin and end with a pedestal. The space between balustrade and columns may be narrow, but it is essential that there be one (fig. 2.43). In cases where such a treatment would seem heavy-handed, a delicate metal guardrail may be substituted for the heavier stone balustrade; if it touches the columns, it will hardly be noticeable. This solution was frequent in the decades around 1800 (fig. 2.44).

OPENINGS IN WALLS

So many classical doors and windows are in the proportion of 1 : 2 that the format of two superposed squares can be called the fundamental classical opening. The reason for this ubiquitous proportion is that it combines simplicity and clarity with the ideal frame for a human being (fig. 2.45).

The practical purpose of doors is entry and egress, but they also present an opportunity to celebrate human beings that classical architects have seized with relish. The Philadelphia architect Alvin Holm summed it up when he declared that everyone who walks through a classical door feels like a hero. Many beautiful classical facades rely on nothing but the happy effects of proportions in their openings (fig. 2.46).

Since openings are perceived as pictures, it is natural to surround them with frames. Frames add to the beauty of doors and windows and to the significance of facades. The typical frame (fig. 2.47) is adapted from the entablature design; depending on the degree of refinement intended, a frame includes one or more parts of a diminutive entablature. A simple frame con-

2.45. A young man framed by a double-square doorway in an early nineteenth-century French house.

2.46. The elegant windows at the Chateau de Bénouville are a study in classical restraint.

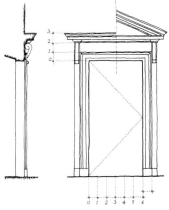

2.47. The frame of a canonical opening.

2.48. One of four pairs of windows on the main block of the Villa Rotonda. Note the consoles.

sists of an architrave wrapped around the four sides of a window or three sides of a door. In more elaborate designs, a cornice is added above, directly on top of the architrave or separated from it by a frieze. The frieze might be richly ornamented or consist of the bare wall surface running between the architrave and a "floating" cornice above. A good proportion for the width of the architrave is 1/6 the width of the opening. The same dimension may be given to the frieze and to the cornice if they are present. A pediment may be added to the cornice, and its form may be triangular, segmental, or "broken." The latter creates a fine setting for a bust or other precious ornament. This is a valid approach for both exterior and interior walls.

An opening may be enhanced by adding a pair of *consoles* under the cornice, which must be lengthened if it is to sit squarely on them. Consoles are narrower than the architrave (fig. 2.48). It is indeed a rare classical building that does not include openings in the 1 : 2 proportion, but classical openings come in other proportions, usually decreasing in height, and possibly in width, as they are further removed from the piano nobile (see fig. 1.46).

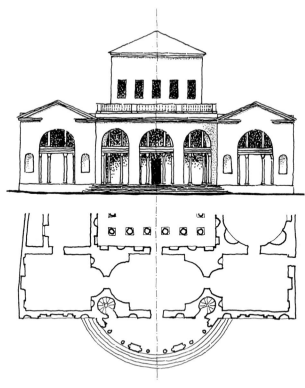

2.49. Assembly Rooms in York, 1730. Lord Burlington. Thermal windows let light into the building. The columns underneath are purely ornamental, and the curved wall in the center is a screen.

2.50. Chiswick House, near London, 1725–29. Lord Burlington with William Kent. Palladian window with a thermal window above in the drum.

Circular windows, or *oculi*, have their place in the classical vocabulary. Two other designs must be mentioned for their significance and striking appearance. One is called the thermal window because it made its first appearance in Roman baths (fig. 2.49). It has the advantage of admitting light into a room without affecting the lower part of the wall. The other is the Palladian window, which consists of a three-light opening with the middle one round-headed and wider than the lateral ones (fig. 2.50). It is spectacular and should be used sparingly.

ARCHES AND VAULTS

Throughout history, the challenge of covering enclosed spaces has been met in a variety of ways. A wall could be built relatively easily by piling stone upon stone, but spanning a large space required ingenuity, especially when the width of the space exceeded the length of available timber. The answer was the arch and then the vault, brilliant and paradoxical inventions that make use of small objects—bricks or stones—to cover large spaces.

A vault can be made by placing a series of identical arches side by side (fig. 2.51). Arches and vaults can assume many shapes, but classical builders have favored pure geometric forms. Usually, the formal vocabulary is limited to the straight line with the "flat arch" and the semicircle with the *barrel vault*. A number of barrel vaults intersecting one another at right angles can cover a series of square or rectangular spaces. Four supports are required for each unit but a support can serve up to four vaults. This type of vaulting is called *cross vaulting* (figs. 2.52, 2.53).

Vaults transmit considerable loads to their supports, but we perceive them in an entirely different way: they seem to "soar." In spite of their simplicity, or more probably because of it, barrel vaults and cross vaults have produced

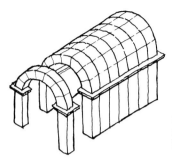

2.51. Diagram of a semicircular arch and a barrel vault.

2.52. Two intersecting barrel vaults create a configuration called a cross vault.

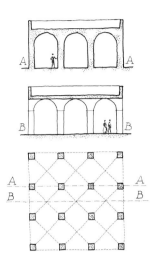

2.53. Plan and cross sections of nine squares covered by cross vaults. The vaults are formed by the intersection of three barrel vaults running left to right and three others running front to back. The six intersecting barrel vaults rest on sixteen supports. The cross section A-A is drawn through a row of piers and the cross section B-B is drawn between two rows of piers.

2.54. Arc de Triomphe, Paris, begun in 1806. J. F. T. Chalgrin. Barrel vault.

2.55. Panthéon, Paris, 1764. Jacques-Germain Soufflot. An elliptical vault with penetrations in the crypt.

spectacular results (fig. 2.54). Elliptical vaults take less vertical space, but the lateral stress on the walls is enormous (fig. 2.55). There are more complex vaults, but the simple ones described here can satisfy many design problems.

THE DOME

The dynamics of spaces defined by barrel vaults and cross vaults can be said to be mainly horizontal. A dome, on the other hand, creates a vertical pull: we tend to stop and look up when we enter a domed room. Many domes cover a square space or, more accurately, a cubic space. The reconciliation of the two forms presents an interesting problem which, in classical architecture, is usually solved as follows:

Consider a cube surmounted by a half-sphere. The diameter is such that the sphere is in contact with the four upper corners ABCD of

2.56a. A cube with half a sphere resting on it at four points ABCD.

2.56b. The intersection of the half-sphere by the extended faces of the cube leaves four semi-circles. Between them are the pendentives.

2.56c. A dome is usually supported by a drum resting on pendentives.

2.56d. A drum and a lantern enhance the uplifting impression of a dome.

2.56e. The saucer dome is made visible by the simple insertion of a circular molding above the arches.

2.57. A comparison between a dome over pendentives and a pendentive or sail vault dome. The dotted line on the right represents the artificial boundary of a saucer dome.

the cube (fig. 2.56a). If we extend the vertical faces of the cube and allow them to section off portions of the sphere, four semicircles appear. What remains of the spherical surface is a dome, called a *pendentive* dome or *sail vault*. The pendentives themselves are four spherical triangles (fig. 2.56b). A smaller dome is generally built on top of the pendentives, and in most cases a cylinder, referred to as a *drum*, is inserted between the dome and the pendentives. The drum is a good place for windows, and the heightening of the interior space greatly enhances the effect (fig. 2.56c). Frequently, another opening is created at the very top of the dome for additional light, and a *lantern* is placed over it to keep the weather

out. This is a formal necessity. The intersection of the vertical axis with the outer surface of the dome is critical and must be visible. The exterior appearance of a dome is generally much improved by the addition of a lantern (fig. 2.56d). The *saucer dome* is a direct application of the pendentive dome. When a molding tangent to the top of the pendentives is placed on the spherical surface, the illusion of a distinct dome is created (figs. 2.56e, 2.57).

Not surprisingly, the symbolism of the cube, representing the earth, and the symbolism of the sphere, representing the universe, have made the combination of the two forms a natural for the design of sacred buildings (figs. 2.58, 2.59, 2.60).

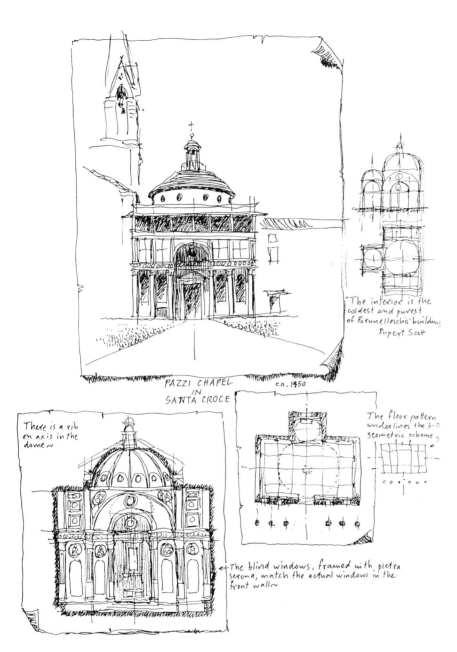

"The interior is the coldest and purest of Brunelleschi's building
Rupert Scott

PAZZI CHAPEL
IN
SANTA CROCE   ca. 1450

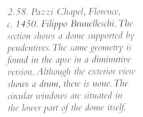

There is a rib on axis in the dome~

The floor pattern underlines the 3-D geometric scheme

←The blind windows, framed with pietra serena, match the actual windows in the front wall~

2.58. Pazzi Chapel, Florence,
c. 1450. Filippo Brunelleschi. The
section shows a dome supported by
pendentives. The same geometry is
found in the apse in a diminutive
version. Although the exterior view
shows a drum, there is none. The
circular windows are situated in
the lower part of the dome itself.

2.59. S. Maria della Consolazione, Todi,
near Perugia, begun in 1509. Attributed
to Bramante or Baldassarre Peruzzi.
A remarkable essay in pure geometry, it
consists of a cube surmounted by a cylinder
capped by a half-sphere. Semi-domes are
applied to all four lateral faces of the cube.

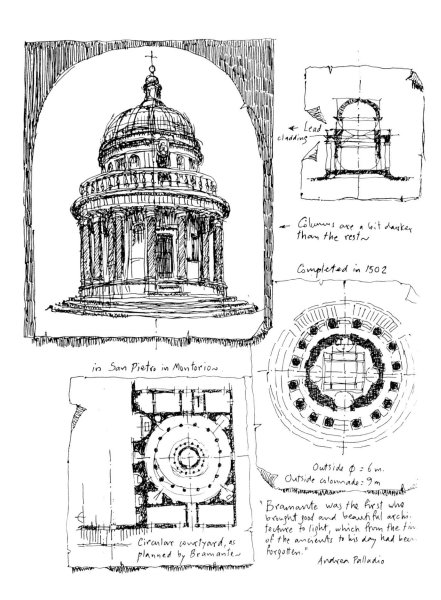

← Lead
cladding

← Columns are a bit darker
than the rest~

Completed in 1502

in San Pietro in Montorio.

Outside Ø = 6 m.
Outside colonnade = 9 m.

"Bramante was the first who
brought good and beautiful architecture to light, which from the tim
of the ancients to his day had been
forgotten."

Andrea Palladio

Circular courtyard, as
planned by Bramante~

2.60. Tempietto at S. Pietro in
Montorio, Rome, completed in
1502. Bramante.

2.61. Pendentive domes at the Mercato
Vecchio, Florence. 1568. Giorgio Vasari.

2.62. Pendentive domes in the twin arcades
of Place Louis XV, completed c. 1763. J. A.
Gabriel.

This does not mean, however, that domes cannot be used in secular building programs. At the Mercato Vecchio in Florence (fig. 2.61) and at Place Louis XV (now Place de la Concorde) in Paris (fig. 2.62), a series of small pendentive domes cover arcades.

ROOFS

Roofs have always had an important role in architecture: they have enormous expressive power. To protect buildings as well as their occupants, roofs must extend beyond the outer walls. It is the lateral extension and the height of a roof that gives us such a comforting feeling at first sight (fig. 2.63). The slope of a roof is determined by the climate and by the roofing material, but, in their eagerness to emulate Italian models, classical architects have occasionally sacrificed roofs. The roofs of neo-Palladian buildings are often hidden, but many architects of the seventeenth and eighteenth centuries integrated high and steep roofs in their designs. Among those, Louis Le Vau and François Mansart stand out. In ordinary, anonymous buildings, prominent roofs are commonplace (fig. 2.64). One of the best ways to give unity to a building is to put a roof over it and to give all the slopes the same slant.

Let us look at a simple, square building. It is normally capped with a pyramidal roof. When the four faces of the pyramid have the same slant, the apex A is at the center of the roof plan (fig. 2.65). Intersections of the roof planes are drawn at a 45-degree angle in plan regardless of the height of the apex. It is on the elevation that the true slope is revealed; as a consequence, any number of different elevations (A1, A2, and A3) can share the same plan.

When the parts of a building differ in height, they might have discrete roofs that do not intersect. Drawing the roof plan presents no difficulty (fig. 2.66). But if the eaves of a roof are all at the same level, the height of the roof increases in proportion

2.63. Old roofs in Basel, Switzerland.

2.64. The entry facade of the eighteenth-century Thénissey chateau, in Burgundy. Architect unknown. The monolithic form of the roof shelters the entire building.

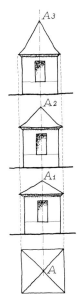
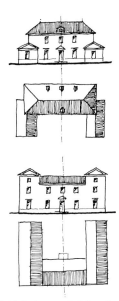

2.65. Triangular faces of a regular pyramid lean at the same angle; therefore, the apex is at the center of the square plan. The roof plan is the same regardless of roof slopes.

2.66. In these two buildings, the wings and the center are of different heights. Each part has its own roof.

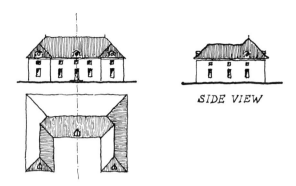

SIDE VIEW

2.67. When the slopes are all the same, the height of the roof depends on the width of the building parts.

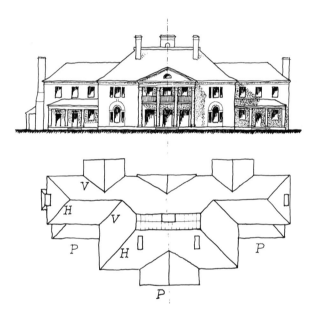

2.68. Farmlands, Cooperstown, New York, 2000. Fairfax & Sammons. On the roof plan, the intersections of roof planes are drawn at 45 degrees, indicating that the slopes are identical. Hips are marked "H" and valleys "V." The roof planes of the porch and pediments are shallower. They are marked with the letter "P."

to the width of the building, and there will be intersections between the roof planes (fig. 2.67). These intersections are either convex (*hips*) or concave (*valleys*). With practice, one learns to "read" a roof plan, that is, to form a mental picture of the building in three-dimensional space (fig. 2.68).

Mansard roofs are well adapted to wet climates. High enough to accommodate one or two more stories, such roofs convey a pleasant domestic feeling (fig. 2.69). As is often the case, a simple graphic method generates a harmonious form in space, for the profile can be fitted in a semicircle bisected by 45-degree lines (fig. 2.70).

Dormers add variety and can contribute to the unity of a design when they are faced with the same material as the wall below (fig. 2.71).

The shape and the relative height of roofs can express the hierarchy of the different parts of a building. At Vaux-le-Vicomte (fig. 2.72), cubic forms reinforce the four corners while the dominant mass in the middle of the garden facade is capped with a dome.

ORNAMENT

All cultures around the world have used ornaments in a meaningful way for millennia, but after the industrial revolution, ornamentation became an emotionally charged issue. Modern architects have looked at ornament with suspicion, considering it immature, immoral, or in bad taste. In 1892, Louis Sullivan expressed hostility to ornamentation, or to what he thought was bad ornament, when he advised architects to refrain from using ornament altogether for the next fifty years.

Ornament is an integral part of classical architecture. Columns are both structural and ornamental, and windows are functional and ornamental at the same time (fig. 2.73). Similar relationships exist between all things classical, large and small, from decorative drawer pulls and door bells to large urban compositions (fig.

2.69. The buildings of the Notre Dame market in Versailles. The buildings are wide enough to allow for a second story under the upper part of the mansard roofs.

2.72. Vaux-le-Vicomte, near Paris, construction interrupted in 1661. Louis Le Vau. On the garden façade, cubic forms underline the four corners while the oval room in the center is covered with a dome.

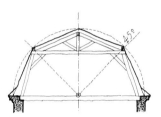

2.70. A simple method to determine the cross section of a mansard roof.

2.73. Ionic capitals at Hendricks Interfaith Chapel, Syracuse University, Syracuse, New York, 1929. John Russell Pope.

2.71. Two classical designs for dormers; the one below is shown out of context.

2.74. Doorbell button at Villa Gamberaia and a name plate in a street in Florence, both made of "pietra serena" and forming an integral part of the walls.

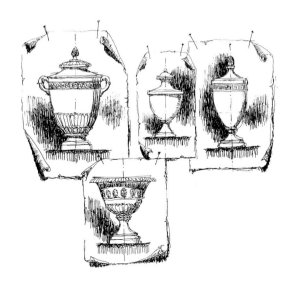

2.75. Urns, vases, and finials.   *2.76. Two obelisk designs.*

2.74). Classical ornament takes many forms: urns, vases, fountains, benches, topiary, pools, obelisks, finials, arbors, sculpture—allegorical, mythological, symbolic, or purely decorative— and even pavilions (fig. 2.75). Obelisks (fig. 2.76) are especially powerful as symbols of time: they stand for the seasonal cycles, the ebb and flow of fortune, life, death, and rebirth.

Applied ornament includes shields, friezes, wreaths, masks, trophies, frames, garlands, reliefs, swags, scrolls, medallions, mosaics, lettering, and more. The context is perhaps the most important issue; an ornament out of place is not only a mistake in itself, it can ruin an entire design.

It is their uselessness that makes ornaments important. When Oscar Wilde said that only luxury was indispensable to him, he was using a paradox to make a point. More recently, Walter Gropius insisted that spiritual needs were as important as physical needs. Beautiful ornaments have, like music, the power to make us feel happier.

Nearly alone among the architects of his generation, Frank Lloyd Wright incorporated ornaments in his buildings, even in the simplest and least expensive and in the face of declining craftsmanship and rising costs. Each of his Usonian houses was given an original design for cut-out plywood panels that were multiplied as many times as necessary to animate clerestory or vertical windows. Glass sheets were sandwiched between two sheets of plywood (figs. 2.77, 2.78). This proves that a resourceful mind can overcome stringent economic constraints; that the decorative effect of a simple motif relies on repetition, and that mechanization does not prevent effective ornamentation. These points were understood in the early nineteenth century. Using geometric forms and two-fold symmetry, designers had managed to create handsome patterns specifically conceived for mass-production in cast iron. The resulting pieces were destined to replace expensive wrought-iron elements, but it is worth observing that they did not imitate them (fig. 2.79).

2.77. *Medical building, San Luis Obispo, California, 1955. Frank Lloyd Wright.*

2.78. *Pope-Leighey house, Falls Church, Virginia, 1940; moved to Woodlawn Plantation, 1964. Frank Lloyd Wright.*

2.79. *Cast-iron panels in an early nineteenth-century door, Troyes, France.*

2.80. *Statue on a pedestal in the garden of the Palazzo Medici-Riccardi, Florence.*

The representation of the human figure is the ultimate ornament in classical architecture, the architecture of humanism. The beautiful body becomes a metaphor for human virtues. It is to honor their status that statues are given prestigious settings; they are enshrined in niches, elevated on pedestals, or framed by pediments.

Classical buildings use symmetry, regularity, and every possible symbol to convey an impression of solidity and immutability. It is against that background that stone and bronze figures (fig. 2.80) are asked to suggest just the opposite: the animation of life. Those that seem to be in motion or about to start moving are compelling, and there are few that take a rigid pose.

CHAPTER 3

THE WELL-DEFINED SPACE

To enclose a space is the object of building; when we build we do but detach a convenient quantity of space, seclude it and protect it, and all architecture springs from the necessity.

—GEOFFREY SCOTT

THE ONE-ROOM BUILDING

The simplest possible building contains a single room—the basic spatial unit of classical architecture. To focus on the formal issues, we will assume that, in general, the building does not have a precise function but instead lends itself to many possible uses. It might be a sentry box, a garden pavilion, a summer house, a tea house, or a folly. Regardless of its name, it must be an ornament to its site. Substantial estates often had one or more such rooms, where time would be spent working in peace, conversing with friends, enjoying music, or drinking tea. Depending on the climate, these small buildings were either open to cooling breezes or closed to provide a snug shelter.

The variety of programs offers an array of formal possibilities. To organize the discussion, let us first consider square plans. Although a square building invites four identical facades, site conditions might suggest otherwise (fig. 3.1). Reflection in water always enhances the ornamental effect of a pavilion. The use of an order adds sophistication to a plain rusticated base. So will a dome (fig. 3.2). Ornamental urns or finials will emphasize the center and/or the corners, and the interior space can easily be transformed into an octagonal room (fig. 3.3). Another transformation of the plan—from square to cruci-form—can have tremendous spatial consequences: the interior acquires subsidiary spaces and the four facades, moved forward, appear to be almost detached from the main body (fig. 3.4). Pavilions can be built on polygonal or circular plans, and covered with domes or pyramidal roofs (figs. 3.5, 3.6).

Moving away from the pleasure pavilion does not mean that aesthetic standards must be compromised. The eight aedicules erected around the Place de la Concorde in Paris (fig. 3.7) functioned as sentry boxes guarding the major gate to the city and as shelters for stairs leading to the dry moats surrounding the square. In spite of their small size, they played an important role in marking the corners of an immense urban square, and they served as bases for dynamic groups of sculpture celebrating royalty. In the nineteenth century, the original graceful figures were replaced with pompous representations of morose women. The moats now are filled in, but the stairs are still used for access to an underground parking garage.

One-room buildings can be used in pairs to frame an entrance or a vista. Many designs look better when replicated because they relate to an additional, outdoor space between them and form a complete composition. We tend to look for sets of three parts, and we unconsciously give the middle part a dominant role, even if it is a

3.1. A square pavilion, probably from the nineteenth century, in Switzerland. The pedimented portico on the water makes a pleasant shelter to enjoy the view.

3.3. An adaptation of a c. 1726 design by James Gibbs.

3.5. An octagonal pavilion near Lausanne, Switzerland.

3.6. Music Pavilion in the gardens of the Petit Trianon, Versailles, 1778. Richard Mique.

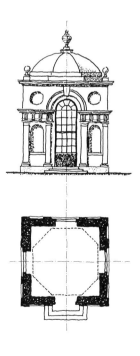

3.2. A pavilion closely following a design by James Gibbs.

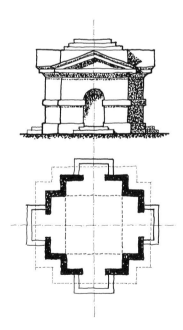

3.4. Design by Ledoux for a customs post in Paris, c.1783.

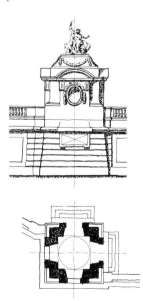

3.7. One of eight aedicules designed for the Place Louis XV, now the Place de la Concorde, completed c. 1763. J. A. Gabriel.

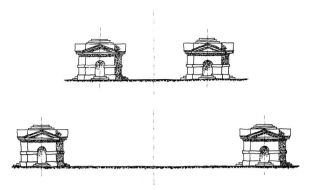

3.8. Ledoux's design for a customs post was conceived to form a gateway.

3.9. A simple pavilion marks the corner of an eighteenth-century garden at the chateau of Villotte St. Seine, Burgundy.

void. This illustrates Josef Albers's pronouncement that, in the visual arts, one plus one equals three. Let us look again at the design by Ledoux for a customs post (see fig. 3.4). It was originally conceived as one of a pair, and, if we place it side by side with a clone, we immediately see that the effect is much more impressive (fig. 3.8).

When pavilions are used in pairs, the distance between them is critical. The top drawing shows the minimum permissible distance, which equals 1.5 times the width of one building. Making that space narrower would seem to crowd the opening. Determining how far apart the buildings can be before they cease to form a design unit is more difficult. It depends on the distance from which the composition can be seen without turning one's head. In the bottom drawing, the space is four times the width of one building.

The effect of a pavilion depends in large part on its site. Even a plain building can look beautiful if it participates in the space-making of the setting. Here a simple cube with a pyramidal roof (fig. 3.9) marks the corner of a square garden—an outdoor room. Its hard geometry echoes a pair of large topiaries framing the entrance to another part of the garden.

In 1938, five years after the death of the poet Anna de Noailles, her friends and admirers commissioned Emilio Terry to build a memorial to her in Evian on a strip of land adjoining her parents' estate. Entered by a discreet gate from the road that now bears her name, the site slopes sharply toward the lakeshore; a shady walk leads down to a circular platform where a bend of the axis reveals the pavilion that is the heart of the garden (fig. 3.10). It is a hexagonal brick structure sheltering a cinerary urn. Although the reflecting pool is now empty, the vast expanse of the lake is visible through the open arches of the pavilion. A path around the pool leads to a terrace framed by two exedra. Sheltered within, circular benches invite meditative rest; the gentle sound of water against the rocks induces a peaceful and reflective mood.

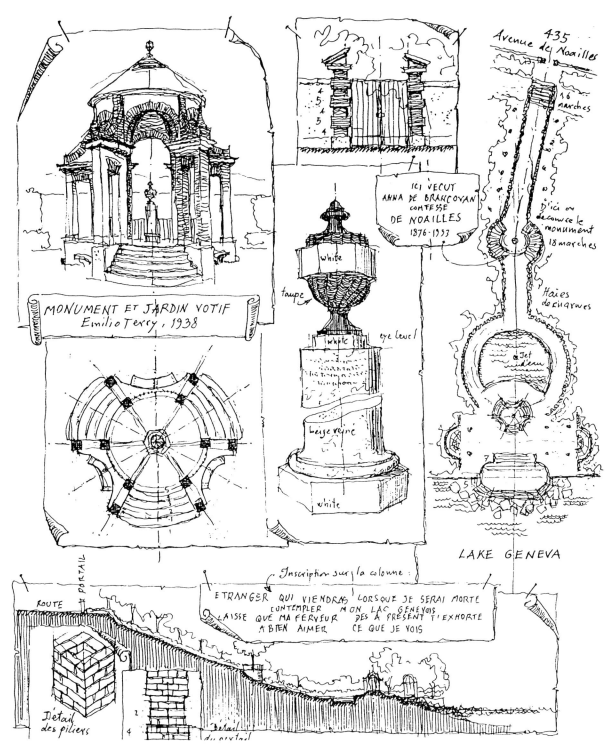

435
Avenue des Noailles

16 marches

D'ici on decoure le monument
18 marches

Haies de charmes

Jet d'eau

LAKE GENEVA

ICI VÉCUT
ANNA DE BRANCOVAN
COMTESSE
DE NOAILLES
1876-1933

white

taupe

white

eye level

beige veine

white

MONUMENT ET JARDIN VOTIF
Emilio Terry, 1938

ROUTE

PORTAIL

Détail des piliers

2
4

Détail du portail

Inscription sur la colonne :
ETRANGER QUI VIENDRAS LORSQUE JE SERAI MORTE
CONTEMPLER MON LAC GENEVOIS
LAISSE QUE MA FERVEUR DÈS A PRÉSENT T'EXHORTE
A BIEN AIMER CE QUE JE VOIS

3.10. *Votive garden and monument to Countess Anna de Noailles, Evian, 1938. Emilio Terry.*

Fundamental design lessons can be learned from the study of these simple buildings. Pavilions enclose a small space, but they also play an important role in their relationship to outdoor spaces in the city and the country. The number of doors and windows, their size, and their location are in great part determined by their role in the context. They can be the centerpiece of an open space, mark its corners, or frame an entrance. They can be open or closed, rustic or refined, austere or cheerful, depending on their function, the climate, and the location.

OUTDOOR ROOMS

The corollary of the one-room building is the outdoor room. The differences are clear—the obvious one being the missing roof—but they have much in common.

In *Architecture: Choice or Fate*, Leon Krier pointed out that there are only two kinds of urban spaces: "Public spaces can be built only in the form of streets (linear spaces) and squares (nodal spaces)." That is to say, there are places to congregate and circulation spaces. The same observation applies to gardens, both public and private. Inside buildings, there are rooms in which to engage principally in sedentary activities, and corridors to go from one room to another. A crude but useful metaphor for designers is to think of people in terms of liquid flowing through pipes or standing still in pools.

Four elements go a long way toward the making of a successful outdoor room, in urban or natural settings: regular shape, firm enclosures, few openings, and a point of interest. Piazza SS. Annunziata in Florence (fig. 3.11) is a plain rectangular space. Spatial unity is reinforced by repetition of elements in the enclosure. Three of the four sides carry loggias, the earliest designed by Brunelleschi for the Ospedale dei Innocenti in 1419. Michelozzo followed his design closely in 1454 for the facade of the church as did Sangallo the Elder in 1516 for the west side of the piazza. Instead of asserting a personal style, each designer continued the work of his predecessors to achieve coherence.

The five streets converging on the square have been consolidated into three significant points of entry. The most important is from Via dei Servi, on axis with the church and providing a link with the Duomo, the most important building in the city. The others are found in the corners. Within the square itself, there are three "objects of interest." On the main axis is an equestrian statue of one of the Grand Dukes, facing south toward the Duomo (figs. 3.12, 3.13). On either side are two fountains, placed to screen the entrances on the north side from Via dei Servi and reinforce the impression of a closed square, suggesting a forecourt to the church.

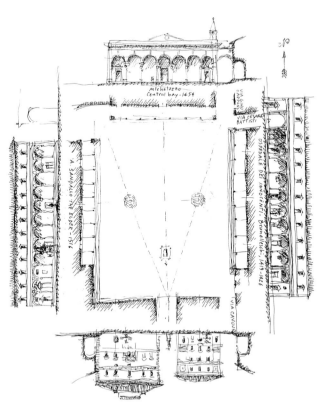

3.11. Piazza SS. Annunziata, Florence.

"....a bronze Grand Duke stands at the centre of the arcaded Piazza
SS. Annunziata and staxes down a monumental axis worthy of
Baxoque Rome."
        Rupert Scott

3.12. Looking north from Via dei Servi, with the statue
of the Grand Duke in front of the church.

" To the south, Brunelleschi cupola and the Duomo are seen at their most
impressive — a cliff of green and white marble sheared and scarred by
a pattern of buttresses, walls and windows, by patches of dark shadows and
splashes of livid colour, rises from the end of the street, creating a
contrast in scale that is always breathtaking, no matter how often it is seen."
        Rupert Scott

3.13. Looking south from Piazza SS. Annunziata on Via dei Servi,
with the Duomo at the end.

Urban rooms cannot be conceived without thinking of streets at the same time. An urban composition of great symbolic power is Amalienborg, in Copenhagen (figs. 3.14, 3.15). It consists of one short street connecting the sea, a source of wealth for the Danes, to the church. At one end, is the infinite vista over the sea, and at the other, a small square dominated by a massive church that screens the exit at the back. In between there is an airy octagonal space formed by four interconnected palaces now occupied by the royal family. The only object in the square is the equestrian statue of a king at the exact center, where it is visible from the two intersecting streets. The four facades reflecting one another across the square in absolute symmetry give the impression of a palatial interior court.

The relationship between a formal outdoor room and the objects, large or small, that furnish

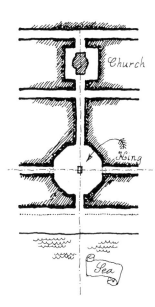

3.14. Amalienborg, Copenhagen,
begun in 1749.

3.15. One of four identical palaces
surrounding the Amalienborg. An elaborate design on the pavement enhances
the connection between the enclosures
and the monument in the middle.

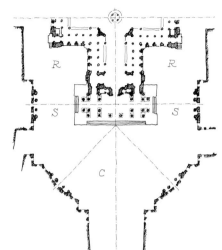

3.16. Design for the context of Ste. Geneviève church, now the Panthéon, Paris, 1764. Jacques-Germain Soufflot. "C" indicates the exedra, "S" the squares, and "R" the rectangles.

3.17. One of the two remaining buildings designed by Soufflot. Together, the curved facades form an exedra. They were built to house a school of law and a school of theology. Labrouste's library, built in 1839, can be seen in the background.

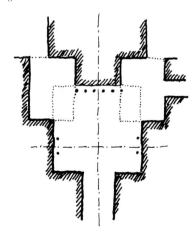

3.18. An alternative design from 1775 for the Place du Panthéon shows three overlapping rectangular areas.

it requires sensitive handling. A large building does not necessarily demand a huge open space. The Parisian Panthéon, built as the Church of Ste. Geneviève, stands today in a large and ill-defined space where it seems to be "rattling." One would not wish for the removal of such a remarkable building as Henri Labrouste's Bibliothèque Ste. Geneviève, but one might regret the loss of Jacques-Germain Soufflot's original design (fig. 3.16), where the shape of the enclosure entered into an intense dialogue with the church. The buildings on either side of the porch reflected the lateral elevations of the porch itself, and the distance between them is approximately one hundred feet, or half the width of the porch. Only the curved buildings forming an exedra in front of the building are standing today (fig. 3.17), just enough to give an idea of the architect's vision. In this design, Soufflot achieved perfect balance in making the surrounding space and the object within equally figural. The plan shows five well-defined regular shapes: two rectangles, two squares, and one semicircle. An alternative design for the square shows the same concern for equilibrium between context and object with only three clear geometric shapes in the plan, all rectangular (fig. 3.18).

The Place d'Armes in Dijon is part of an exceptionally sucessful urban sequence (fig. 3.19). The city's most vital street, Rue de la Liberté, connects Porte Condé (now Porte Guillaume), to the church of St. Michel (fig. 3.20). The climax occurs in front of the seat of government, formerly the ducal palace and later Palais des Etats. J. H. Mansart was put in charge of the plan in 1688, and the project was completed almost one hundred years later following his design. The citizens of Dijon were as affectionate towards a medieval tower as the Romans had been towards the tower at the Campidoglio. In both cases, a tower became the point of departure for the design. Mansart created a rectangular forecourt for the palace surrounded by new buildings on three sides. He then cleared a

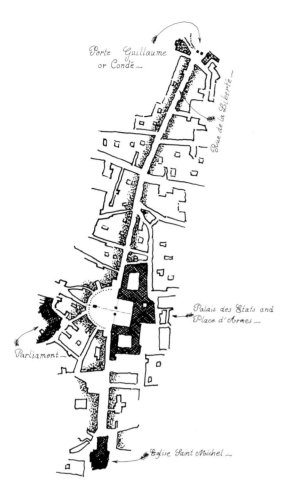

3.19. Rue de la Liberté in Dijon begins at the Porte Condé and terminates at the Eglise St. Michel. The street intersects the parade ground in front of the Palais des Etats, the seat of Burgundy's government before the revolution. The medieval tower is represented by a small white square in the gray mass of the Palais.

3.20. Porte Condé, built in 1783.

3.21. The monumental gate in the enclosure, opposite the Palais, was more significant as a frame to the statue of the king than as the opening into a very minor street.

3.22. The west wing of Palais des Etats seen, through the enclosing arcade, from the street that led to the Parliament buildings.

space for a semicircular parade ground and built an arcaded wall to screen the remaining buildings (fig. 3.21). For further unity, the walls of Rue de la Liberté were given similar blind arcades all the way to the city gate.

The focal point of the composition was an equestrian statue of Louis XIV looking towards the palace from the back of the parade ground. Long since destroyed, the statue stood in front of a monumental gate that served as a frame rather than an opening (fig.3.22). In contrast, the nar-

3.23. Counter-clockwise from lower left: The facade of Palais des Etats, showing the fifteenth-century tower on axis; one of the sentry boxes; the extremity of one of the wings overlooking Place d'Armes; a section of the arcaded screen wrapped around Place d'Armes; varied wrought-iron balcony designs; schematic plan of the courtyard and the semicircular parade grounds, intersected by Rue de la Liberté. The monument to Louis XIV is at the bottom of the plan.

PALAIS DES ETATS
J. H. Mansart architect
1681-1786

row but important street between the Parliament buildings and the palace is barely acknowledged because it intersects the parade grounds at an awkward angle. The similarity of spatial concepts in classical interior and exterior design is clear. Porte Condé is the entry to the sequence. Rue de la Liberté is the corridor leading to the suite of rooms formed by the Place d'Armes and the palace courtyard (figs. 3.23, 3.24).

If the definition of open spaces in the country can be more ambiguous, the means available are more varied. The terraced gardens of Villa Medici in Fiesole (fig. 3.25) are clearly defined by retaining walls, and each terrace forms an outdoor room. The steep drop between the two is mediated by a pergola at mid-height. A small stream running down the slope links the three levels and feeds a pool at the center of the lower terrace. Surrounded by four shade trees and framed by two square formal gardens, the space around the pool becomes a comfortable "room within a room" (fig. 3.26).

The English architect Sir Edwin Lutyens liked to conceive outdoor spaces as a series of related

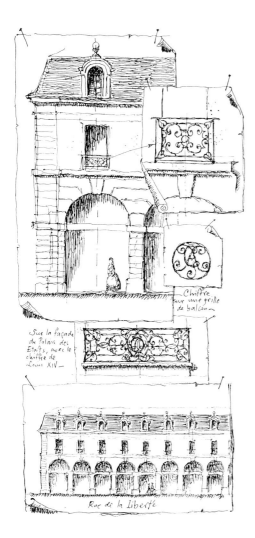

3.24. To emphasize the continuity of the spatial sequence originating at Porte Condé, a consistent design of mostly blind arcades was applied to the street walls and to the enclosure of Place d'Armes.

3.25. Villa Medici, Fiesole, 1461. Michelozzo Michelozzi. Cross section through the upper and lower terraces.

3.26. The lower terrace at the Villa Medici. The vegetation covering the mediating pergola can be seen on the right.

3.27. Gardens at Hestercombe, Somerset, 1908. Sir Edwin Lutyens.

3.28. Hestercombe. Sunken garden and pergola.

3.29. Hestercombe. Raised walk at the north edge of the sunken garden.

rooms. This can be seen in Hestercombe, Somerset (fig. 3.27), designed in 1908 with his friend and colleague, the landscape designer Gertrude Jekyll. The terrace on the south side of the house overlooks the largest space of the garden, a square plateau surrounded by raised walks and bound by high walls in the best classical tradition (fig. 3.28). The sunken parterre in the middle (fig. 3.29), a room within a room, is a little world of its own. A pergola (fig. 3.30) sheltering a fragrant walk forms the south edge. From there the view over meadows appears to be infinite.

In the upper right corner of the plan there is a circular space called the rotunda. Private and restful with a small pool in the middle, the place can be enjoyed from a bench sheltered in a small

3.30. Hestercombe. View from the pergola over a vast expanse of meadows.

3.32. Hestercombe. Small door between the rotunda and the orangery.

3.31. Hestercombe. Rotunda with the pond and the seat in the niche.

3.33. Hestercombe. The orangery forms the backdrop of an outdoor room.

recess in the wall that is given a monumental appearance in elevation (fig. 3.31). The rotunda is the antechamber to a long and narrow terrace revealed through a small doorway in the wall (fig. 3.32). This is a secret garden. Pushed against the hillside on the north, a small building with the character of an orangery (a conservatory to shelter boxed trees in winter and display them in summer) is also a room within a room (fig. 3.33). The building also forms the background of the outdoor room in which it stands. Downhill is an extensive view over more meadows.

Greywalls, in Scotland (fig. 3.34), also by Lutyens, is conceived as a series of outdoor rooms. Here, Lutyens gave a distinct identity to each room but maintained unity with a contin-

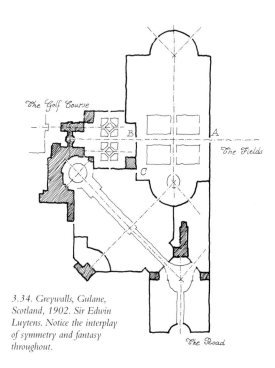

3.34. Greywalls, Gulane, Scotland, 1902. Sir Edwin Luytens. Notice the interplay of symmetry and fantasy throughout.

3.35. View of the house through an opening in the wall (C on the plan).

3.36. The last axis of the sequence originates in the house and directs the eye to a small but significant motif (A on the plan).

3.37. Sketch of the house from the rose garden (B on the plan).

uous wall of constant height. The shapes of the rooms vary, and the openings are distributed to offer varied and dramatic views (fig. 3.35). The main paths coincide with axes of symmetry. The final axis of the sequence begins at the fireplace of a small, circular sitting room in the house and ends at a Janus-like aedicule. An opening through the outer wall with a view over the fields extends the axis to the horizon, while a bench looks back towards the house, showing its best side (figs. 3.36, 3.37).

A design that epitomizes the classical approach to the design of a room open to the sky can be found in the public garden at the Gobelins in Paris (fig. 3.38). Designed by the architect Jean-Charles Moreux before World War II, it includes all the amenities to make parents and small children happy, distributed according to pure logic and geometric rigor. An obelisk anchors the place and signals its center. It is set in a small pool that is irresistible to children. Trellised exedra reinforce the corners, giving a sense of privacy and sheltering benches. The side enclosures, alternating with wide

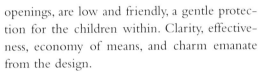

3.38. An outdoor room realized with simple means. Jean-Charles Moreux.

*3.39. The chapel of the Invalides, Paris, 1679–1706.
J. H. Mansart.*

openings, are low and friendly, a gentle protection for the children within. Clarity, effectiveness, economy of means, and charm emanate from the design.

On a monumental scale, the chapel of the Invalides (fig. 3.39), designed by J. H. Mansart, is a superb object in its own right, but imagine how glorious it would look enshrined in the urban context it deserves. A project of the seventeenth century shows the chapel framed by curved wings suggesting open arms, their forms extended by a dry moat around a large podium (fig. 3.40). Five avenues converge toward the podium, accessible by three narrow gates preceded by formal "outdoor vestibules." Double rows of trees give grandeur and formality to the setting.

The most important formal problem facing the architect is the definition of space. Good solutions depend a great deal on the quality of the boundaries. A large portion of this book addresses the question of what makes good boundaries, but we must now consider the essential role that drawing plays in the design process.

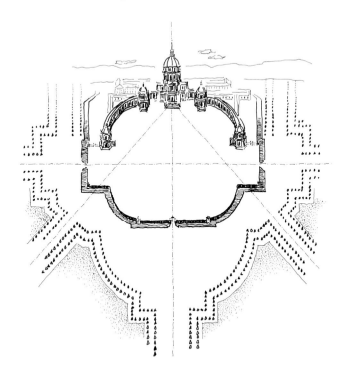

3.40. Proposal for an outdoor room worthy of the Invalides chapel.

CHAPTER 4

DESIGN AND DRAWING

If you want to be an architect, start by becoming a painter.
—C. N. LEDOUX

THE VALUE OF DRAWING

In the sixteenth century, Leon Battista Alberti observed, "I have often conceived of projects in the mind that seem quite commendable at the time; but when I translated them into drawings, I found several errors in the very parts that delighted me most, and quite serious ones." It is painful to find out that the beautiful designs we have in our head are often disappointing when we put them down on paper. Alberti is not the only one to have made the discovery, but he may have been the first with enough candor to admit it. In architecture as well as in all the visual arts, the eye is the best judge, as long as it is an educated eye. But how does one train one's eye? The best way is by drawing. Experience has shown that the best designers are also the best draftsmen because they have educated their eye by dedicating themselves to a rigorous training, by observing things closely, and by making the effort to represent them accurately. This requires thought and sustained attention. One is forced to make comparisons, to check alignments, to devise methods of verification. Mechanical reproduction cannot replace on-site studies. The geometer and architect Robert Greenberg accurately summed up the value of drawing: "With a camera, the picture is on paper; with a sketchbook, the picture is on the brain."

For the architect, there are two different types of drawing: visualization sketches and orthogonal projections, that is, plans, cross sections, and elevations. Visualization sketches come first, followed by plan studies. Visualization sketches should be freehand, unrestricted by tools, either the T-square or the computer. The plan is the generator, as Le Corbusier remarked, but it is nothing more. It is in the cross section that the third dimension can be studied, and it is there that the spatial quality of a design—the essential quality of architecture—is determined. Sectional drawings follow plan studies. Elevation drawings come last, as the result of plan and section studies, as a verification, so to speak, of the previous phases. Elevations, or facades, are important because they are visible to all.

The three drawings—plan, cross section, and elevation—are equally important for different reasons. They should be done in turn, in this order, and the cycle should be repeated as many times as necessary. A too-common belief is that a good plan automatically leads to a good elevation. This is a dangerous illusion, and one should never polish up any of the three drawings of a set until they all are as good as one can make them and perfectly coordinated with one another.

I am speaking metaphorically here. Even the simplest building will require more than three drawings, but at every stage of the design process

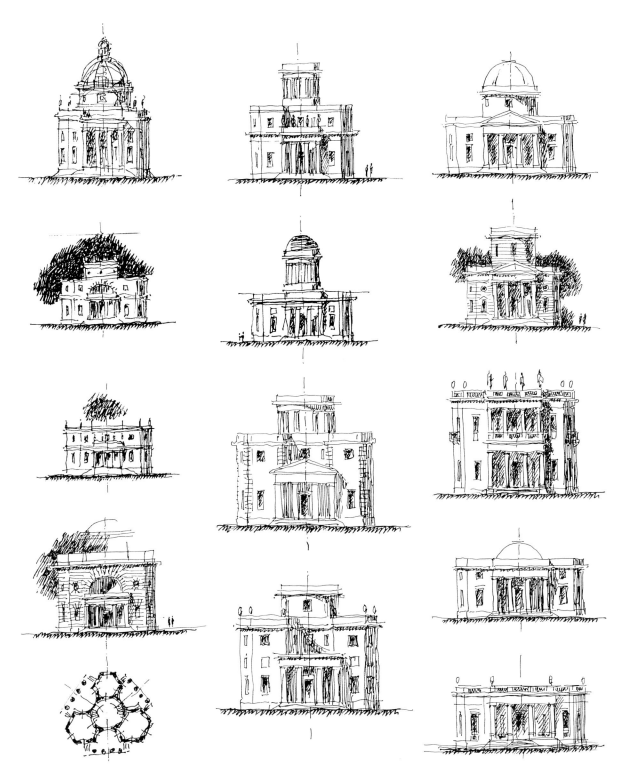

4.1. Speculative elevations by the author based on a plan by Ledoux.

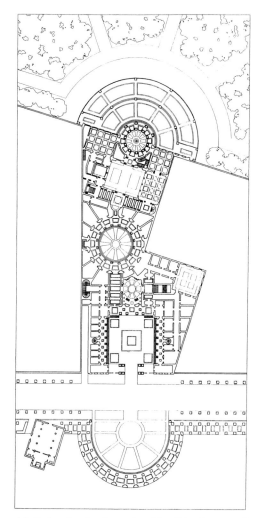

4.2. Section of an American embassy. Tom Chin. Compare with a finished drawing based on the same program (fig. 8.18).

and at any scale at least one set of drawings should be done for a design to be considered finished.

Some people, including many architects, are under the misapprehension that the discipline of the classical language of architecture impedes design flexibility. Let us then consider a simple plan and see how many elevations can be derived from it. One of Ledoux's most unusual plans, for one of the customs posts he designed around Paris, consists of two overlapping Y-shaped configurations. Three hexagonal rooms alternate with exedra around a circular space

housing stairs. What elevations might be compatible with such a plan? Fig. 4.1 shows quick exploratory sketches of the external appearance of the building. A more thorough study would include investigation of the cross sections.

The building might have one, two, or three stories; the circular stair on center might suggest a tower emerging above the building; a dome might cap the tower; the porticos might be treated like superimposed loggias, and so on. It would be difficult, but not impossible, to use a steep, visible roof because of the complexity of the plan.

Rendered drawings are typically produced at the end of the design process to show clients how the building will look or to promote the work of the architect. However, renderings would be even more helpful as part of the design process. Today, architectural drawings are mostly line drawings—"wire drawings" in modern parlance. These are incomplete since they do not include color to indicate the materials envisioned for the building and its context. A line drawing is only the armature of a design. A good rendering is not just a pretty picture; it is a necessary step in a conscientious design process. It is a faithful representation of the building in its setting, complete with materials, the effect of light on the forms, and the expression of the third dimension, i.e., depth and layering. As Le Corbusier said, "The use of color is an architectural statement as powerful as a plan or a section."

Le Corbusier believed that the sky and the trees were part and parcel of the urban designer's materials. This is also true for the architect and the landscape architect. A line on paper remains a line unless there is a clear graphic representation of the materials on either side of that line. Without it, how could the total effect of a design be judged (fig. 4.2)?

Finally, the use of color is pleasurable, and some of the capable draftsman's enjoyment is sure to be shared by those who will look at the finished drawing. As Gordon Cullen, author of *The Concise Townscape*, has written, "Without the ingredient of sensuous enjoyment the practice of architecture must inevitably degenerate into little more than a sordid routine, or at the most the exercise of mere intellectual cleverness."

THE WATERCOLOR WASH TECHNIQUE

The American Renaissance architect Eugene Clute stated, "The ultimate purpose of any rendering should be the effective and evocative depiction of the architectural object in its setting, no more and no less." Architecture is a visual art, and its purpose is to make the world more pleasant to live in. Ledoux advised those who want to become architects to begin their career as painters. Another good piece of advice was given by Camille Pissarro, a post-impressionist painter, who said that a picture cannot possibly show everything. In fact, he said, very little indeed can be shown in a painting. In other words, be selective, and show only what is important. Also, keep in mind that a design can never be exactly represented in any form, model or drawing. A drawing is not a photograph any more than an architectural model is a miniature; both are interpretations.

Nevertheless, a good line drawing is indispensable to start with. Vary the line weight and firmly outline three-dimensional forms and openings in walls. The tendency among beginners is to draw every single line regardless of the size of the drawing. This cannot be done on a small drawing: you must learn to edit, that is, to choose among the lines those that define substantial forms, and draw them. Ignore or eliminate the others; they will only create confusion.

Over the last three hundred years, classical architects have perfected a drawing technique adapted to the expression of their designs. Although known as "watercolor wash," it is not a painter's technique, nor does it call for watercolor paints. Watercolor wash is a drawing skill that can be mastered with close attention and a little conscientious practice.

Basic Principles

•Values should control your use of color. As you begin to consider color, ask yourself how a black-and-white photograph of your drawing will look. Better yet, make your first renderings with shades of gray to gain experience in your perception of values. Ten shades of gray ranging from black to white will meet all your needs. This is called the gray scale. Use it thoughtfully. On an elevation the darkest value (or color) should be found in the openings. On a section, however, what you see through the openings is the outside, and that is what should be shown. On a section, as in a plan, the darkest value should be for the *poché*, that is, the solid parts of the building through which the section is cut: the walls, roofs, and ground line.

• Colors should enhance and clarify the three-dimensional forms. Select in advance all the colors you will be using and place them close together on a color sample board to observe their interaction. Use light and dull colors on large areas and reserve bright colors for accents. Intensity seems to increase proportionally with the size of the colored area.

• Shading is the best way to show the layering of surfaces from front to back in buildings that consist of solid surfaces. It was once highly developed, but it is no longer taught in architecture schools. Rendering shadows is a sophisticated technique. Adopted for the sake of convenience, the conventional location of the sun is such that light rays can be drawn at a 45-degree angle in plan as well as in elevation. If you are just beginning, cast the shadows only in plan drawings. This can be done easily by sliding down a tracing of the plan at a 45-degree angle. Suppose the walls to be cut off at the height of the window sills. Go over the outline of the shadow in pencil and color the area with a light gray wash. Remember that the light source is the sun and that, in a plan, shadows would appear on the ground plane. Depending on the orientation of the final drawing, whether pinned on a wall or reproduced in a

ELEVATION

PLAN

4.3. Without their shadows, two squares drawn from above look identical. The square on the left is just a weightless horizontal square, but that on the right is the top face of a half-cube. The shape of the shadows shows the difference. The height of the two squares above the ground is the same; it can be measured by the length "h" of the shadows.

publication, the shadows should be drawn below the object (fig. 4.3). In this technique, horizontal lines cast shadows parallel to themselves on the ground plane, and vertical lines cast shadows at a 45-degree angle. On elevation drawings, use strong, contrasting values on the foreground, and lighter ones as objects recede further and further into the background. Do not attempt to cast shadows on elevation drawings until you have received proper instruction or you fully understand the technique of shadow casting. Do not attempt to communicate depth at all in sectional drawings. Instead, concentrate on surface articulation and on the color scheme of each room.

Materials Required for Rendering

• Two-ply, 100 percent rag watercolor illustration boards, cold press and white or off-white, with some grain. Cut the boards to suit your needs. Save the scraps to practice the wash technique, test your colors, and finalize your color selection.

• Permanent and transparent acrylic-based artists ink. You only need a few basic colors to mix and obtain any tone: two at the most of the primaries, red, yellow, and blue (cobalt and Prussian). You will also need sepia. Black is unnecessary since it can be obtained from a mix of blue and sepia. White is also unnecessary because the medium is transparent and the white of the paper will show through several layers of ink diluted in water.

• A good watercolor brush that makes a perfect point and holds water well. Pure sable brushes are the best; they are expensive, but they last a lifetime if well cared for. Do not waste your money on several small brushes, even of good quality. All you need is one good brush, two at the most. It is important that the brush be big enough, at least an inch from the tip to the handle. A less expensive alternative to pure sable is called a "quill mop," made of pure squirrel.

• A large and stable water container, with approximately a two-pint capacity. If the container is too small, the water will soon become muddy. If not wide enough to be stable, the container might accidentally be knocked over.

• A large mixing tray.

• Watertight, transparent containers to keep mixed colors for as long as they are needed. It is very difficult to match a color if you run out of it before you are finished. You might need ten or fifteen containers.

• A clean rag to wipe your brush dry.

• A natural sponge for emergencies and to clean your boards before you start applying the color washes on the drawing. Wet the sponge and drag it lightly over the entire surface of the board.

• A supply of extra illustration boards for practice.

How to Practice

The goal is to learn to cover each area with a perfectly even layer of color.

• Outline varied shapes in pencil on a practice board. Begin with small areas, and increase their size and complexity as you develop confidence.

text continues on page 105

C.1 (fig. 4.9). Plan, section, and elevation of a one-room building. Chris Campbell.

C.2 (fig. 4.10). Plan, section, and elevation of a landing stage with a pair of one-room buildings. The overlap of the three drawings makes an effective one-board presentation. Colin Lowry.

C.3 (fig. 4.11). Elevation of two pavilions connected by an arcade. Jesse Benjamin Nicholson.

C.4 (fig. 4.12). A one-room pavilion within an outdoor room. Joel Kline.

C.5 (fig. 4.13). Plan of four pavilions connected by porticoes in a formal clearing. Jessika Creedon.

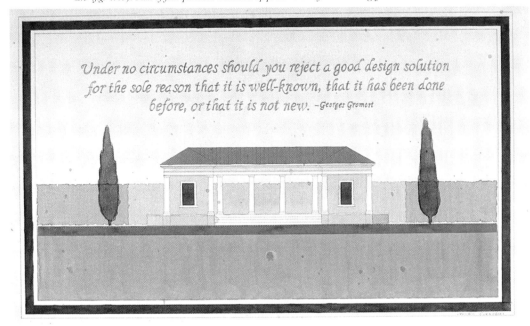

C.6 (fig. 4.14). Elevation. Jessika Creedon.

STUDENT PROJECTS FOR RESTRICTED SITES
See chapter 8

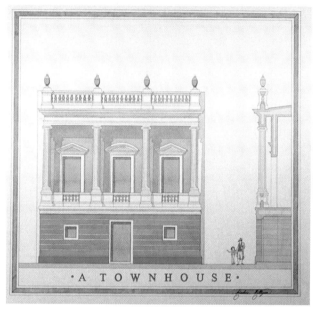

C.7 (fig. 8.1). Town house. Street facade. Ariadne Milligan. Ferguson, Shamamian & Rattner Architecture Prize, 2002.

C.8 (fig. 8.2). Town house. Plan of main room and elevation of one of the lateral walls. Ariadne Milligan.

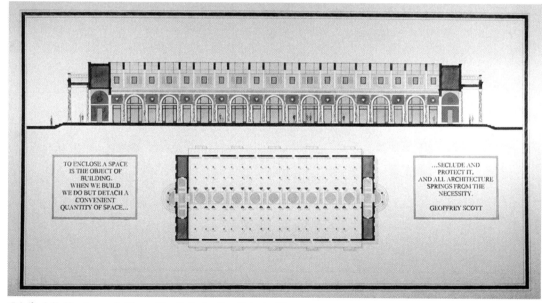

C.9 (fig. 8.3). Hopping arcade. Plan and longitudinal section. Katherine Hogan.

C.10 (fig. 8.5). French hôtel. Longitudinal section with the entrance on the left. James Wisniewski.

C.11 (fig. 8.7). French hôtel. Elevation of the main building from the garden with section through the orangery and the residence. Joel Kline.

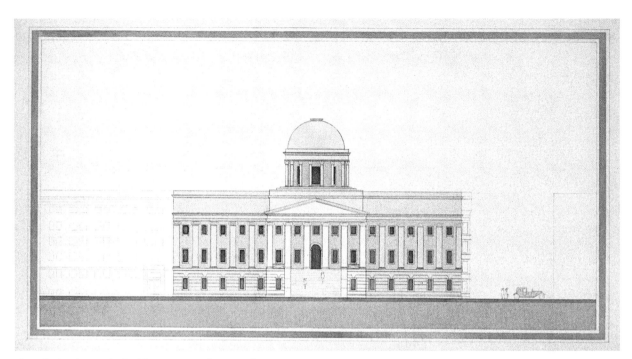

C.12 (fig. 8.11). Main facade of the institute. Matthew Manuel.

C.13 (fig. 8.14). Facade of the institute. Christopher Pizzi.

C.14 (fig. 8.17). Elevation of the public square in front of the consulate. Grady J. Dagenais.

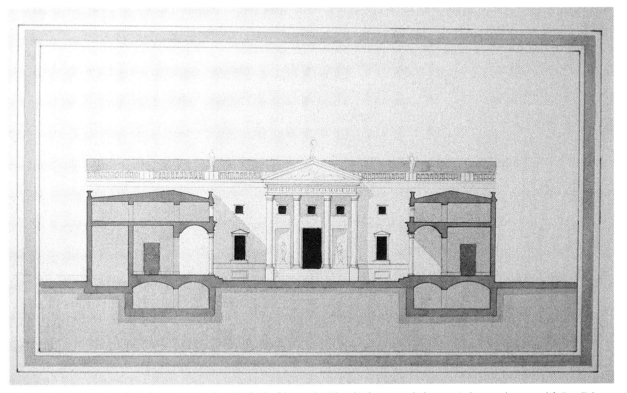

C.15 (fig. 8.18). Section through the forecourt showing the public facade of the consulate. The vehicular ramp to the basement is shown on the extreme left. Scott Delorme.

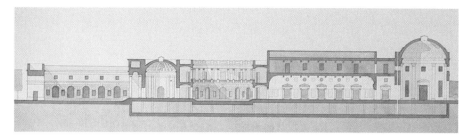

C.16 (fig. 8.20). Section through the embassy compound. Rick Colson.

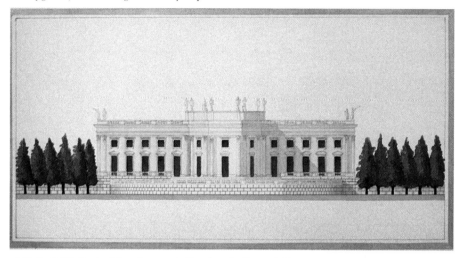

C.17 (fig. 8.21). Facade of the embassy overlooking the park. Gregory Malette.

C.18 (fig. 8.24). Section through the main building, showing the circular court open to the sky. Gregory Malette.

STUDENT PROJECTS FOR OPEN SITES
See chapter 11

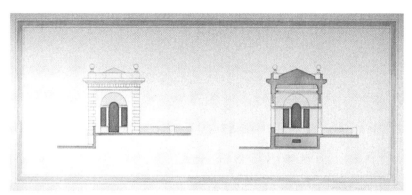

C.19 (fig. 11.2). Section and elevation of a corner pavilion. Matthew Manuel.

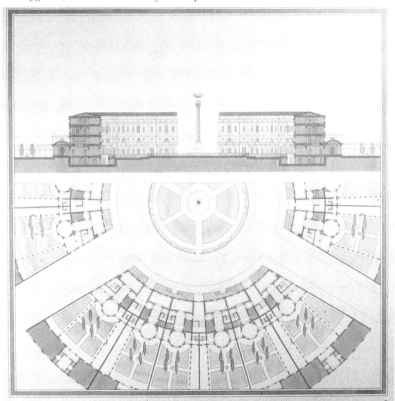

C.20 (fig. 11.4). A circular residential square. Elevation/section and half-plan. The opening to the arcaded street is beyond the freestanding column in the middle. Services spaces are shown in pale red. Jim Bouffard.

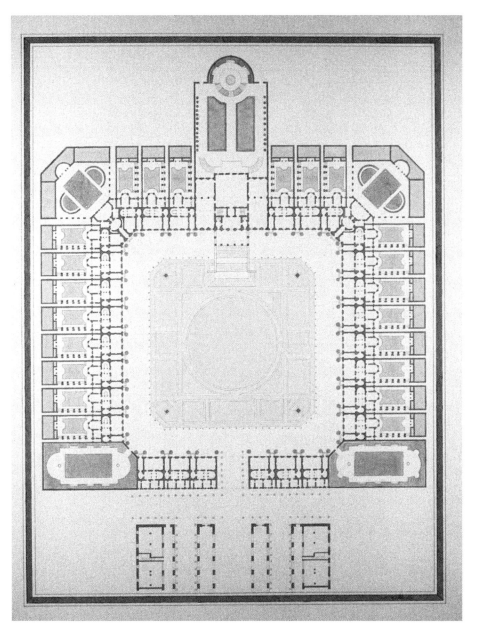

C.21 (fig. 11.5). A square urban room. General plan at the piano nobile level. The beginning of the arcaded street is shown at the bottom of the drawing. Sue Robbins.

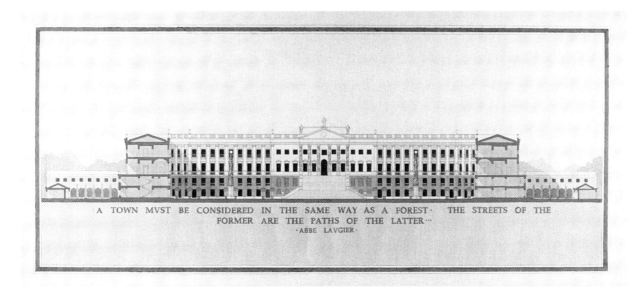

A TOWN MVST BE CONSIDERED IN THE SAME WAY AS A FOREST· THE STREETS OF THE FORMER ARE THE PATHS OF THE LATTER···
·ABBE LAVGIER·

C.22 (fig. 11.6). Cross section of the square, facing north. Sue Robbins.

C.23 (fig. 11.11). Plan of the hospice. Robert Laterza.

C.24 (fig. 11.13). From the top down, entrance facade, view from the ocean, cross-section on the main axis, with the entrance on the right and the ocean on the left. Peter Rust.

C.25 (fig. 11.14). Axonometric drawing of the villa and its enclosed garden. The forecourt with the two garages is at the bottom. Trevor Lavoie.

C.26 (fig. 11.21). Plan and elevation of the summer house. Robert Parise. Collector's Estate.

C.27 (fig. 11.22). Elevation of the summer house. The structure is raised on a podium. Cory Berg.

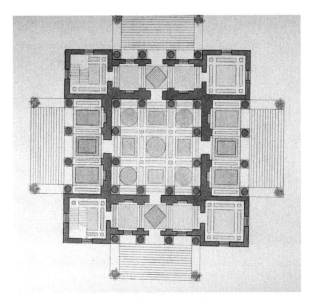

C.28 (fig. 11.24). Plan of the villa. Douglas Neidhart.

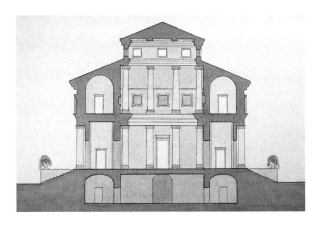

C.29 (fig. 11.25). Section of the villa. Douglas Neidhart.

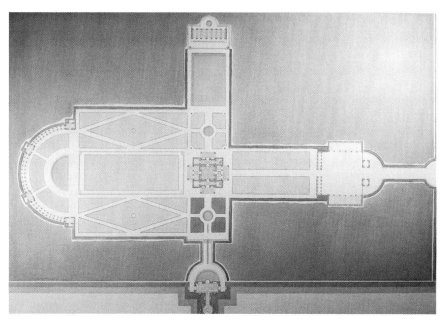

C.30 (fig. 11.27). General plan of the gardens. Douglas Neidhart.

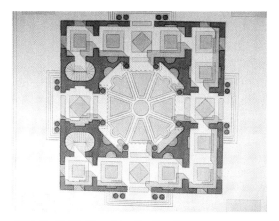

C.31 (fig. 11.28). Plan of the villa. Cory Berg.

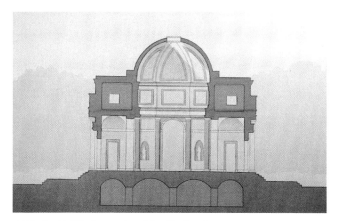

C.32 (fig. 11.29). Cross-section of the villa. Cory Berg.

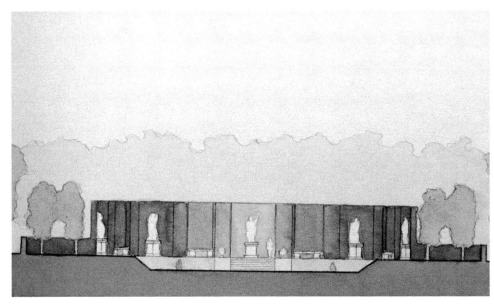

C.33 (fig. 11.31). An exedra facing the villa on the west side of the gardens. Cory Berg.

C.34 (fig. 11.32). Elevation of the villa. Shawn Kirk.

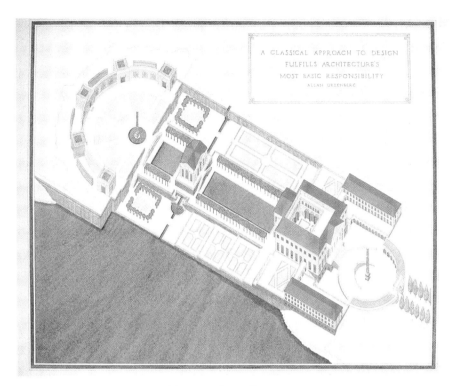

C.35 (fig. 11.33). Axonometric view of the compound. Steve Fernaays.

C.36 (fig. 11.35). Axonometric of the main building and the court of honor. Marcell Graef.

C.37 (fig. 11.37). The view from the loggia of the main building focuses on the summer houses and includes the sculpture studios. Adam Kehr.

C.38 (fig. 11.38). The main house seen from the summer house. Samantha Divak Eio

C.39 (fig. 11.39). The main house seen from the summer house. Mark Degnan.

C.40 (fig. 11.40). Section through the main building. The large room overlooking the gardens is on the right. Christian Bolliger.

C.41 (fig. 11.44). The garden facade with the cliff on the right. Underneath, a half-scale drawing of the entrance side. Colin Lowry.

C.42 (fig. 11.45). Three houses wrapped around a common forecourt. The cross section through the side houses shows the facade of the house in the middle. Each house has a private garden at the back. Timothy Houde.

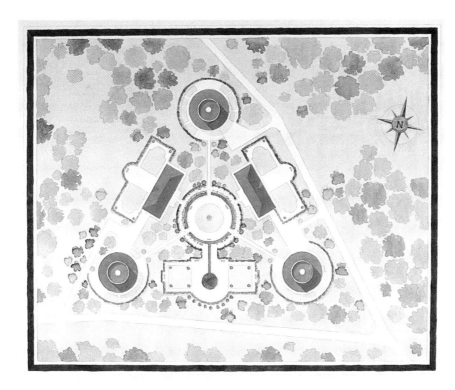

C.43 (fig. 11.47).
A cluster of five
houses. Blake Guyer.

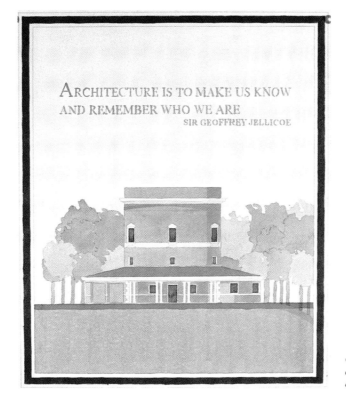

C.44 (fig. 11.48). Elevation
of one of the houses based on
a cylinder. Blake Guyer.

C.45 (fig. 11.49). Plan of a private garden with the facade of the adjacent house. An herb garden occupies the rectangular space on the right. The context must be imagined filled with dense vegetation. Rachana Ky.

C.46 (fig. 11.50). Garden facade of one of the houses. Eric Godin.

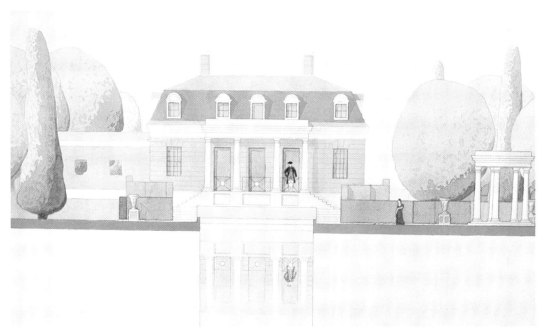

C.47 (fig. 11.52). Private facade of a house. Maher Sweid.

C.48 (fig. 11.53). Half-plan of one of the outdoor rooms with elevation of a summer house. Maher Sweid.

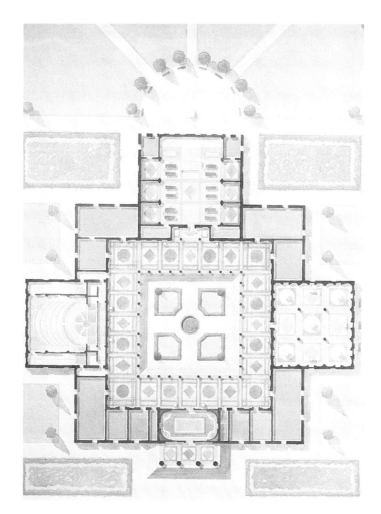

C.49 (fig. 11.56). Plan of an athenaeum. Enrique Vela. Ferguson, Shamamian & Rattner Architectural Prize, 2002.

C.50 (fig. 11.57). Entrance facade. Enrique Vela.

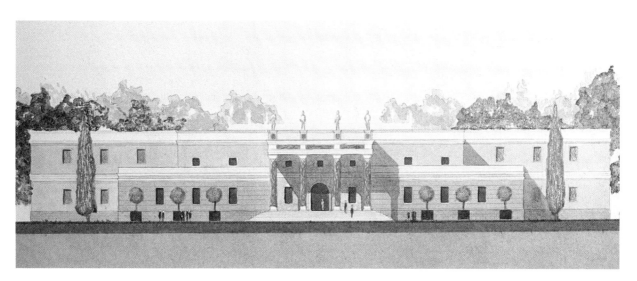

• The board must be secure on the table and slope toward you. When the wash almost runs down the board, the slope is correct. You will soon learn to judge what slope works best. Do not rely on your free hand to hold the board; you will need that hand for other purposes.

• Orient the board so that the length of the area to be colored is vertical, and the width horizontal. This will make your task much easier. Practice over areas of varied shapes, including L- and U-shapes. When the area to be colored changes directions, rotate the board so that the slope always faces you and your strokes continue to be as short as possible.

• Load the brush to capacity. Remember that a good brush does not drip.

• Starting at the top, drag the brush lightly across the area, all the way to the opposite edge (figs. 4.4a, 4.4b). Do not go twice over the same stroke. If you need to refill the brush, resume the stroke where you left off.

• Reload the brush and repeat, making sure that the new stroke overlaps slightly with the previous one. The wash of the previous stroke will be still wet and will run into the new one by itself. This will produce the smooth effect you seek. Do not interrupt the process until the entire area is done. Do not allow the brush to go over the pencil lines or the effect will be messy. If you cannot control the brush perfectly, it is better to stop short of the lines and let some of the white of the paper show.

• When you reach the bottom of the area to be covered, squeeze the brush dry in the color container. You might need that color again. Then use the brush to pick up the extra wash left on the paper by your last stroke.

• Give the area just colored plenty of time to dry completely. Do not attempt to fix any problem until the board is perfectly dry.

• Proceed carefully. Begin with light values. It is always possible to darken an area but it is impossible to make it lighter. It is normal to go over the same area more than once to obtain a satisfactory color or value. Never lose sight of the overall effect you are hoping to achieve. Remember that every additional coat makes the color darker.

• Before attempting to fix a problem, make sure you know what it is you hope to achieve. If you are not pleased with the uneven texture of your wash work, another coat will not improve matters.

If at first your performance fails to meet your expectations, do not become discouraged. Excellent work has been done by beginners after unpromising first attempts. The key to success is persistence and disciplined practice.

4.4a, 4.4b. Drag the loaded brush from left to right. The wash will gather at the bottom, waiting for the next stroke.

Color Selection

You probably need a maximum of ten tints to indicate all the materials used in your design. Once you have made your complete selection, put a patch of each color in close proximity to the others to see how they interact. This will be your color sample board. Adjust the colors until they work together in harmony. Then mix enough of each color for the entire set of drawings and store in a container.

Be conscientious about your color selection. There is no point in using color if it does not make a positive contribution to your design.

Color on Plans

• POCHÉ: The convention is to represent poché in light red. A dull orange or light reddish-brown is acceptable. You will need at least two shades, a medium-dark shade for plan and section cuts and a lighter shade for residual spaces.

• WALKING SURFACES: For the sake of clarity, all floors, paths, steps, terraces, should be uncolored, with the paper reading as white (fig. 4.5). This recommendation applies to both interior and exterior conditions. Nothing should be allowed to interfere with the flow of space.

• GRASS: Light yellow-green. For some reason, many beginners favor a blue-green that is not found in nature. Resist the temptation, and add yellow! The painter Pierre Bonnard believed that there could never be too much yellow in a landscape.

• HEDGES: Dull green, darker than the grass.

• TREES: Varied shades of yellow and green.

• WATER: Blue-gray.

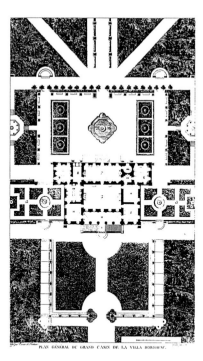

4.5. Plan of the casino with entourage at the Villa Borghese in Rome from Charles Percier and Pierre Fontaine, Choix des plus célèbres maisons de plaisance de Rome et de ses environs, Paris, 1820. In this print, white is reserved for walking surfaces.

Color on Elevations

• BUILDING ARMATURE: A good way to present your design clearly is to make a distinction between the wall surface and the trim. Most facades consist of a marriage between a visual armature and a field. The armature is the three-dimensional framework of columns, entablatures, quoins, steps, and so on. The field is the wall surface within the armature. In your first design and drawing efforts, leave the armature uncolored, i.e., paper white. It is a reasonable thing to do because white is the color of fine building stone. Then select the appropriate brick or stucco color for the field. Balustrades, stone ornaments, and sculpture will generally also be white. Another advantage of a white armature is that it separates adjacent color areas. This will prevent the mistake of juxtaposing two different hues of equal value. This does not mean that all your designs should include a white armature. This is simply a helpful way to articulate designs and make them clear.

• FIELD: Brick or stucco, yellow to terra cotta colors.

• ROOFS: Gray-blue for slate; terra cotta color for tiles; verdigris for copper.

• WINDOW OPENINGS: Dark blue-gray; a shade that suggests that the sky is reflected in glass.

• RETAINING WALLS AND RUSTICATED BASE: Light grayish brown.

• TREES: Varied shades of yellow-green for both foliage and tree trunks. Use lighter shades as trees recede in the background.

Color on Sections

• ARMATURE: White, as on the exterior elevations. White paint is more likely to be used than stone in interiors.

• OPENINGS: Leave them paper white. An alternative is to represent what would be seen of the outside scenery, but it might be confusing. Some beginners use the same dark color as they did on the facades. This is a mistake: openings look dark only when seen from the outside.

The Frame

Frames can greatly enhance architectural drawings. In addition to isolating a drawing from its surroundings, a frame celebrates a picture; it leaves no doubt as to its uniqueness and conveys your pride in a job well done. To give unity to a set of drawings, all boards should have frames of the same color. Take this as an opportunity to enrich your palette. Use gold, or any other strong, suitable color (fig. 4.6).

Corrections

Mistakes or accidents occur at all levels of experience. Before you throw away a drawing on which you have labored for hours, consider "transplant surgery." If the problem is localized, that area can be neatly cut along pencil lines and removed. Replace it with another piece of exactly the same shape and tape it in the back. Seams look very much like pencil lines, and a

neat patching job will not be noticeable. Wisdom suggests that you complete the replacement drawing before you cut the other one out (fig. 4.7). There is no limit to the size of a patch. An entire drawing might be cut out of the frame and placed inside a new one if it turns out to be inadequate or if the margin happens to be damaged.

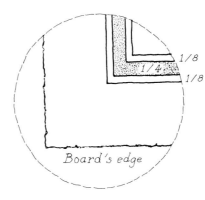

4.6. A simple frame drawn on the sheet will anchor and enhance a drawing. The pencil lines should be firmly drawn, so that they can be clearly seen at some distance. Color the middle strip only, which is 1/4 inch wide. The margin outside the frame should be greater on a small board than on a large one.

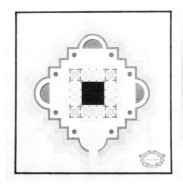

4.7. In this case, the portion to be corrected was at the very center of the drawing. A new floor pattern, shown at the bottom, was designed and later inserted. See also fig. 4.13. Jessika Creedon.

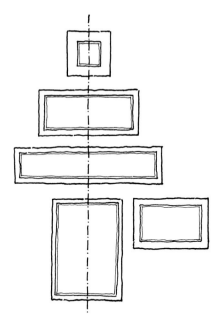

4.8. In a formal presentation, all symmetrical sheets should be placed on the same axis of symmetry. Asymmetrical sheets are placed on the side.

Pin Ups

To understand an architectural design and to evaluate it, all the drawings should be seen together (fig. 4.8). Place them on a wall in such a way that your eye can easily go from one to another; plans find their place logically under matching elevations because we look down at the ground and we look up at facades. Ideally, sectional drawings should be placed beside elevations.

Some circumstances prevent the ideal ordering of the drawings, particularly in competitions, where the format is imposed or wall space is limited. Nevertheless, logic must prevail. For instance, a plan should always be placed under a matching elevation, i.e., the elevation that corresponds with the lower edge of the plan. To do otherwise would require an observer to mentally turn the plan around.

Why such emphasis on draftsmanship, upon presentation? Because, as the early twentieth-century American architect H. van Buren Magonigle noted, it is "by means of drawings the eye is trained to appreciate values of light, shade and color—and it is with light and shade and color the architect deals all his life."

Drawing takes time, but the result is worth it. Make time for drawing. It will do wonders towards educating your vision and refining your taste. Georges Gromort wrote, "Some students draw faster than others. Learn to estimate how many days you need to complete your final drawings. You must naturally work on your design as long as possible, but you must absolutely know when to stop. Wisdom consists of expressing all that your design has to give, at the point where it is in its development. For this to be possible, it must be properly drawn and rendered. It is foolish to let poor time management ruin a design. Take into account, every time, the scale of your drawings—especially the facade—and the size of the boards."

Before leaving the subject, I must reiterate the importance of shading in drawing classical forms. A detailed rendering of a simple Doric column with its entablature, correctly drawn, demonstrates the expressive power of shading and its subtlety (see fig. 2.1). Observe the smooth transition between the lighted side of the shaft and the shaded side; notice the highlight from top to bottom on the left; see the effect of reflected light, especially dramatic on the metopes. The purpose of shading is not to present a realistic rendition of the lighting conditions of a specific facade, but to accurately represent the modeling of that facade. (More detailed advice can be found in Henry McGoodwin's *Architectural Shades and Shadows*, originally published in 1904 and reprinted by the American Institute of Architects in 1989.)

An architectural project should be drawn accurately in all its aspects for evaluation. For this to happen, design and drawing must occur simultaneously.

FOUR SIMPLE DESIGN PROBLEMS

The following programs were written for second-year students majoring in architecture. Functional requirements were kept simple to allow students to concentrate on aesthetic and formal issues. The buildings and their context require equal attention. Naturally, the programs may be adapted to suit your needs.

Since the obvious is sometimes neglected, a few reminders may be helpful:

• A room is a space clearly defined by a floor, a roof, and four walls.

• The functions of the walls are to enclose, protect, and support.

• The main function of a roof is to protect an interior space as well as the walls that enclose it.

• Openings: Doors allow passage in and out of rooms and buildings. Windows let light in and let you see out. They also ventilate interiors.

A One-Room Building

The first program, a study in the well-defined plan, calls for a small building. Freestanding and with four identical facades, this building should aim to be the most beautiful ever designed. This may be an unrealistic goal but, as Frank Lloyd Wright observed, one should aim for the ideal. The site is a lake shore in a privately owned, large and beautiful landscape. The structure must provide a comfortable summer shelter where a few people—adults or children—can sit, rest, talk, make music, read, play, or have tea. In other words, this is a place to be enjoyed in a civilized way.

• The space within will measure 8 x 8 feet. It will be raised a step or two above the ground. There will be an opening on each of the four walls.

• The walls, 24 inches thick, will be made of solid masonry. All four sides carry the same design. Classical columns frame the openings on the outside and enhance the four facades.

• The openings only receive curtains, not doors or windows.

• The roof may be flat or pyramidal; the underside may be flat or vaulted.

• The floor pattern is made of colored marbles arranged to underline the shape of the space within; the design will echo the articulation of the ceiling

DRAWING REQUIREMENTS
Floor plan, section, elevation at 1/4 inch scale.

DESIGN SOLUTION
In this proposal (fig. 4.9), thin engaged columns carry a diminutive entablature. Pediments suggest a cruciform plan. Arcuated openings and balustrades—on three sides only— give an inviting look to the building.

A Pair of Pavilions

Design a pair of identical, freestanding, one-room buildings for a lake shore in a large and

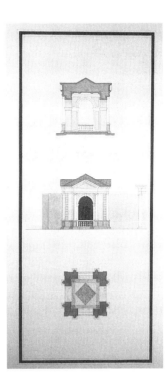

4.9 (see also C.1). Plan, section, and elevation of a one-room building. Chris Campbell.

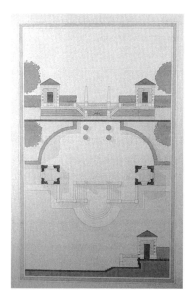

4.10 (see also C.2). Plan, section, and elevation of a landing stage with a pair of one-room buildings. The overlap of the three drawings makes an effective one-board presentation. Colin Lowry.

4.11 (see also C.3). Elevation of two pavilions connected by an arcade. Jesse Benjamin Nicholson.

4.12. A one-room pavilion within an outdoor room. Joel Kline.

beautiful park. The pavilions provide a comfortable summer shelter for a few people to wait for a boat. The buildings stand at the top of an eight-foot cliff; they frame a landing stage, which consists of wide steps against which small craft are moored.

This is a variant of the first problem. A major difference is that instead of one building standing in isolation, the pavilions frame an open space. Due to its size and its central position, that interval is more important than the buildings.

DRAWING REQUIREMENTS

Floor plan, section through the stairs, and general elevation at 1/8 inch scale.

DESIGN SOLUTION

The strategy for this project (fig. 4.10) is to convey hospitality. The modest architecture of the pavilions gives more importance to the space between them. A semicircular hedge frames that space in an "open-arms" gesture.

In a slightly different program, the shore is only three feet above the water level and the pavilions are to be connected by an arcade or a colonnade. This leads to a dramatic change of character, and the design looks like a monumental gateway (fig. 4.11).

A Room within a Room

Design an outdoor room around a one-room pavilion. The outdoor space will be understood as an extension of the space within the pavilion. Activities of the users include sitting, resting, talking, making music, playing, having tea, and generally enjoying themselves both indoors and outdoors, depending on the weather and the number of participants.

No specific form or dimension are given by the clients. The site is well drained, and the ground is covered with coarse sand. A path through the woods leads to a single point of entry on the south. A gateway consistent with the architectural language of the pavilion will express the character and the function of the place.

First phase: General plan; longitudinal section through the door and the gate; transverse section showing the south elevation of the pavilion, all at 1/8 inch scale.

Second phase: Some of the most informative and elegant architectural drawings ever made were those of the seventeenth century, which combine true plans and true elevations into one single drawing. A good source is *Views of the Gardens at Marly* (Emmanuel Ducamp, ed., Alain de Gourcuff, Paris, 1998). Study them and present your design in one drawing combining plan and elevation. Make sure the plan is entirely shown and that nothing drawn in elevation—gate, pavilion, fountain, statues, stone furniture, enclosures—hides any part of it.

DESIGN SOLUTION

The outdoor room is enclosed by a wood trellis painted green (fig. 4.12). Dense vegetation growing up behind the trellis suggests that the space is a clearing carved out of the woods. There are alcoves, or intimate recesses such as exedra for varied, peaceful activities and a sheltered walk around the site. Outdoor furniture consists of fixed stone benches and tables. A small fountain and classical sculpture animate and embellish the outdoor room and contribute to a mood of cheerful and relaxed enjoyment.

In order to show the most important aspects of the design in a single drawing, the pavilion is represented by its facade. The walk surrounding the site, treated as a pergola, is shown realistically in the upper half of the drawing and as a plan in the lower half.

Rooms within Rooms within Rooms

Design a formal clearing to accommodate a complex structure made of four one-room buildings connected by porticoes wrapped around a square open-air space. The program requires indoor and outdoor rooms connected by roofed-over spaces without walls, so that users

4.13 (see also C.5). Plan of four pavilions connected by porticoes in a formal clearing. Jessika Creedon.

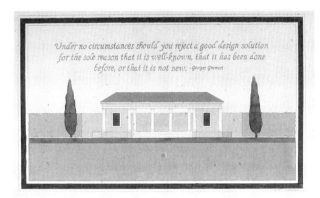

4.14 (see also C.6). Elevation. Jessika Creedon.

could experience a complete range of architectural spaces, from most open to most secluded. The purpose of the design is to provide a venue for large parties involving musical entertainment and dancing. The corner pavilions could house any number of functions including catering facilities, restrooms, storage, and so on.

DRAWING REQUIREMENTS

Plan, section, and elevation at 1/8 inch scale.

DESIGN SOLUTION

A high hedge defines a great variety of spaces (figs. 4.13, 4.14). Tall cypresses and small pools animate the enclosure. Different floor patterns distinguish the three types of space within the structure: enclosed, roofed, and open to the sky. The elevation shows one of the colonnades between two of the corner pavilions.

CHAPTER 5

INTERIOR ARCHITECTURE

If, as the philosophers maintain, the city is like some large house,
and the house is in turn like some small city, cannot the various parts of the house—
atria, loggias, dining rooms, porticoes, and so on—be considered miniature buildings?

—L. B. ALBERTI

The previous chapter focused on the essential design problems of the one-room building, the outdoor room, and the relationship between the two. Classical architecture revolves around these issues. Now we will look at the design of larger buildings and explore the interrelationships of rooms and the articulation of the surfaces that enclose them.

When we enter a building, we form a rapport with it, consciously or not. Whether we normally pay attention to our surroundings or not, the opportunity for so doing is greater inside because our pace usually slows down. In this first contact with a building, the quality of the architecture is determinant. The facade should have already suggested the character of the building, and the vestibule should confirm it.

VESTIBULES AND STAIRS

The vestibule, foyer, or entry hall is the most public part of a building. Whatever its size, it is unique in function, and its form, location, and treatment should reflect this status. The door through which we enter is likely to be the main opening of the facade, and it is probably found in the middle. Once in the vestibule, we find ourselves in a space that is both a room and a circulation space. A vestibule is a place of orientation and decision. It is also a transitional space, mediating between the outside and the inside. This is why its architectural treatment is often that of an exterior space and built of stone (fig. 5.1).

If there is a stair, it must be considered in conjunction with the vestibule. If the principal living spaces are on the next floor, the stair should be visible and inviting; it should probably be placed on axis with the front door. If the upstairs rooms are secondary, the stair should be on the side, and perhaps screened from view.

Either way, stairs have such a unique form and a special role that they deserve a space all their own. In grand buildings, they play a ceremonial role and should be the main focus of the vestibule (fig. 5.2). Double stairs with open wells belong to palaces and public buildings that handle large crowds. So do wide and straight stairs.

At the Théâtre de l'Odéon in Paris (fig. 5.3), a pair of straight stairs leads to a two-story octagonal space covered by a dome. The original design provided access to a café on each side, accessible through bridges spanning lateral streets.

The celebrated stair of the Grand Théâtre in Bordeaux (figs. 5.4, 5.5) is on axis with the vestibule in a 30- x 30-foot space. Treated in stone and most dignified, it is nevertheless almost intimate in feeling because of the handling of natural light, which seems to caress its walls.

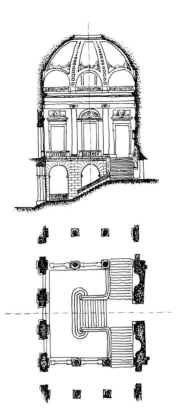

5.1. The gallery leading to the Royal Opera at Versailles is executed in stone as if it were an outdoor space.

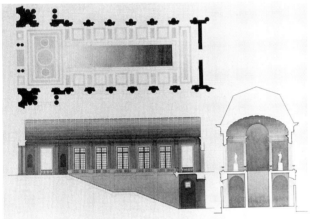

5.2. Plan and section of a stair in a museum. Student project by the author in preparation for admission to the Ecole des Beaux-Arts.

5.4. Grand Théâtre, Bordeaux, 1780. Victor Louis. Second-floor plan and section.

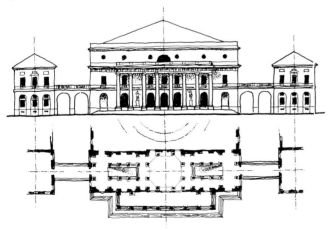

5.3. Théâtre de l'Odéon, Paris, 1780. Peyre and De Wailly. A dramatic effect was created on the upper floor by an octagonal opening in the ceiling and a dome above it.

5.5. Flight of stairs leading to the first tier of boxes at the Grand Théâtre in Bordeaux. The heavy rustication of the lower part of the walls is a treatment suitable for an exterior space.

Courtyard

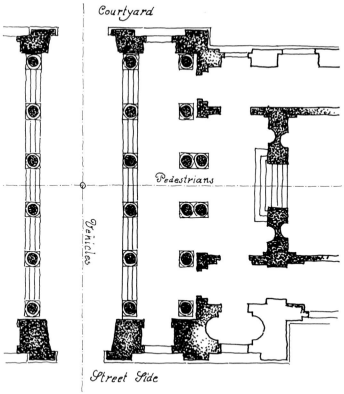

Pedestrians

Vehicles

Street Side

5.6. *Hôtel de la Monnaie, Paris, 1775. J. D. Antoine. Half-plan of the vestibule showing vehicular access and the steps leading to the split stair.*

5.7. *Hôtel de la Monnaie. The covered drive running through the vestibule from left to right. Access to the staircase is at a right angle, to the left.*

5.8. *Hôtel de la Monnaie. The twin upper flights of the split stairs.*

COURTYARD

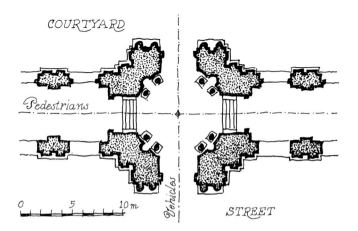

Pedestrians

Vehicles

STREET

0   5   10 m

5.9. *Palais du Luxembourg, Paris, begun 1615. Salomon de Brosses. Plan of the open pavilion where visitors arrived.*

5.10. *Palais du Luxembourg. Entrance pavilion seen from the street.*

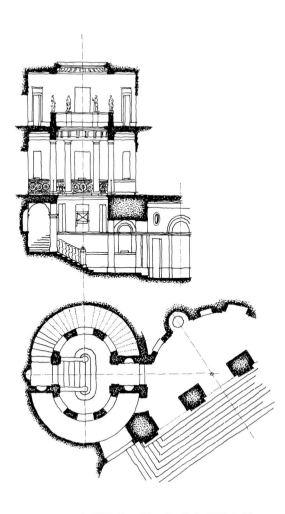

5.12. Stair at Hume House, London, 1775. Robert Adam. The straight lower flight ends at the first landing to be continued by two semicircular flights.

5.11. Stairs to the Bibliothèque Mazarine, Paris, 1824. L. M. Biet. Plan and section.

5.13. Stairwell at Hume House. Although the stair leads only to the first story, the stairwell is three stories high and capped with a dome and skylight.

When a vestibule is accessible to vehicles, passengers disembark under shelter. In that case, the stair must be placed on the side. In the vestibule of the Hôtel de la Monnaie in Paris, an impressive colonnade frames the one door leading to the stairs on the right side. To achieve grandeur and symmetry, an identical colonnade is repeated on the other side of the covered drive (figs. 5.6, 5.7, 5.8).

Another interesting arrangement is found at the Palais du Luxembourg, built in 1615 for Queen Marie de' Medicis. Passengers arrive in a domed pavilion (figs. 5.9, 5.10) framing a view of the large courtyard beyond. From there, a long gallery takes the guests around the courtyard to the main rooms of the palace.

The nineteenth-century stair leading to Bibliothèque Mazarine, also in Paris (fig. 5.11), relies on an ingenious combination of curved forms and straight lines to lead visitors from the courtyard to a split stair—actually a half stair—cradled in a quasi-elliptical enclosure. Robert Adam used a similar plan in 1775 for the stair of Hume House in London (figs. 5.12, 5.13), where a greater elegance prevails in the decoration.

5.14. *Petit Trianon, Versailles, begun in 1753. J. A. Gabriel. On the south facade, the middle door, undifferentiated from the others, leads to the vestibule.*

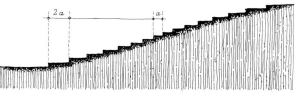

5.17. *The first eight steps of this diagram were observed in the gardens of Vaux-le-Vicomte, begun in 1653 by André Le Nôtre and restored in the early twentieth century. The treads increase progressively until their length is double. The eight upper steps were added on the drawing to show how their length would decrease in a longer flight.*

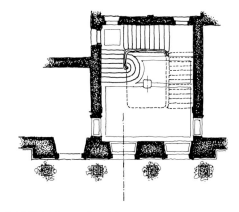

5.15. *Petit Trianon. Plan of the stair at ground level. The lower steps face the entry door but the room itself is off-center.*

5.18. *Farnsworth House on the Fox River, Illinois, 1950. Mies van der Rohe.*

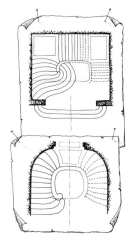

5.16. *Plan of rococo stairs contained in an enclosure no wider than 12 feet. Far from being disconcerting to the user, the relaxed, sinuous curves send a message of welcome.*

5.19. *Tayloe House and Office, Williamsburg, Virginia, mid-eighteenth century.*

Formality coexists harmoniously with informality at the Petit Trianon at Versailles. Built for the king but conceived for his private enjoyment, the informal stair is found within the vestibule itself. The entry door is correctly located at the center of the facade (fig. 5.14), but the vestibule is off-center and only the first steps of the stair align with it. The stair itself curves to one side in the typical domestic fashion of the period (fig. 5.15).

The art of building comfortable stairs has suffered in contemporary design. The sensuous curves of rococo stairs (fig. 5.16) may appear gratuitous and self-indulgent, but they are carefully designed to accommodate the gait of the users. Those who have climbed such stairs can testify that they are safe and easy to negotiate, either going up or coming down. A particularly neglected refinement is the variation of step dimensions within a single flight of stairs. It was common practice in the seventeenth and eighteenth centuries to increase the treads and shorten the risers of the first and last steps to ease the transition from horizontal to incline and vice versa (fig. 5.17).

5.20. Petit Trianon, Versailles. A stair is seen at the end of the enfilade.

THE ORDERING OF ROOMS AND THEIR SHAPE

We erect buildings principally as shelter. In the twentieth century, the use of glass was often intended to create the illusion that the natural environment was brought inside (fig. 5.18). A traditional building creates a sense of security with four walls, a roof overhead and solid ground underfoot (fig. 5.19).

Knowing where you are is fundamental in architecture. A classical building lets you know this by first making it clear whether you are indoors or outdoors and then by giving every room a distinctive and memorable shape. As we have seen, simple geometric figures derived from the square and the circle are favorites; rooms are contrasted with one another to reinforce the uniqueness of each. While differentiating each room, the classical architect must also ensure the unity of the whole and establish a clear relationship between rooms with a simple plan. Doors are lined up for visual continuity, creating enfilades terminating on a focal point—a door, a window, or a fireplace, for example (fig. 5.20).

Next comes the design of the inside surfaces. As noted earlier, opposite walls contribute to the unity of the space they define by "reflecting" one another. This applies to the floor and the ceiling as well. If a room is vaulted or covered with a dome, the floor responds with a two-dimensional reflection of it (fig. 5.21). If the room is a plain rectangle, floor and ceiling receive a grid approximating the subdivision of the walls (fig. 5.22). It is not necessary to match divisions line for line; widths may vary but the number of subdivisions must be the same. What is essential is a

5.21. Panthéon, Paris, 1764. Jacques-Germain Soufflot. The floor design reflects the circular form of the dome above and the five rings of coffers that articulate it.

5.22. Vizcaya, Miami, Florida, 1914–16. F. Burrall Hoffman; Paul Chalfin, artistic supervisor. In this room, ceiling and wall conform to the same general subdivision, but the ordering patterns are not rigidly lined up.

set of compatible patterns, and the better trained the eye of the designer, the better the result.

Wall articulation is a way to give presence and significance to a large and undifferentiated surface. That is achieved by dividing the surface into a series of juxtaposed, regular areas that can be apprehended by the eye in sequence, one at a time. Articulation takes its clues from the openings in the walls. Few walls are totally devoid of openings; there is at least a door, a window, or a fireplace. If a wall is absolutely plain, it will be modeled after the one on the opposite side.

Once an opening is made into a wall, the remaining area around it resembles an O, a U, a T, or an L. The eye feels uncomfortable with asymmetrical, off-balance shapes; it prefers squares and rectangles. The articulation of a wall thus consists of dividing the entire surface into a series of squares and rectangles placed side by side within a simple regular grid (fig. 5.23). A dado replaces the pedestal in a room without actual columns. Encircling the room like a belt, the dado seems to hold it together. Curves are friendlier than angular shapes. They can be introduced in the form of round openings or arches. Arches have the power to emphasize the preeminence of openings, which can be actual passages or just frames (fig. 5.24).

There are many ways to make the articulation of a wall visible, starting with paint and a good color selection. Moldings can create superb effects. More expensive materials include oak paneling, gilt, marble, carvings, frescoes, or paintings on canvas integrated in a wall, but a good articulation scheme is more important than the materials.

Built-in furniture is part of the walls. In dining rooms, hallways, and libraries, tables are usually freestanding, but they too are part of the architecture. They introduce an important datum: the positions of our elbows when we are seated. That height should be matched by the dado. In the seventeenth and eighteenth centuries, it was customary to line chairs up against

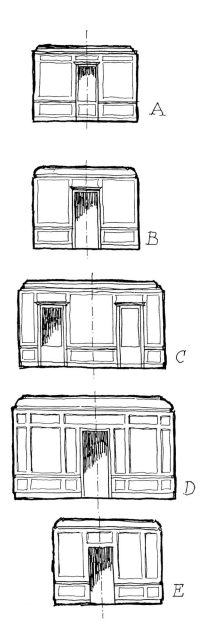

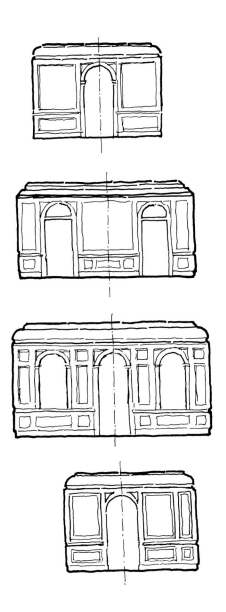

5.23. The articulation of a wall takes its cue from the openings. A door or a window on center allows for a comfortable balance, as in A and B. Where the door at the center is too narrow to dominate the entire wall, the panel above can be stretched over the side panels to suggest a larger element, as in D. When the opening is off-center, the impression of another opening must be introduced to achieve a symmetrical design, as in C. When this cannot be done, symmetry must control as much of the wall area as possible, as in E, where the narrow panel on the right contributes to the regularity of the wall pattern.

5.24. Arches celebrate the entrance of a person into a room. The curve of an arch can fit in the rectangular grid of an articulated wall.

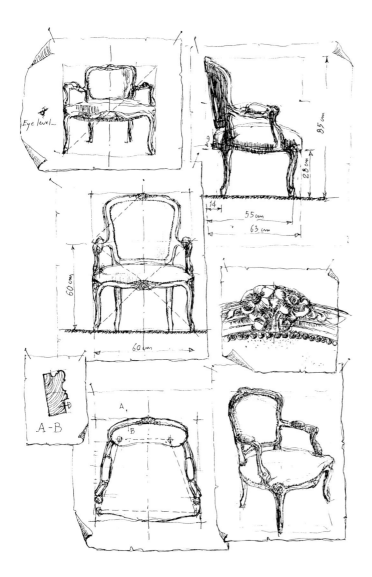

5.25. Multiple views of a mid-eighteenth-century French armchair.

the walls when not in use to give an impression of peace and order to people entering the room. Chairs can easily be moved wherever they are needed. Having to adapt to the human body, chairs are also the most complex of all architectural forms (fig. 5.25).

The ordering of rooms obeys functional and circulation requirements. A look at a few buildings of moderate size shows the simple shapes of rooms, their variety and the nature of their interrelationship. Chiswick House, on the outskirts of London, is a square building measuring approximately 70 feet. Entrance from the forecourt is on the west side, at the bottom of the plan (fig. 5.26). The main axis goes from there through the entire structure into the garden, as do the parallel companion axes and the north-south cross-axis, which reaches out beyond the walls to anchor the building in the landscape. Secondary axes, parallel to the cross-axis, terminate at fireplaces. There are two main circulation paths. One is cruciform originating at the core, under the dome. The other is peripheral, beginning and ending at the entrance hall. The axes are lines of vision that give visitors a clear sense of where they are in the building by allowing a glimpse into adjacent rooms.

The overwhelming importance given to the central room is shown in the section. Planned as a gathering space, it is more than twice the height of the other rooms, which display paintings. The ground floor, where the library is located, is half the height of the piano nobile.

Bagatelle, in the Bois de Boulogne, measures about 60 feet in its greater dimension. Unlike Chiswick House, it is a two-sided building, with a front and a back (fig. 5.27). Both were "day villas," conceived for the exclusive enjoyment of the owners and their friends. Here again we can appreciate the formal variety of the spaces and the richness of both the lines of vision and circulation patterns. A circular form was also given to the assembly room, but for a different reason. At Chiswick, clerestory windows admit light

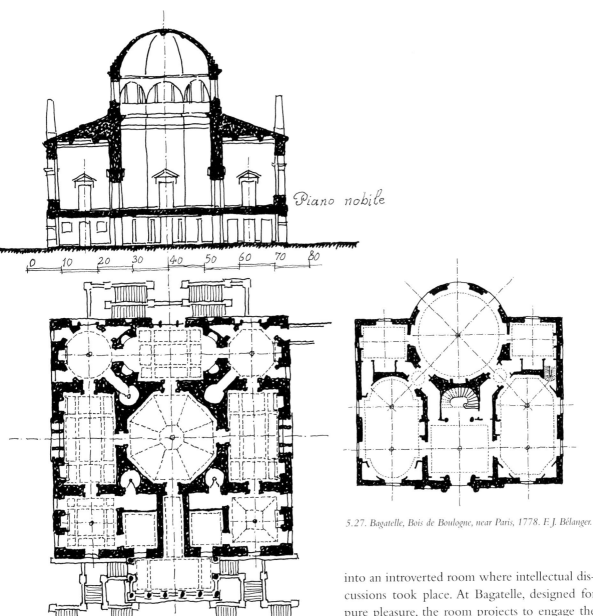

Piano nobile

0   10   20   30   40   50   60   70   80

5.26. Chiswick House, near London, 1725–29. Lord Burlington with William Kent.

5.27. Bagatelle, Bois de Boulogne, near Paris, 1778. F. J. Bélanger.

into an introverted room where intellectual discussions took place. At Bagatelle, designed for pure pleasure, the room projects to engage the garden visually and physically. The difference in the shape of the large rooms on either side is subtle. The ends of one room are polygonal while the ends of the other are semicircular. One reason for this is the search for variety. A more important reason is to avoid possible confusion. One must know exactly where one is, and no two rooms should be identical.

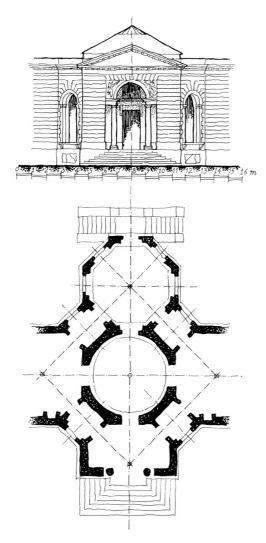

5.28. Music Pavilion, Montreuil, near Versailles, 1784. J. F. T. Chalgrin. Plan and entrance facade of the original building.

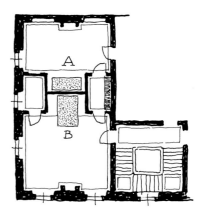

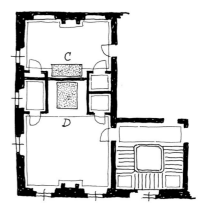

5.29a, 5.29b. A basic alcove contains a bed and little else. The bed can be hidden during the day, and small spaces on either side can be put to multiple uses.

The plan of the Music Pavilion of Montreuil (fig. 5.28) shows another variation on the day-villa theme. As at Chiswick, the circulation scheme involves two circuits, one cruciform and the other peripheral.

Whether wrapped around the outside of a building or the interior of a single room, walls present the same challenges. They must be organized and they must communicate the char-

acter and the function of the space they enclose. Important differences between indoor and outdoor surfaces reflect scale and materials.

BEDROOMS AND ALCOVES

Regardless of their form or their size, the two types of rooms that have the most specific

5.30. An alcove is a good way to give focus to a room.

5.31. This alcove includes a fireplace and other amenities. It is, in fact, a small bedroom widely open on a more public room. Curtains allow for privacy when needed. Musée Magnin, Dijon, France.

requirements are the most public and the most private: the vestibule and the bedroom. Both types have reached a high level of sophistication in the hands of traditional architects. Perhaps the most useful and pleasant feature in a bedroom was the alcove. In its simplest form, the alcove is just a recess for a bed (figs. 5.29a, 5.29b). It has advantages and charms of its own; it gives intimacy and it can save on heating costs. It is an ingenious way to combine sleeping accommodations with the other requirements of home life. The bed can be protected by curtains or a set of doors so that the room may be put to other uses during the day. The alcove is so convenient that it was found throughout Europe, in both modest farmhouses and palaces. Closet-like spaces on either side can satisfy a variety of needs, becoming bathroom, dressing room, home office or passageway. If adequately lighted and ventilated by a window, a residual space can be made into a small study or a sleeping room for an infant. In the embryonic form of a niche, the alcove can frame a bed or a couch (fig. 5.30) or it can be as large as a small

bedroom with a fireplace and other amenities (fig. 5.31).

Rooms are naturally placed in a certain order to satisfy functional requirements, but they are given identity by their shape, size, and proportions. The articulation of walls, floors, and ceilings also contributes to that identity. A good room is defined by walls all around, but its relationship to the context is also important. That is made clear by the vistas and enfilades revealed through door openings.

CHAPTER 6

FACADES

The architect's responsibility extends beyond the client's brief into the public realm so that his buildings, whether small or large, give public performances to the user and passersby—the audience of today and tomorrow.

—SIR RICHARD ROGERS

Not all buildings have a facade. A jumble of building blocks (fig. 6.1) may present a picturesque sight, but it does not have a facade, a "face." A true facade resembles the face of a geometric solid in the sense that it is nearly a plane surface. This is an important condition in smaller buildings because a small facade depends even more on flatness for unity. There will be projections and recessions, but the wall plane will be clearly identified.

COMPOSITION

In some ways, the facade of a building is like the human face; to a certain extent, it can be read. As Henry Hope Reed, the founder of Classical America, has observed, "Man does not build for himself anymore than he smiles for himself alone; the facade is designed out of respect for the beholder, a form of architectural courtesy to the man in the street." Unlike a human face, a facade is static, and it is usually regulated by a rectangular grid.

It is easy to verify these observations by looking at classical buildings. Robert Adam's Fishing Room (fig. 6.2), on the grounds of Kedleston Hall in Derbyshire, is about 20 feet wide. In spite of the proportionally large exedra carved out of

the facade, the wall plane maintains a powerful presence.

The French Pavilion at Versailles (fig. 6.3) derives its name from its location in the French garden. Facing the west side of the Petit Trianon, it consists essentially of one large circular room. Four smaller square rooms attached to it give the building a cruciform plan. The result is an imaginative design with sixteen wall planes. Of these, five can be seen from the Petit Trianon. It is the symmetry of the alternately receding and projecting planes that gives coherence and unity to the undulating facade. Situated in the middle of the garden, the pavilion presents the same inviting "open arms" gesture to the four cardinal points.

At the Pavillon de l'Aurore in Sceaux (fig. 6.4), the circular room is clearly revealed on the outside by a dome. Instead of four square rooms there are only two, attached to the right and to the left, and the front is identified by a pair of stairs leading to a terrace stretching across one of the long sides.

William Kent's Queens Temple (fig. 6.5) is backed up against dense plantings in Kensington Gardens. There are three large, identical arches in the front, but the middle one is given prominence by the much larger structure in which it is found. Visual unity is achieved in an inventive way: three

6.1. Chartrené in the Anjou region of France. Once a prosperous farm or manor, the building has been modified over the years in response to changing needs.

6.4. Pavillon de l'Aurore, Sceaux, near Paris, 1672. Claude Perrault.

6.2. Fishing Room, Kedleston Hall, Derbyshire, 1769–72. Robert Adam.

6.5. The Queen's Temple, Kensington Gardens, London, 1734. William Kent.

6.3. The French Pavilion on the grounds of the Petit Trianon, 1751. J. J. and J. A. Gabriel.

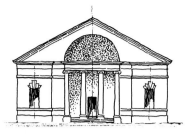

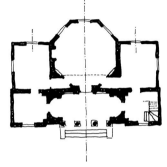

6.6. The Ingreste
Pavilion, Staffordshire,
c. 1750. Attribution
uncertain.

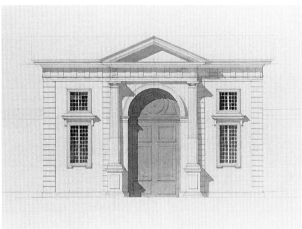

6.7. The entrance to a French hôtel. Design by the author. The shadows cast
by the capitals are inaccurately drawn.

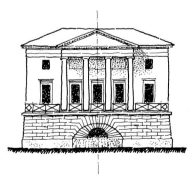

6.8. Country house
adapted from a drawing
by an unidentified nine-
teenth-century architect.

identical pediments whose sloping sides appear to be aligned suggest a fourth, larger triangle stretching across the three parts of the building.

The Ingreste Pavilion in Staffordshire (fig. 6.6) is also a two-sided building, but the front and the back form a striking contrast: there is a projecting octagonal room on one side and a recessed loggia on the other. A gigantic pediment capping the entire structure unifies the three parts of the composition. This is a two-story building deliberately presenting itself as one story. It is also an instance where either side can be considered the front: the concave elevation with the main entrance or the convex with the best view.

Until the late 1960s, the entrance pavilion to a French hôtel (fig. 6.7) was a typical project for students seeking admission to the Ecole des Beaux-Arts. The shallow facade of the building makes a contribution to the street wall. The division of the structure in two solid parts framing an opening dramatizes its function as a passageway to an important building. The large opening is dignified by a pair of columns and a pediment.

Buildings in the country tend to spread out laterally while urban constructions grow taller from a narrow base. Cities are supposed to be places of more intense activity; therefore, the erect, dynamic thrust of urban buildings contrasts with the horizontal stretch of country buildings, which suggests repose.

Let us examine two houses that illustrate this convention and symbolize their respective context. In spite of a substantial rusticated base raising a middle-size residence above the ground, the country house (fig. 6.8) is wider than it is tall. Water gushing from an arched opening in the base indicates a close involvement with the site. Of approximately the same period—that is, the early part of the nineteenth century—a town house (fig. 6.9) adopts the same three-tier composition: rusticated base, body, and roof. But the overall proportions are reversed, and the height is twice the width.

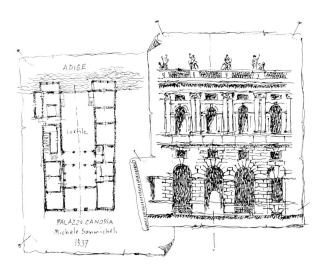

6.9. Town house facade adapted from a design by C. Normand.

6.10. A classical town house in New York City.

6.11. Palazzo Canossa, Verona, 1537. Michele Sanmicheli. Central portion of the facade.

Disregarding a fundamental classical canon, the horizontal line of the balustrade in a Manhattan town house (fig. 6.10) divides the height of the facade in half. The design is a chaste interpretation of Sanmicheli's Palazzo Canossa in Verona (fig. 6.11), where the height is also divided in half. Sanmicheli has been cited for his propensity to "break the rules," but it seems to me that Sanmicheli was so fluent in the classical language that his designs would not shock the most demanding classical critic. The facade of Palazzo Canossa is perfect, and so is that of the Manhattan town house.

A large building in a narrow street tends to be overwhelming, and it can never be seen as a whole. The solution adopted by the architect of 28 rue des Saints Pères in Paris (fig. 6.12) was to divide his design into five narrow, distinct sections, held together compositionally by horizontal lines and a consistent formal vocabulary.

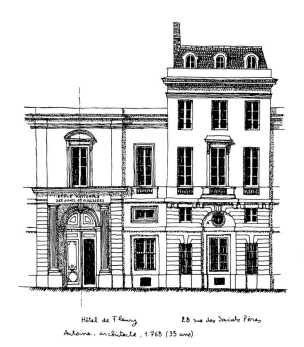

6.12. 28 rue des Saints Pères, Paris. Sometimes attributed to J. D. Antoine. Half elevation of the street facade.

6.13. *The thirteenth-century facade of the basilica forms the background of Piazza San Marco, Venice.*

6.14. *The square in front of Santo Spirito, Florence.*

FACADES AS BACKDROP

Victor Hugo argued that although a building belongs to its owner, its public facade belongs to the man in the street. The poet had a point: a facade can only be seen well from the outside. Classical and medieval facades were designed to address the community and serve as backdrops to social and civic activities, either staged or spontaneous. Every day of the year, there now are throngs of tourists who act their part on fabulous stages in Siena or Venice (fig. 6.13). In Florence, a few trees and some benches make the small space in front of Santo Spirito a delightful place to sit (fig. 6.14). The center of the stage is animated by the gentle play of water in a fountain. The provincial simplicity of the church makes a fitting background for the public space in front of it.

In the same vein, the facade of Santa Maria di Visitapoveri, on the island of Ischia in the bay of Naples, completes the courtyard. This tiny space is lined with stone benches where paupers sat, waiting for alms. However unlearned, the design of the facade (fig. 6.15) makes a charming contribution to the outdoor extension of the church nave.

Designed for an aristocratic patron, the Giardino del Cavaliere (fig. 6.16) is also striking for its simplicity. Built on the edge of the Boboli gardens in Florence, the charm of the place lies in the obvious lack of a wish to impress visitors. But there is drama in the site, an elevated terrace on the edge of a cliff with a lovely panoramic view of the Tuscan hills to the west and south. The garden is entered through a single opening in the north wall. The sober facade of the building on the east matches the long and flat rectangle of the garden. Horizontal and vertical surfaces bear simple designs executed with economical means—geometric patterns of low plantings for the garden and stucco for the building. Accessible only on foot, this peaceful place is a haven for those who walk between the rose beds or sit on the parapet in the shade of a few trees.

Palladio's Villa Barbaro (fig. 6.17) was intended to impress visitors. Located in the rich

6.15. *Santa Maria di Visitapoveri on the island of Ischia in the Bay of Naples.*

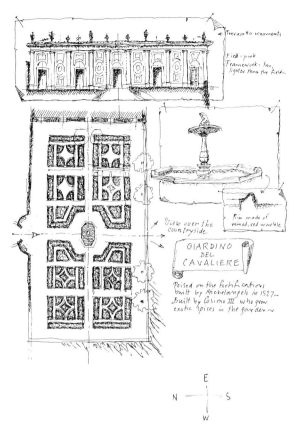

6.16. *Giardino del Cavaliere, Florence, originally built as an herb garden for Cosimo de Medici.*

6.17. *Villa Barbaro, Maser, 1549–58. Andrea Palladio.*

6.18. Campidoglio, Rome, 1536–78. Michelangelo.

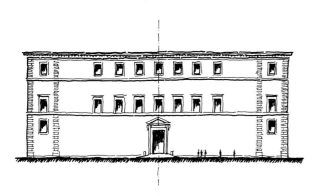

6.19. Palazzo della Sapienza, Rome. Probably designed by Giacomo della Porta.

plains of the Veneto, the design is stretched out for maximum effect. The approach road was built through the fields, and great attention was paid to the animated silhouette of the villa. The center and the extremities of the facade are taller than the rest, and connected by lower arcades. As guests came closer, at the slow pace of their horses, the building grew bigger and more details were revealed. Approaching a building indeed can be a form of theatrical performance. The ensemble combined the functions of a summer retreat and a working farm. Appropriately, the residential part is in the middle; it dominates the composition in height and in architectural treatment. Its status is indicated by a large pediment carried by a giant order, while the wings that shelter the farm buildings are plainer.

The Campidoglio in Rome (fig. 6.18) is one of the great urban compositions of all time. The U-shaped facade is discontinuous, but from the bottom of the stairs it hints at a tantalizing outdoor space. The broad stair itself is an invitation to go up. More or less rebuilt to Michelangelo's design, the pre-existing tower is essential because its vertical thrust anchors the design.

The facade of the Palazzo della Sapienza (fig. 6.19), the original university in Rome, sends an esoteric message. Clearly divided in three parts horizontally and vertically, the composition is established in a solid classical framework. The first tier consists of a forbidding wall that reveals nothing of the interior. In fact, it is misleading. Of the three openings, two are windows placed high above ground. A 15-foot door in the middle dwarfs all who enter. Was all this intended to intimidate those seeking wisdom?

There is no functional reason for the seven windows on each of the upper two floors, but in the occult language of numerology, the figure seven is the threshold of wisdom. This is supported by enduring popular beliefs: besides the seven pillars of wisdom, it is said that a child reaches the age of reason at seven; the crisis point of a marriage is supposed to occur in the seventh year; a broken mirror announces seven years of misery; most people cannot remember more than seven items from a list; only seven identical objects in a row can be perceived at one glance; and according to the Bible, the Creation took seven days.

Finally, does the progressive reduction in floor heights also carry a message? Might it symbolize a selective process in the number of students reaching sapience? Today, education is a universal right, but the ancients believed that knowledge might be dangerous in certain hands and should be cautiously passed on to those mature enough to make good use of it.

A facade that recedes invites the participation of the space in front of it in the design. An example of this is Collège des Quatre Nations in Paris (fig. 6.20). There may not be a more impressive design conceived on a more awkward site. Here the architect designed an ensemble which, seen from across the Seine, is one of the great ornaments of the city. A giant colonnade surmounted by a great dome forms the monumental core. Curved wings spread out to embrace a great outdoor space from which the river view can be enjoyed. Unfortunately, vehicular traffic along the river is now so heavy that pedestrian crossing is all but impossible.

Sheer size and an animated roofline are important factors in a building's presence, but they are no guarantee of success. The west facade of the Ecole Militaire (fig. 6.21) is separated from the Seine by the Champ-de-Mars, an empty space over 3,500 feet deep, where the Eiffel Tower was erected in 1889. Begun in 1751, the ambitious project for a military academy was severely curtailed by political discord and funding difficulties. Of the five pavilions originally envisioned for the 1,000-foot facade, only the central block with its square dome was built as designed. The photograph shows the abrupt termination of the main body of the building at the point where another muscular pavilion should

6.20. Collège des Quatre Nations, now Institut, the seat of the Academie Française, 1662. Louis Le Vau.

6.21. Ecole Militaire, Paris, begun in 1751. J. A. Gabriel. West facade.

6.22. Royal palace at Versailles, begun 1661. Louis Le Vau and J. H. Mansart.

6.23. Rue Royale, Paris, 1772. J.A. Gabriel.

have been erected. In spite of amputation, the building retains an amazing presence in an open space of awesome dimensions.

INFINITE FACADES

A facade that cannot be seen in its entirety may be called infinite. This is the case at Versailles, where the side overlooking the gardens is half a mile long. The gardens are huge in proportion, but they are fragmented in such a way that only a portion of the palace is visible frontally.

When commanded by Louis XIV to triple the size of the palace, J. H. Mansart simply replicated the beautiful design of Le Vau's original building. As noted earlier, the theme for the garden facing the new north wing is winter, incorporating tall and dark shade trees and appropriate iconography. For the garden facing the south wing, the theme is summer, celebrated by an abundance of flowers and a huge orangery. The regularity of the long, low facade of the palace in the background maintains the unity of the gardens (fig. 6.22).

Similar situations are found in urban contexts. A street is a circulation space connecting two nodes. It often is a long and narrow urban corridor, and its walls are mostly seen in perspective. In the best cases, their horizontal lines converge on an urban landmark as if they pointed toward it. Rue Royale in Paris (fig. 6.23) was conceived at the same time and by the same mind as Place de la Concorde, which it connects with the Church of Madeleine. While there is much to be said in favor of the picturesque spirit of medieval streets, often built and rebuilt over centuries, the homogeneity of a coordinated design ensures a greater sense of order and dignity. The termination of the Rue Royale by the Madeleine, completed in 1842, is rather cold and pompous, but the wide steps in front of the colonnade provide a wonderful stage for grand weddings and other pageants.

While the street walls are more interesting than the end wall of Rue Royale, the opposite is true of Rue de Birague, which leads to the Place des Vosges. In spite of heterogeneous constructions, the street has kept its original, regular shape. What we see at the end of the street is not a monument but a gateway (fig. 6.24) to the royal square built in 1612. Called the King's Pavilion to honor Henri IV, who ordered the construction of the square, the gateway is in fact a house. Taller than the other houses that surround the square and placed on the main axis, it faces the Queen's Pavilion on the opposite side. All thirty-six buildings in the square share the same colorful design of brick, stone, and slate, and they are further united by a continuous covered arcade. Although very large at 500 x 500 feet, Place des Vosges is perceived as a semiprivate space, as popular today as it was four hundred years ago.

The inward-looking, circular enclosure of the Place des Victoires (fig. 6.25), also in Paris, is another form of infinite facade. J. H. Mansart designed the supremely elegant wall in 1685. There are, unfortunately, too many interruptions, one of which is extremely wide, and the continuity of enclosure is lost.

Size alone does not determine whether a facade can be said to be infinite; more critical is the distance from which it is seen. The garden facade of the château at Bénouville (fig. 6.26) is by no means a small one, but it faces a limited space from which it fills the entire visual field of an observer.

PROPORTION, ARTICULATION, AND MEANING

Since the Renaissance, a considerable amount has been written on proportion. The fascination with certain recurring mathematical figures is justified by our forefathers' belief in the perfection of God's creation. The ratio 1.618 is found

6.24. One of the gateways to the Place des Vosges, completed in 1612. Attribution uncertain.

6.25. Place des Victoires, Paris, begun in 1686. J. H. Mansart.

6.26. Château de Bénouville, Normandy, 1768–77. Claude Nicolas Ledoux

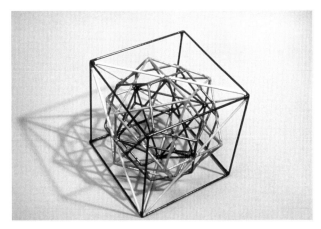

6.27. The five perfect polyhedra nestling in one another. The lattice form of the model makes the interrelationship of edges, nodes, and faces visible. Model and photograph courtesy Professor Pieter Huybers, Delft Institute of Technology.

6.28. The cross on the tallest of the three towers of the chapel in Ronchamp, completed in 1953. Le Corbusier.

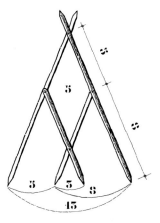

6.29. Diagram of the four-point compass. Opening ratios are identical to the division of every branch in the instrument.

so often in the natural world and in geometry that it has earned the name "Golden Number." This ratio is found in the five Platonic polyhedra, also called "perfect" because each one is made of a set number of identical and regular figures: square, equilateral triangle, or pentagon. The tetrahedron has four (triangular) faces; the hexahedron—more familiar as the cube—six (square) faces; the octahedron, eight (triangular) faces; the dodecahedron, twelve (pentagonal) faces; and the icosahedron twenty (triangular) faces. There are very interesting relationships between the faces, edges, and nodes of one perfect polyhedron and another, and the golden number is present in these relationships (fig. 6.27).

Through geometry, many great architects have endeavored to compose their buildings to reflect the ways of nature. Palladio, for example, strove to give his rooms dimensions taken from the square, including the diagonal of a half-square, which is also in the golden ratio. Le Corbusier used a method of his own invention, which he appropriately called the "Modulor," to coordinate the dimensions of his designs. But, in the preface to his book describing the system, he was careful to warn the reader that no system could be a substitute for talent, that is, for a sharp, well-trained eye.

An anecdote will confirm this (fig. 6.28). When putting the final touch to his chapel at Ronchamp, he used his eye to determine the dimensions of the slender cross that crowns the tallest of the three towers. A worker stood up there, holding two sticks at a right angle, while Le Corbusier gave him directions from the ground. Only when he was satisfied with the adjustments did he call the man down. Then and there, he adjusted the dimensions of the cross to fit precisely in his "Modulor" scale.

A "compass of proportion," also called "four-point compass," was used by architects, painters, and sculptors as well as masons and carpenters from the end of the sixteenth century until the

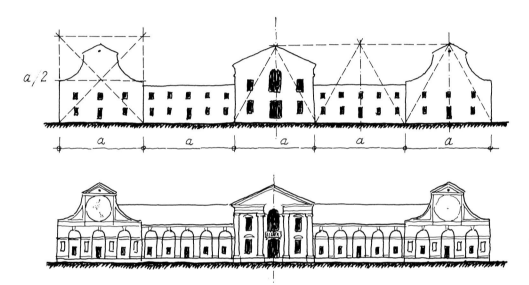

6.30. Although Durand reserved square grids for plans in his Précis, they are also used in the coordination of his facades.

6.31. Analysis of the facade of the Villa Barbaro.

mid-twentieth century. Made of four arms hinged in the proportion of 5 and 8, the distance between the points of the compass will also be 5 and 8, regardless of the angle between the arms. While the dimensions of the compass are fixed, the distance between the openings vary, but the ratio remains constant. The diagram (fig. 6.29) shows how 8 and 13 are obtained. That gives us the rule by which the series can be extended upwards and downwards to: 1, 2, 3, 5, 8, 13, 21, 34, etc. This leads to the Fibonacci series where (5 : 3), (8 : 5), (13 : 8), (21 : 13), etc. are nearly equal and average 1. 618, the golden number.

Many architects have designed beautiful buildings with the help of proportional systems. Others seem to have arrived at similarly good results instinctively. There are also rationalists like Auguste Choisy, a historian who favored simple

ratios like 3 : 2 and 3 : 5, or J. N. L. Durand, who relied mostly on square grids for the coordination of his designs (fig. 6.30).

Most people would agree that certain proportions are more pleasing to the eye than others. And it is a fact that, in most cases, these proportions are based on simple relationships. The differences between those who believe in the "magical" powers of the golden number and those who do not may not be irreconcilable. After all, a rectangle in the proportion 5 : 3 is very close to 1.618.

Proportions can best be studied in the design of facades. By looking closely at the elevation of the Villa Barbaro (fig. 6.31), we discover that it is divided in five parts of equal width (a). If we trace a square with (a) for the side, the center of that square determines the height of a significant

6.32. Analysis of the street facade of Hôtel d'Hallwyl.

line stretching across the entire facade. Drawing equilateral triangles on (a) gives us the apex of the three pavilions.

Similar observations can be made about the facade of Ledoux's Hôtel d'Hallwyl (fig. 6.32), where the overall diagram consists of two squares separated by the width of the door. The center of the squares gives us the location of a strong horizontal shadow line, cast by a cornice stretching from end to end of the building. The width of the door relates to the rest through an equilateral triangle whose height is that of the building and whose base is half the length of the facade. Lastly, the division of the width in five equal parts determines the height and width of the square recess in which the colonnaded frame of the door opening is inserted.

Investigations of this sort are easy to conduct and quite revealing. It is gratifying to engage in them, with the understanding that a geometric diagram underlying a design only provides a framework. The articulation that follows is just as important. The top drawing of Villa Barbaro contains the essentials of the design, but it seems uninspired. The next drawing, which includes the arcuated screen, makes all the difference. The final touch is given by the temple front on the central block, which definitely establishes the hierarchical logic between the parts.

We can also see the process from diagram to fully developed architecture at Hôtel d'Hallwyl. In the middle drawing, a radical transformation is made by the insertion of a triumphal arch at the center of the facade. Finally, the striation of the joints on the wall surface gives unity to the background. Note that these lines, horizontal and vertical, are an abstraction of their structural origin; only the radiating voussoirs of the arch express the logic of construction (fig. 6.33).

Before leaving this brief overview of proportion and articulation, let us mention a companion principle, the need in any composition for a dominant element. We have already seen that the need for a focus may be partially fulfilled by location, size, or shape. Palladio and Ledoux show us other ways to satisfy the same need when they use symbols: a temple front at Villa Barbaro or a triumphal arch at Hôtel d'Hallwyl.

A dominant element can only be significant if it is seen against a neutral or subdued background. At Villa Barbaro, the links between the three pavilions serve as foils. At the Hôtel d'Hallwyl, it is the entire surface of the wall. Observe how, though clearly distinct, the triumphal arch motif is finely integrated into the wall. In his wonderful essay on the theory of architecture, Georges Gromort makes the case for the same principle, but he uses the term "law of contrasts" instead of "law of dominant element," the latter being more precise. The difference is only one of degree, but "contrast" suggests conflict or opposition. "Dominant element" implies two aspects of one cohesive entity, like the recto and verso of a medal. The essential in architecture is harmony between the parts, and the suggestion of conflict is contrary to harmony. It is true that many buildings derive their visual interest from the opposition of two elements, but the opposition must be moderate, not jarring.

The law of contrasts or dominant elements might also be called "the law of difference." Except when mimesis protects a species from predators, nature gives a distinct look to each of her creations. Natural things that are different look different because nature loathes confusion. And so does good architecture. A capital is different from the base of a column for the same reason that a human head is different from a foot. Conversely, things that have the same purpose, like columns in a colonnade, should be identical.

ARCADES AND COLONNADES

Today the term "arcade" is used in many senses. What interests us here is the covered passage

6.33. Hôtel d'Hallwyl. The main entrance from the street.

6.34. Arcade along Rue de Rivoli, Paris, built 1812–52. Charles Percier and Pierre Fontaine.

found in front of a wall and behind a series of open arches. Palladio recommended that all city streets be lined with arcades. He praised them for the protection they gave pedestrians from the sun, from rain and snow, and also from traffic. They continue to do so, five centuries later.

Rue de Rivoli (fig. 6.34), lined with a variety of shops, is one of the more popular streets with

6.35. *The twin palaces on the north side of Place de la Concorde, Paris. There is a two-story loggia above the arcade at ground level.*

6.36. *Place de la Concorde. Interior of the arcade.*

6.37. *Place des Vosges. The arcade.*

tourists and other shoppers in Paris. It is a one-sided street facing the Louvre palace and the Tuileries for a good part of its length. Thick piers separate strollers from the traffic. The arcade is surmounted by several stories of luxury apartments and professional offices.

Rue de Rivoli terminates at the west in an arcade of a different character. Bordering Place de la Concorde on the north side, it is connected with no business with the exception of Hotel Crillon. There, strollers can enjoy a quieter walk on the way to the Champs-Elysées and its gardens (figs. 6.35, 6.36).

Place des Vosges (fig. 6.37) is surrounded on all four sides by an arcade deep enough for the restaurants to spread their tables out for alfresco lunch and dinner in the summer months. The view over a large garden dotted with fountains and benches under tall trees is restful. Vehicular traffic is limited by the narrow entrances to the square.

Even more secluded, the garden of the Palais-Royal (fig. 6.38) excludes traffic entirely. In fact, it is so well insulated by a solid mass of tall buildings around it that even the noise of traffic does not penetrate. Since entry is gained only through a few pedestrian entrances, many Parisians are not even aware of this oasis at the very heart of the city. Arcades make strolling around three sides of the gardens, past many interesting shops, a very pleasant experience.

An open colonnade at the south end of the garden marks its boundary; it indicates a change from public garden to official function. The courtyard on the other side is part of Palais d'Orléans (fig. 6.39), the seat of Conseil d'Etat, the French equivalent of the Supreme Court of the United States. The colonnade runs around the four sides of the courtyard, now disrupted by an "installation" of truncated columns.

The term "arcade" is used for a covered passage regardless of the nature of the structural supports, which might be piers or columns. One of the most celebrated public buildings of the second

6.38. Palais-Royal, Paris, a 1774 housing and business development on the site of Palais d'Orléans. The public garden.

6.39. Courtyard of the Palais d'Orléans, built c. 1770 and reconstructed several times. Contant d'Ivry. Colonnade, 1831. Pierre Fontaine. The public garden begins on the other side of the colonnade.

6.40. Ecole de Chirurgie, Paris, 1769–74. Jacques Gondoin. Partial view of the arcade joining the wings of the complex on the street side. The side of the main gate can just be glimpsed on the right. The first column on the left and the fourth one are engaged into a corner of the wall.

6.41. "The Lawn" at the University of Virginia, Charlottesville, 1817–25. Thomas Jefferson. Three of the pavilions with the continuous arcade in front of them.

half of the eighteenth century was the Ecole de Chirurgie (fig. 6.40) in Paris. It is a dignified U-shaped complex wrapped around a courtyard visible from the street through four rows of Ionic columns forming an arcade. There are fifteen bays from end to end, all approximately of the same width, but, although perfectly correct, the design is unusual. The columns facing the street in a row are handled in three different ways. They are either engaged in a wall, freestanding, or engaged in a corner. Moving from left to right, there are four engaged columns, then two freestanding columns, then two more engaged columns before the arch of the gate in the middle. Since the facade is symmetrical, the sequence continues in reverse order on the other side. The photograph shows that the first column on the left and the fourth one are engaged in a corner of the wall.

Arcades are also found outside cities. The University of Virginia (fig. 6.41), conceived by Thomas Jefferson as an "academical village," was built on what was then a rural site. The centerpiece is a domed library from which two opposing arcades run southward, framing a

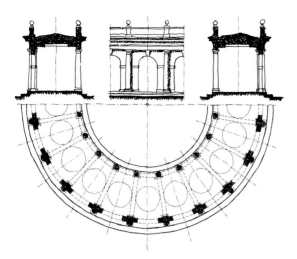

6.42. A circular arcade. Half-plan, cross section and partial elevation of the outside wall.

200- x 600-foot lawn and, originally, a view over the hills at the south end. The arcades connect ten pavilions, five on each side, each housing a classroom on the ground floor and living quarters for a professor above. The spaces between the pavilions are occupied by student rooms built along the arcades. To serve as illustrations for lectures on architecture, Jefferson made ten different designs for the pavilions. But he sensed that the arcades should be perfectly regular from end to end to give unity to the entire complex.

Arcades can be detached from a larger building and open on both sides. Circular arcades (fig. 6.42) present an interesting problem because the

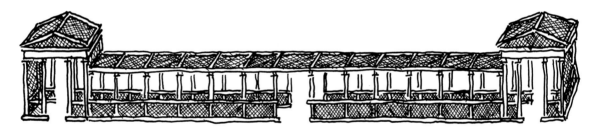

6.43. A rustic arcade in the country after Jacques Androuet Du Cerceau.

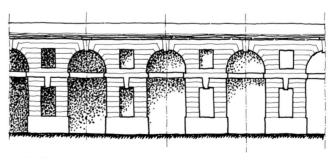

6.44. Openings necessary in one- and two-story buildings can fit in the same wall pattern.

length of the curve is greater on the outside than on the inside. Consequently, the openings will be larger on the outside than on the other. A colonnade on the shorter side and a wall on the other will solve the problem. The ends of the cross-beams sitting on the columns will be received by pilasters applied to the wall and engaged columns of the same size will be applied to the outside. The outer wall will absorb the difference in length, and the openings on both sides will have the same width.

Arcades in the country (fig. 6.43) may be plain wood structures whose charm greatly relies on the plants they support. Solid enclosures may be replaced with lattice to filter the bright summer light.

The great merit of arcades and colonnades is to endow buildings and streets with regularity. Many arcades are only two-dimensional features. Such is the case at the Place d'Armes in Dijon (see fig. 3.21) and at the circular Place des Victoires in Paris (see fig. 6.25). Arcaded walls can accommodate both high- and low-ceilinged rooms with a variety of openings. Where openings are not needed, their outlines will appear as simple recesses in the wall (fig. 6.44).

Another type of arcade is the shopping gallery with shops on both sides. Such arcades are usually entered from the ends, which can be locked up at night. Security becomes less of an issue, and the shop fronts can include large expanses of glass. Natural light must come from above, which explains why this type of arcade began to appear when glass and metal became affordable in the nineteenth century. Shopping arcades are attractive because they are safe, climate-controlled, and removed from traffic (fig. 6.45). In Paris it is possible to hop from one arcade to the next and browse for hours (fig. 6.46). The Galleria Vittorio-Emanuele in Milan is among the largest, composed of two pedestrian streets intersecting at a right angle. The glass dome at the crossing reaches a height of 160 feet (fig. 6.47).

6.45. An elegant nineteenth-century shopping arcade in London.

6.46. Galerie Vivienne, Paris, 1828.

6.47. Galleria Vittore-Emanuele, Milan, 1867.

CHAPTER 7

MASSING

Architecture is inhabited sculpture.

—CONSTANTIN BRANCUSI

The word "massing" describes the arrangement of architectural volumes into a coherent whole. Many factors, including function, site, climate, local culture, aesthetics, and building technology determine the arrangement, and the relative influence of these factors varies greatly.

Massing is the arrangement of volumes in space, and it requires a minimum of three drawings to be understood. As we know, the plan shows the location of the rooms and the circulation pattern in a building, the section indicates the relative height of the rooms, and the elevation shows the exterior appearance of the building. Only the sequential study of the three drawings makes it possible to form a mental picture of the building. Massing is that mental picture.

THE DOME AND
THE COURTYARD:
THEIR ROLE AND THEIR PLACE

In an ornamental pavilion for the park at Croome Court in Worcestershire (fig. 7.1), Robert Adam imagined a witty massing that contains no rooms. The core of the building conceals a small spiral stair leading to the roof terrace. The massive masonry block seems to have been created for the sole purpose of carving out four exedra, which offer views of four different landscapes. The design is an abstract sculpture dominated by the pure geometry of squares and circles. The tower and the dome, the columns and exedra, the niches (all nineteen of them) are circular. They modify and enrich the half-cube of the building mass. The concavity of the exedra is held in balance by the convex, semicircular steps and by the cylindrical structure on the upper level. In elevation, the diagonal of a square equivalent to that of the plan controls the size of the tower, the height of the main block, the axes of the niches, and the location of the columns and their height.

Each drawing, plan, section, or elevation, reveals something that cannot be shown in the others. Louis XIV's chateau at Marly was a perfect square in plan with four identical facades, but the regularity of the facades belied the spatial complexity of the cross section (fig. 7.2). How could visitors anticipate that the huge door in the middle of each facade opened into a small vestibule? And once arrived in the three-story salon at the center of the palace, how were they to understand how natural light could flood the room from windows that should have been buried in the mass of the building? The facade announced a solid and compact building block, and the last thing to be expected was a circular

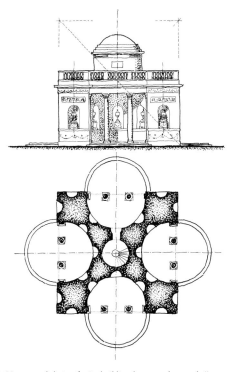

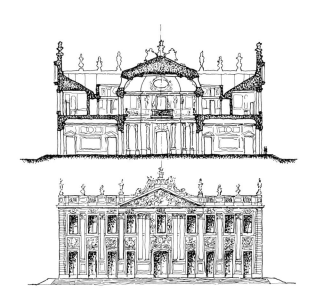

7.1. *Unexecuted design for "a building between the woods."*
Robert Adam.

7.2. *Royal Pavilion, Marly, near Paris, 1679–82. J. H. Mansart with*
Charles Le Brun.

terrace around the main salon on the second
floor. Here the architect performed a bit of
magic. Marly was created for the king's entertainment and the adulation of his entourage. The
spatial organization—the massing—was deliberately handled in a theatrical way, suggesting the
miraculous. The basic concept, or *parti*, of a larger
space at the core with smaller rooms revolving
around it is an archetypal design solution for
classical buildings. The central space reveals the
essence of the whole building. Open to the sky
or covered by a roof, it is the ideal location for
the principal function of the building. At Marly,
it is for the worship of the all-powerful king. In
another, much admired twentieth-century
design, the library at Phillips Exeter Academy by
Louis Kahn (fig. 7.3), the six-story void at the
core has no purpose other than to show the

7.3. *Library, Phillips Academy,*
Exeter, New Hampshire, 1971.
Louis Kahn. One of the four
undifferentiated facades.

7.4. *At the Exeter library, the*
book stacks surround the hollow
core of the building.

7.5. *Monticello, Charlottesville, Virginia, 1771–1809. Thomas Jefferson. The west front, with the dome reflected in the fishpond.*

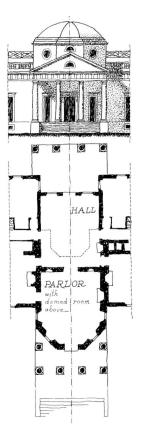

7.7. *Monticello. Interior surface of the dome.*

7.6. *Plan of the central part of Monticello. The dotted line in the hall indicates the outline of the balcony that links the private rooms of the house on either side of the double-height public rooms.*

book stacks for their symbolic significance. Wrapped around on several stories, they can be fully seen from the center, through enormous circular openings on all four sides (fig. 7.4). The outer layer of the building, around the stacks and next to the windows, is filled with study carrels.

From the outside, neither Marly nor the Exeter library reveals the presence of a major space within. Other classical buildings do announce that fact, usually with a high dome, which is the most effective way to disclose the presence of an important room within. That is the reason for the dome Thomas Jefferson built at Monticello (fig. 7.5). The dome is there only for visual emphasis; it is built over the most important room of the house without being integral to it. That room, which is the parlor (fig. 7.6), was built many years earlier. It is a rectangular room with an octagonal bay, which may have suggested the idea of a dome to Jefferson. The use of the space inside the dome itself remains unclear (fig. 7.7).

Jefferson is clearly one of the great American architects. Should we fault him for having treated the interior and the exterior of Monticello in a somewhat unrelated manner? Certainly not, since he is in good company: St. Paul's Cathedral in London, the Invalides in Paris, and the Capitol in Washington, D.C., all have two domes, one in keeping with the interior space and one at the much larger scale of the urban context and intended to be seen from afar. A domed parlor would be extravagant in a domestic program but, without the upward thrust of the dome, the hierarchy of the Monticello concept could not be read on the outside, and the exterior would be undistinguished.

Roofed over or not, large spaces at the core of buildings play a similar role. Free of the structural constraints of a roof, a courtyard can be given any size or shape. Should we, as designers, ask ourselves if the shape of a courtyard must bear some relationship to the overall shape of the

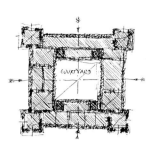

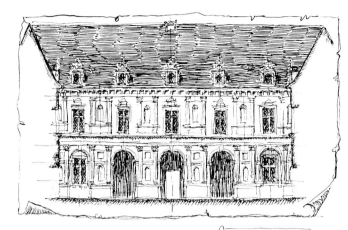

7.8. Chateau at Ancy-le-Franc, begun 1541. Attributed to Sebastiano Serlio or Francesco Primaticcio. The courtyard as it is today.

building around it? Does unity of design require a recurring formal theme, or should surprise and variety prevail? The square is the formal theme at the chateau at Ancy-le-Franc in Burgundy (fig. 7.8). The square courtyard at the center is the most magnificent "room" in the building. Curves are also used, but sparingly.

In 1532, Antonio da Sangallo and Baldassare Peruzzi began the construction of a fortress at Caprarola (fig. 7.9), twenty-five miles north of Rome. The pentagonal shape of their foundations determined the shape of the summer residence commissioned in 1546 by Cardinal Alessandro Farnese II, but the courtyard (fig. 7.10) was given a more conventional, circular shape. The architect was Vignola. How did he articulate the wall of the courtyard? A circular wall is usually divided into eight, twelve, or sixteen parts to maintain a reference to the front, back, and sides in a non-directional, circular space. Vignola decided on ten arches, half of them in reference to the five faces of the building exterior and five more for the corners. The arches alternate with ten pairs of columns. At Caprarola it is with numbers that the relationship between inner and outer enclosures is expressed.

It is a question of design ethics whether, in the absence of a dome, a courtyard—a hollow core—should remain hidden from the outside. Would it be more "honest" to let it stand out

7.9. Villa Farnese, Caprarola, 1557–73. Vignola. View from the village main street.

7.10. Villa Farnese. Circular courtyard.

7.11. *Customs post at the Barrière St. Martin, Paris, 1783–87. Claude Nicolas Ledoux.*

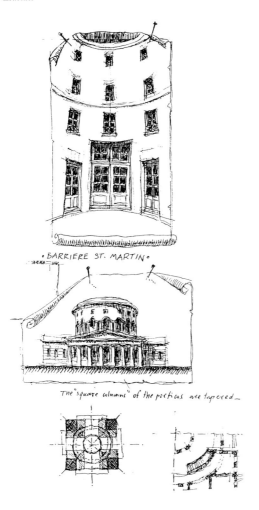

·BARRIÈRE ST. MARTIN·

The "square columns" of the porticos are tapered.

7.12. *Customs post of La Villette. Courtyard.*

above the roofs and reveal it as the dominant element of a composition? In other words, is it perverse to express with a solid form the existence of a void? Ledoux thought it was permissible, and he did just that, with a flourish, on several occasions. The results are evident in the well-preserved building of the Barrière St. Martin in Paris, one of the last remaining of the fifty customs posts he designed for that city (fig. 7.11). It overlooks the harbor at the end of a canal, and a raised, circular arcade (fig. 7.12) was used to monitor the boat traffic in the harbor. The arcade is carved out of a massive circular tower arising from a large square base. The core of the tower is a four-story courtyard, tall and narrow, not much more than a lightwell. It is nevertheless the major space of the building, and it presents itself as a huge tower.

FRONT AND BACK

Domes are special design elements that dominate an architectural composition when they are placed at the center, as at the Villa Rotonda or Chiswick, or in the middle of a facade, as at Monticello. In the latter case, the facade with the dome becomes the main facade. Does this mean that the main facade of Monticello is at the back? Is it not customary to call principal facade the front one, the one you see first? These are good questions.

As we have seen, classical architecture is anthropomorphic to the extent that buildings, like people, have a front and a back. So far so good, but front and back are not as clear in architecture as they are with people. In a public building, the principal facade conveys a civic image to the public. When the main side faces the public realm, it should be designed accordingly. At the Collège des Quatre Nations, the circular chapel occupies the middle of the facade facing the royal palace across the river, and the dome leaves no doubt as to the importance of the official religion or that of the urban context (see fig. 6.20).

The rectangular plan of the chapel designed by Liberal Bruant for the Invalides could not accommodate a dome. Three years after its completion in 1676, J. H. Mansart began to design a new church on a Greek cross plan to carry a dome. The new church, completed in 1706, is a powerful presence on the vast public square (see fig. 3.39).

Civic buildings are public by definition. Domestic buildings are built for the enjoyment of a family and, ideally, the private side faces a garden. It is said "to turn its back" on the public realm and, logically enough, the front is on the other side. There will be more "eyes" on that side, that is more openings, or larger ones. That side is the main facade. Monticello illustrates this well, as does Bagatelle (fig. 7.13). Both have a major room that seems to be pushing the wall out towards the garden. At Bagatelle, the room is circular and divided into eight bays to relate to the orthogonal grid of the building. Only three of the bays open out to the garden. The other five are inside to indicate that, in spite of the projecting wall, the room is firmly anchored in the building. This arrangement allows the extra two bays to give access to the rooms on the right and left sides.

FREESTANDING DOMES

Domes may crown a structure complete in itself. Bramante's supremely elegant Tempietto in Rome is a prime example (see fig. 2.60). Built on the presumed site of St. Peter's martyrdom, its impeccable proportions have been justly praised. With an outside diameter of 20 feet, the dome itself is tiny but, seen from the arched entrance to the courtyard in which it stands, the building and its dome convey a monumental impression. Had the courtyard been built as planned by Bramante, the circular building would have been

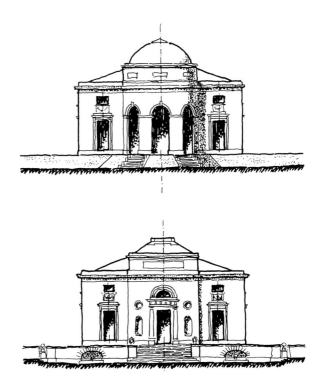

7.13. Bagatelle, Bois de Boulogne, near Paris, 1778. F. J. Bélanger. The main facade, overlooking the garden, is at the top. The entry facade is at the bottom. See also the plan of the building (fig. 5.27).

7.14. Radcliffe Library, Oxford, 1740–48. James Gibbs.

7.15. Temple of Love in the gardens of the Petit Trianon, 1748. Edme Bouchardon.

surrounded by a colonnade of the same shape and the total effect would have been more coherent. As it is, the rectangular shape of the enclosure does not relate well to the Tempietto.

James Gibbs's Radcliffe Library in Oxford (fig. 7.14) is a large and beautiful building. It was sometimes criticized for its circular plan, judged absurd and wasteful for a library, but a conventional rectangle would not have fitted in the site selected for the construction.

The Temple of Love at Versailles (fig. 7.15) was built for the visual pleasure of Marie-Antoinette. Sheltering a statue by Edme Bouchardon of Eros carving a bow from Hercules's club, the domed folly stands on a small island on axis with the east facade of the Petit Trianon. Better known as a sculptor than as an architect, Bouchardon belongs, like Brunelleschi and Michelangelo, to a distinguished group of artists who excelled in both fields.

MULTIPLE COURTYARDS

Large buildings are called "complexes" for good reason. They require a multitude of corridors, galleries, hallways, stairs, lobbies, and elevators. The size and shape of the many rooms vary. Every floor requires its own plan, and several sectional drawings are needed to make the design understandable. The facades are diverse, and each must have its own drawing. The massing of building complexes is also difficult because large rooms require proportionally greater height, sometimes reaching two or three stories. Furthermore, courtyards are necessary if a complex is to "breathe."

The function of courtyards is to admit light and fresh air into the rooms, but the larger ones may also be honorific spaces strategically placed in a processional sequence, alternating with important rooms and playing a similar role. They are outdoor rooms in a literal sense. Major spaces, open to the sky or not, seem to be carved out of

7.16. Hôtel de la Monnaie. Principal façade overlooking the Seine. The giant colonnade on center corresponds with the major space in the complex.

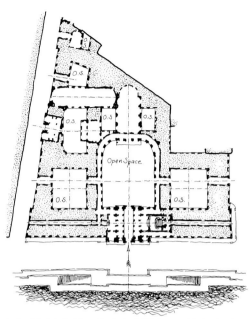

7.17. Hôtel de la Monnaie, Paris, 1775. Jacques-Denis Antoine. Plan showing the interrelationship of major spaces. Courtyards are labeled O.S.

the building fabric. This is made clear in the plan of the Hôtel de la Monnaie in Paris (figs. 7.16, 7.17), where the largest space is on the main axis, leading to the chapel at the rear. There are seven other courtyards, hierarchically gradated in order of size, shape, location, and regularity.

The plan of a mid-eighteenth-century private residence in Avignon (fig. 7.18) shows the degree to which a complex design depends on courtyards. The architect turned a narrow and irregular site bound by jagged party walls to his advantage by stretching the building along the boundaries and making the main outdoor spaces regular and symmetrical. The most important rooms are placed between the garden and the middle court, where they can enjoy cross ventilation, an important factor in the warm climate of southern France.

The site of Hôtel d'Hallwyl is a perfect rectangle, almost a double square, and Ledoux's plan (see fig. 1.3) is entirely made up of rectangular shapes. The two major rooms—forecourt and garden—are nearly the same size and their proportions are identical. This design encapsulates in the clearest possible way the massing of the French hôtel building type, which consists of three parts: a forecourt, a building, and a garden, in that order.

7.18. Hôtel de Villefranche, Avignon. François Franque. Note the shifting axes of symmetry on the plan.

7.19. House in Versailles built in 1746 for Madame de Pompadour. View from the street.

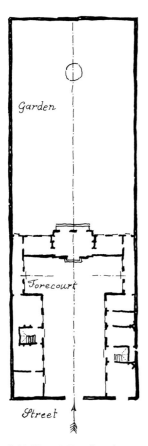

7.20. House in Versailles. Schematic plan.

Madame de Pompadour, mistress of Louis XV, chose this model for the public facade (fig. 7.19) of the small hôtel she built in Versailles for her secretary, a Mr. Colin. Located on a street side like many others built in French cities, the building is a minimalist interpretation of the type. The plan (fig. 7.20) shows just a suite of three rooms rather than a building block in the middle of the site and additional rooms along three sides of the forecourt. This must have been a delightful place to live in, with eight bays looking out into the garden on the south, which occupies more than half of the site.

OPEN ARMS

The main door of a typical French hôtel occupies the place of honor, in the middle of the street facade. To exploit the drama of the situation, the void of the doorway is encased in a solid wall that blocks the view to the house. Just as the wall frames the door, a pair of symmetrical buildings frames the wall. These buildings are placed as far apart as the property's width allows.

In the country, where there is more land available to spread out, wings are thrust forward in a gesture of welcome. Between them is a well-protected space that acts as an outdoor vestibule. This can be seen in François Mansart's chateau at Maisons (figs. 7.21, 7.22). The other facade is elongated to give as many windows as possible a good view of the elaborate formal gardens. To further improve the viewing conditions, the gardens are on a lower plane.

The open-arms gesture was brought to a high level of drama at Sceaux, another seventeenth-century chateau near Paris, unfortunately no longer extant. An engraving by Perelle shows the entry sequence in a bird's eye view (fig. 7.23). The forecourt, surrounded on three sides by the chateau itself, opened into another, larger space through a wrought iron grill (B-B.) That second forecourt was hidden behind a wall

7.21. *Chateau at Maisons, 1642. François Mansart. Facade overlooking the forecourt.*

7.22. *Chateau at Maisons. Facade overlooking the gardens.*

7.23. *Chateau at Sceaux, near Paris, 1673–77. Claude Perrault. The entry sequence. Note the two round windows in the sentry boxes, evocative of a pair of eyes watching incoming visitors.*

interrupted by a pair of substantial pavilions. The single opening in the middle was framed by two sentry boxes and preceded by a bridge spanning a symbolic moat (A-A.). There can hardly be a more eloquent boundary in the landscape, and a bridge over it makes a dramatic entrance. It was at this point that the chateau revealed itself. The quadruple allée of trees lining the broad avenue leading to the first gate would have prepared the visitor for an imposing building, but its entrance was carefully concealed until the last moment.

7.24 Fallingwater, Bear Run, Pennsylvania, 1937. Frank Lloyd Wright. The first sighting of the house is through a screen of trees.

7.25. Fallingwater. Bridge to the house.

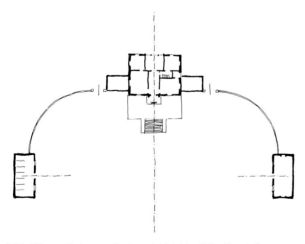

7.26. Ebberston Lodge, near Scarborough, Yorkshire. Colen Campbell.

A bridge can be an interpretation of the open-arms theme. It is one of the most effective means to gather visitors and make them feel that they are entering a new realm. Fallingwater (fig. 7.24), the tantalizing house designed by Frank Lloyd Wright in Pennsylvania, is first glimpsed through a curtain of trees. To reach it, one must cross a stream that was fully exploited by the architect as a ready-made moat. His bridge (fig. 7.25) is more than an extension of the road; it is a place where visitors are subtly invited to stop and contemplate the house. They will soon feel that they are at the threshold of a new experience. The kinship of bridge and house is clear: they are made of the same materials and their horizontal lines echo one another. On the surface of the bridge is a light-colored rectangular area with a recessed light at each corner. In addition, a sharp turn ahead forces the driver to slow down. The architectural message is both gentle and powerful.

The open-arms gesture is also a way for a building to take possession of the land or, perhaps more accurately, to wed land and building into a meaningful unit. A 46-foot-wide house designed by Colen Campbell in 1718 (fig. 7.26) seems to appropriate a space five times wider through the simple device of a low wall connected to a pair of ancillary buildings on either side.

Two wall quadrants were also used to frame the gate to the farm at the Vizcaya complex in Florida (fig. 7.27). Not only do they add grace and dignity to the gate itself; they also impart unity to the cluster of disparate buildings beyond.

FRAMING

The term "framing" describes the decorative elements surrounding a door or a window. Except for the general shape of the opening, our design efforts must be concentrated on the frame. The picture in the frame is the view beyond, which can be another room in the same building or the landscape outside. In any case, the opening must be designed in relation to the view it reveals. In passing through a door or standing before a window, we become the subject of the picture, which is another reason why we should take pains to design a good frame.

As much as a window, a door forms a relationship with the view beyond. The reason for positioning a door must be immediately obvious. Where does the door lead? To what object, into what space? The classical "rule of three" applies here, with the opening as the beginning, the point of interest as the end, and the space between as the middle. By moving from room to room, we experience a building in its totality. Framing allows us to orient ourselves beyond the confines of each room. It is a critical issue in massing and must be carefully considered by architects who wish to achieve homogeneity. This is made clear in a drawing by Percier and Fontaine (fig. 7.28) of the pedimented facade of a pavilion at the end of a pergola, the entrance to which is framed by a pair of *terms*, quadrangular, usually tapering, pillars topped with allegorical heads.

Simple as it is, the idea of framing acquires singular power when it is implemented with imagination. The front door to Hôtel de Noirmoutiers in Paris is the focus of a line of vision originating in the street and coinciding with the axis of symmetry to which all the elements of the composition conform. It is distinguished by its central location and by its unique form as the only fully arched opening in the facade (fig. 7.29). The three-bay motif, the trees in tubs on either side, the balcony, which doubles as a shelter over the main door, and the large pediment capping the central projection of the building all sustain the concept of framing. The space between the street and the building is the middle element of a tripartite sequence. This courtyard is dramatically free of distracting objects, except for a subtle line in the paving leading the eye straight to the door. As for the first element of the sequence, the carriage gate,

7.27. Gate to the farm complex at Vizcaya, Miami, Florida, 1914–16. F. Burrall Hoffman.

7.28. Villa Albani arbor from Charles Percier and Pierre Fontaine, Choix des plus célèbres maisons de plaisance de Rome et des environs, *Paris 1820.*

7.29. Hôtel de Noirmoutiers, Paris, 1722. Jacques Courtonne.

7.30. Piazza del Mercato, Lucca.

7.31. *Château du Tholonet, near Aix-en-Provence.*

7.32. *Château de Villiers, c. 1780.*

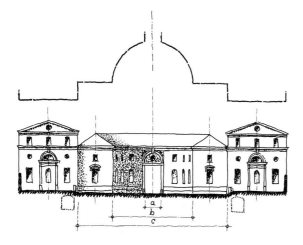

7.33. *Bagatelle. Facade of the service building facing the chateau. Underground corridors between the chateau and the service building frame the sunken court of honor.*

its architrave is curved in a gentle arch similar to those of the openings of the building facade. The keystone over the gate carries a smiling female face, a fitting symbol of the elegant and easy hospitality conveyed by the entire design.

The oval shape of Piazza del Mercato in Lucca (fig. 7.30) was determined by a Roman amphitheater on the site as were the arches surrounding the piazza. As we pass under one of them to enter the space, we face identical openings on the opposite wall. The formal kinship between the figures of the plan and those in elevation results in remarkable homogeneity in spite of the jagged profile of the skyline.

The effect of framing can also be achieved with natural means. The limbs of a double row of trees form an arch over a rectangular pool at the Château du Tholonet, near Aix-en-Provence (fig. 7.31). Reflected in the water, the arch becomes a near circle with the front door of the chateau at the center. Could there be a more successful way to bring together context and object, and give what appears from the distance as a tiny hole in a wall the functional and symbolic significance it deserves?

The sophistication that our predecessors brought to their designs in an effort to obtain homogeneity would be hard to match. In this regard, a series of telling observations can be made about the forecourt of the Château de Villiers (fig. 7.32). Seen from the outside, the rectangle formed by the gap between the masonry piers and their height superimposes precisely with the rectangular facade of the chateau itself. The top of the grille, matching the floor line between the ground floor and the upper story of the pair of pavilions, also appears to coincide with the corresponding line on the main building, although its position is higher. The central projection of the building is perfectly framed by the opening in the gate, and the pediment appears to sit on top of that opening. There is more: the ridge of the roof is optically linked by a common horizontal line with the eaves of the twin roofs of the entrance pavilions.

What of the reverse process? What does the departing visitor experience? The strategy is actually very much the same as that of entering. At Bagatelle, the view from the front door of the house towards the outside embraces the entire width of the ancillary building closing the court of honor (fig. 7.33). A series of receding planes and a progressive reduction in the height of the buildings lead to the actual opening on the forecourts and the world beyond.

THE SKYLINE

It is well known that spires and domes give our great cities their distinctive profile and their unique character. They are the mountains and peaks of the urban landscape. For centuries, domes have been reserved for buildings of great importance. One reason for this is that, in a building technology restricted to timber and masonry, only domes could cover very large spaces (fig. 7.34). Another reason is found in the symbolic significance of the spherical form, suggestive of the universe through a perception of the sky as a vault.

Until recently, London was dominated by the dome of St. Paul's. What would Rome be without the dome of St. Peter's? Or Florence without Sta. Maria del Fiore? Domes and towers are the ornaments of a city; more significantly, they announce the presence of important civic or religious buildings. They are the landmarks which, along with parks and rivers and great perspectives, help us to orient ourselves in a city. For all these reasons they can be said to anchor the city in space and in time (figs. 7.35, 7.36). In smaller communities, gables and pinnacles join domes and towers in animating the skyline. A greater effort should be made to endow modern cities with animated skylines. As Paul Rudolph remarked, "One doubts that a poem was ever written to a flat-roofed building silhouetted against the setting sun."

7.34. Panthéon, Paris, 1755–90. Jacques-Germain Soufflot.

7.35. The skyline in the center of Basel. Insignificant buildings are omitted.

7.36. Hall of Languages, Syracuse University, Syracuse, New York, 1873. Horatio N. White. A single building with three towers is enough to create a lively skyline for part of the campus.

CHAPTER 8

STUDENT PROJECTS
FOR RESTRICTED SITES

The ancients never made the columns in uneven numbers, as you shall not
find any animal that stands or moves upon an odd number of feet.

—L. B. ALBERTI

The material presented in the previous chapters on interior architecture, facade composition, and massing is incorporated in this series of six projects completed by students in my studio. In comparison to the simple projects discussed in chapter 4, these are more ambitious programs, all within urban contexts. They are presented in order of increasing size and complexity. All the sites but one are flat, but the contexts vary widely. Architects quickly learn that some constraints are necessary to produce a design. It is easier to design a building on a site with stringent boundaries because the range of options is more limited than it would be on an open site.

A TOWN HOUSE

The site fronts a public square in a residential area and measures 40 feet between party walls. The facade will fit into a continuous street wall, and it must carry its share of civic responsibility. The program requires a three-story building with a double-height room overlooking the square. An entrance gallery between narrow service rooms leads from the front door to the stairs at the back. The piano nobile consists of an impressive three-space enfilade beginning at the street and ending at a back garden. The stair, lit

from above, marks the middle space of the sequence, functionally as well as spatially. A large, one-story dining room occupies the third space; the floor above contains the bedroom suite.

First phase: Propose a facade respecting classical canons. This includes a lateral division in three bays with the entry door on center, a rusticated ground floor forming a base, the piano nobile as the dominating part with an order to celebrate it and an ornate cap to crown the whole.

Second phase: Design the main room of the town house on a square plan. It will be entered from the stairs at the back and the fenestration will determine the articulation of the walls. The floor pattern will enhance the shape of the room and work in concert with the wall's articulation.

DRAWING REQUIREMENTS
Facade, wall section, plan and wall elevation of main room at 1/4 inch scale.

DESIGN SOLUTION
The author made a reasonable choice in opening the main room of the piano nobile towards the public square with a large loggia which, had it been deeper, would have made a pleasant place to sit in the summer (fig. 8.1). The elegant facade would be an ornament to any street. Square in plan, the main room (fig. 8.2) derives its articulation from the three-bay

facade: the four walls are divided in three parts, but only the back wall reflects the window wall faithfully.

A SHOPPING ARCADE

The building will consist of a central circulation space, a gallery, entered at both ends and lined with shops on either side. Natural light will flood the gallery from above. In this program, the significant facades are those facing each other across a pedestrian passage. Louis Kahn's observation that "a street is a room by agreement" is particularly apt here. The site is non-specific.

A variety of functional and spatial needs must be accommodated. Office and storage space or a mezzanine will be required in most cases; some shops require more floor space than others; others need higher spaces. Provision will therefore be made for flexibility in plan and section. One shop might occupy one bay, while another will need two or three. Delivery and pick up of merchandise will be made in the back of the shops. Security, restrooms, mechanical, and maintenance facilities will be located next to the public entrances of the building.

DRAWING REQUIREMENTS
Floor plan at 1/16 inch or 1/32 inch scale. Longitudinal section at 1/16 inch scale.

DESIGN SOLUTION
The design shown here satisfies the needs for flexibility. An A-B-A-B-A bay system allows for shops with varied widths, and arches alternating with lintels make possible two or three stories with or without a mezzanine (fig. 8.3). The quotation included in the presentation is from Geoffrey Scott's *Architecture of Humanism*: "To enclose space is the object of building. When we build, we do but detach a convenient quantity of space, seclude and protect it, and all architecture springs from the necessity."

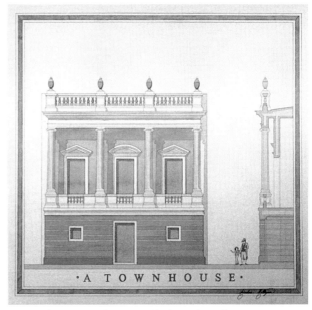

8.1 (see also C.7). Town house. Street facade. Ariadne Milligan. Ferguson, Shamamian & Rattner Architecture Prize, 2002.

8.2 (see also C.8). Town house. Plan of main room and elevation of one of the lateral walls. Ariadne Milligan.

A FRENCH HÔTEL

The objective of this problem is to learn from a tried and true design strategy, that of the French hôtel. How were issues of multiple uses, hierarchy, status, and symmetry handled? How were building forms used to shape and organize figural outdoor spaces?

The program, however, reflects contemporary needs. It assumes that a successful couple engaged in one of the design fields wishes to combine in one compound the facilities for professional activities and family life.

The site is a flat, rectangular parcel measuring 250 x 400 feet. One of the short sides, on the north, fronts an elegant boulevard lined with trees. There is an alley on the south side. The long sides are party walls.

On the north, a forecourt precedes the largest and most important building of the complex, used for exhibitions and entertaining. Two one-story buildings face one another across the forecourt. One building houses the executive offices; the other is a garage. The massing of these buildings is identical, and both facades are arcuated and rusticated.

The main building demonstrates the refined taste of the owners and promotes their designs; the formal garden on the south side functions as an extension of it. Another pair of buildings face one another across the garden. One is an orangery and the other is the family residence. Their massing is identical, although the residence comprises two stories while the orangery consists of one double-height space with service rooms at the back. Trees in tubs are housed there in the winter; in the summer, the orangery becomes another venue for entertaining. Two colonnaded quadrants link the main building with the residence and the orangery.

The formal garden terminates on the south with a pavilion backed against dense planting in the remainder of the site. This structure is used by the children as a playhouse but, like the quadrants, it can provide shelter for guests at a garden party. Finally, two small clearings are carved out of the woods for those in search of solitude or tranquility. Service, maintenance, and catering personnel enter from the alley in the back of the site.

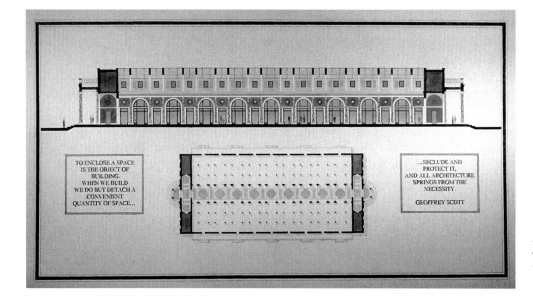

TO ENCLOSE A SPACE IS THE OBJECT OF BUILDING. WHEN WE BUILD WE DO BUT DETACH A CONVENIENT QUANTITY OF SPACE...

...SECLUDE AND PROTECT IT, AND ALL ARCHITECTURE SPRINGS FROM THE NECESSITY.

GEOFFREY SCOTT

8.3 (see also C.9). Shopping arcade. Plan and longitudinal section. Katherine Hogan.

8.5 (see also C.10). French hôtel. Longitudinal section with the entrance on the left. James Wisniewski.

8.6. French hôtel. Main elevation of the south pavilion. James Wisniewski.

8.4. French hôtel. Plan with the main entrance at the top. James Wisniewski.

8.7 (see also C.11). French hôtel. Elevation of the main building from the garden with section through the orangery and the residence. Joel Kline.

DRAWING REQUIREMENTS

Plan of the entire compound; section/elevation of the same taken along the main axis; elevation of the main building from the boulevard or from the forecourt, in which case it will include a section through the lateral buildings; elevation of the main building from the garden, with a section through the residence and the orangery; elevation of the south pavilion. All drawings at 1/16 inch scale.

DESIGN SOLUTIONS

Since the clients' brief was specific about the building requirements and their relationship, the evaluation of the designs rests on the skill with which the general parti was developed. The plan (fig. 8.4) strikes a good balance between buildings and open spaces. Courts and gardens are defined by the buildings and the important ones are treated as figural spaces. A successful hierarchical sequence can be seen in the section (fig. 8.5). The elevation of the south pavilion, framed by trellis, is suitably restful (fig. 8.6). The section through the main garden is from a different student presentation (fig. 8.7). The facade of the main building is grand without ostentation. The entablature of the colonnade is carried across as the unifying feature of the three buildings, from the orangery on the left to the residence on the right.

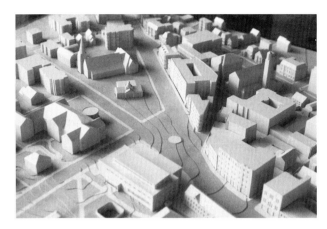

8.8. Scale model of the area. Massachusetts Avenue runs from the lower right corner to the middle of the top edge. Quincy Street emerges from the lower left corner and terminates at Massachusetts Avenue. The building site is beyond the triangular block, just right of the center, fronting on Massachusetts Avenue and reaching back to Bow Street.

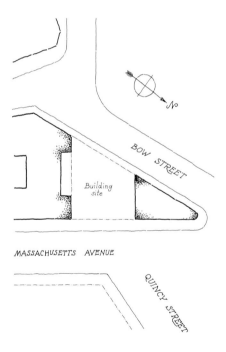

8.9. Schematic map showing the site of the proposed Institute for Classical Architecture at the south end of Quincy Street.

AN INSTITUTE FOR THE ADVANCEMENT OF CLASSICAL ARCHITECTURE

A Harvard alumnus with a commitment to classical architecture and a fortune derived from dealing in classical works of art has endowed the institute and financed the construction of its building.

The site is part of a triangular block between Massachusetts Avenue and Bow Street, adjacent to Harvard Yard. It presents a 60-foot front to the south end of Quincy Street, which is replete with cultural landmarks: Harvard Graduate School of Design, the Fogg and Sackler museums, and Le Corbusier's Carpenter Center across from Henry Hobson Richardson's Sever Hall (figs. 8.8, 8.9). It is assumed that traffic on Massachusetts Avenue and Quincy Street is restricted to emergency vehicles and that the space in front of the site can be developed as a public garden. The main facade, at the end of a street, is highly visible; it should be designed with great care and express suitable dignity. The site is between party walls, and one of the challenges is presented by diverse functions requiring natural lighting in specific ways.

It is the intention of the donor that the building itself be the exhibition, as was Mies van der Rohe's German Pavilion in Barcelona. The difference is that it is not a country that is promoted here but a culture. The facade and the interior will celebrate classical architecture in a literate, tasteful and appropriate manner.

PROGRAM
• Exhibition space for the display of architectural drawings and models. Design competitions will also be judged in this space, which might be two stories in height (2,000 sf).
• Lecture room with a seating capacity of 150. The room might also be used for performances of classical music.
• Library with 500 linear feet of shelving, 30 reader's seats, and a librarian's office.

• Projection room and slide storage (150 sf).

• Conference and seminar room with a seating capacity of 20 (300 sf).

• Studies for institute fellows (6 @ 175 sf).

• Apartments for visiting scholars or lecturers (2 @ 400 sf).

• Office of the president (400 sf)

• Office of the director (250 sf) and two secretaries.

• Publications offices (2 @ 150 sf).

• Kitchen (200 sf).

• Porter's quarters for round-the-clock duty, reception area and waiting room with seating capacity of eight, switchboard, mailroom, duplicating room, storage, elevator, toilets, custodial space, and fire stairs (as required).

Optional

• Bookstore accessible from Bow Street.

• Courtyard, possibly open towards Bow Street, to bring natural light into more rooms or for summer use.

DRAWING REQUIREMENTS

A general plan of the building in context, including the public square, at 1/32 inch scale. Plans of the two main floors; front and back elevations; two transverse sections of the entire building all at 1/16 in scale. Three-dimensional models may be substituted for the elevations.

DESIGN PROPOSALS

Proposal A: A five-bay porch expresses the close relationship between the institute and its context (fig. 8.10). Grand stairs reach out to invite visitors to walk in and experience the public rooms. The layout of the piano nobile pays close attention to the variety of figural spaces obtained in an irregular site and the many ways they can be walked through. The ordering system is based on symmetry and enfilades. The circular space in the middle is capped by a dome that draws attention from Quincy Street to the

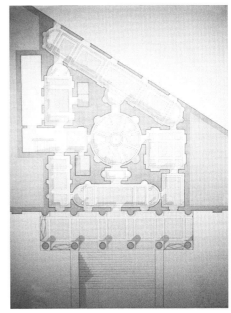

8.10. Plan of the main floor of the institute. Matthew Manuel.

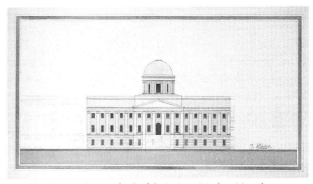

8.11 (see also C.12). Main facade of the institute. Matthew Manuel.

educational character of the institute. The main facade is visually extended right and left by refacing a large part of the adjacent residential block. With this simple device, a more monumental aspect is achieved, consistent with the civic character of the building (fig. 8.11).

Several moves appear to make the public square in front of the institute into a forecourt: the lateral boundaries are lined up with the edges of the facade; the axis of symmetry of the square

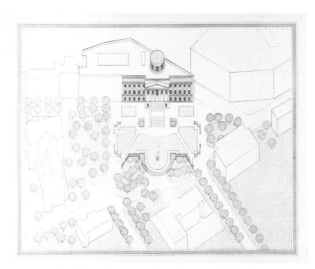

8.12. *True plan of the public square and true elevation of facade of the institute.*
Matthew Manuel.

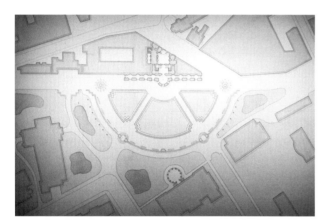

8.13. *Plan of the public square with the ground floor of the institute.*
Christopher Pizzi.

8.14 *(see also C.13). Facade of the institute. Christopher Pizzi.*

is a continuation of the axis of the facade; Quincy Street becomes a pedestrian walk leading into the center of the facade. That focus is energized by the mirror image of the alley (fig. 8.12).

Proposal B: The design strategy is similar to that of Proposal A, but the means employed are somewhat different. Instead of an outdoor stair leading to a porch, a covered walk along the facade creates a zone that belongs to the building as well as to the urban square. A series of benches face the center of the semicircular enclosure and, in response, the center of the facade projects forward (figs. 8.13, 8.14).

Proposal C: The intervention consists of a chaste facade limited to the 60-foot-wide building site. A pedimented portico is set against a well-articulated wall. The only curved element of the facade, an arch is reserved for the entry opening, found at the top of a generous stair. The doorway derives its drama from the contrast with the nearly solid base (fig. 8.15).

AN AMERICAN EMBASSY

This project is based on the architectural design criteria of the Department of State Foreign Buildings Operations. To understand the program, a few definitions may be helpful:

• Ambassador: A diplomatic agent of the highest rank accredited to a foreign sovereign or government as the resident representative of his/her own government.

• Embassy: A mission abroad undertaken officially; the official residence and offices of an ambassador.

• Consul: An official appointed by a government to reside in a foreign country and represent the commercial interests of citizens of the appointing country.

• Consulate: The office or jurisdiction of a consul; the residence of a consul.

• Mission: A team of specialists or cultural leaders sent to a foreign country.

• Attaché: A technical expert on the diplomatic staff of his/her country at a foreign capital.

The embassy compound will be organized in three parts: the consulate, accessible to the public; the missions, which are restricted, and the embassy proper, which is private. The architecture of the compound should create good will by its appearance, expressing such qualities as dignity and neighborly sympathy. Ostentation will be avoided. The design of the complex will use the neoclassical language chosen by the founders of the United States as best expressing their political ideals.

The site (fig. 8.16) was selected in spite of its awkward shape because of its desirable location in the city. Certain restrictions were imposed after lengthy negotiations with the government of the host country, and an understanding was reached on these points:

• There is no limit to the total height of the buildings, but two to three stories should be enough to accommodate the program. It is understood that the floor-to-floor height in a prestigious public building may be 12 to 15 feet. Under no circumstances will any part of the building(s) overlook the adjacent sites.

• The north lot, undeveloped, will eventually be occupied with official buildings.

• The south lot is occupied by a cemetery.

DESIGN CONSIDERATIONS

The consulate will face a north-south street to be created on the west side of the site. The width of the street is limited by the presence of a small structure of archeological interest that must be preserved. The architect of the compound is invited to propose a design for a public square in front of the consulate.

A forecourt facing the street will create a welcoming impression. On a daily basis, security is handled discreetly; in case of temporary difficulties, the courtyard should be capable of being closed off by a substantial screen. Offices and other facilities will be wrapped around the forecourt.

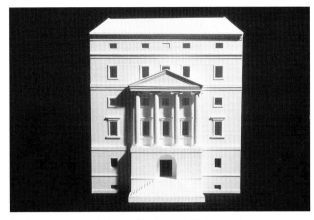

8.15. Model of the main facade of the institute. Christopher Reed.

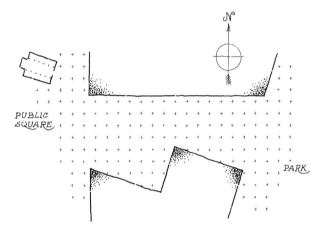

8.16. Schematic map of the building site for the embassy. There is a 10-foot drop from west to east. A 25-foot grid is drawn across the site for reference.

Official receptions take place at night or on weekends in the embassy, when the offices are closed. On these occasions, the forecourt will become a reception area for official guests. Drop-off and pick up of guests must function smoothly. Ample covered space will be provided for greeting guests, waiting, and cloakrooms.

The missions will occupy the center of the site, between the consulate and the embassy itself. The courtyard around which it will be built will act as an organizer for the varied offices and services. It will provide natural light and ventilation to the facilities. Its sober, well-proportioned architecture will be exemplary because it will play an important role in the processional sequence leading to the ambassador's office and the reception rooms. It will occasionally be used for important celebrations and ceremonies.

The embassy is the most exclusive part of the program. General planning requires easy flow through ceremonial spaces and a clear separation between official and private functions. The family quarters should be located on the upper story. Entertaining spaces, such as loggias, terraces, and pergolas, are encouraged.

The reception rooms of the embassy and the ambassador's residence will overlook a public park to be created on the eastern side of the site. The eastern facade will take advantage of the views over the park, but the embassy will be inaccessible on that side. The architect is invited to suggest a design for the park. In exchange, the embassy building is allowed to extend 25 feet beyond the property line. Seen from the park, the facade should express the ceremonial and residential functions of the embassy in terms understandable by, and compatible with, the host country.

SPACE PROGRAM

Consulate: Approximately 3,500 square feet, including reception and adjacent Marine guard room (450 sf), Passport Office suite (1,500 sf),

Offices for Veterans Affairs, Notary, Citizenship (each 150 sf), Support spaces (450 sf).

Missions: Approximately 13,000 square feet, including Deputy Chief suite (750 sf), Political Section (825 sf), Economic Section (1,500 sf), Military attachés (1,400 sf), Communications complex (1,000 sf), Press and Media Sections (3,000 sf), Cultural Affairs (450 sf), Public Affairs (600 sf), Additional offices, reception, conference, support space (3,000 sf).

Embassy: Approximately 10,000 square feet including official spaces (approximately 1,500 sf including Reception Room and State Dining Room, each 450 sf), family and guest quarters (approximately 1,500 sf), service areas (approximately 1,200 sf); chief of missions residence (approximately 1,000 sf); basement service areas (approximately 2,500 sf including garage, staff offices and amenities, mailroom, mechanical room, and storage areas).

DESIGN STRATEGY

The program calls for a large building or, rather, a series of interrelated buildings. Here the integration of the building into the urban and political context requires a thoughtful answer. The slope of the site combined with a somewhat jagged outline presents a challenge to the designer.

There are three major elements in the complex, but their relationship and their integration to the urban context are also important problems, requiring as much attention as the design of the individual buildings. To guide the process, I divided the twelve-week term into ten phases, with a group review at the end of each.

WEEKS 1 AND 2:
MISSIONS AND COURTYARD

We began with the missions building, which occupies the center of the site, at its narrowest point. The courtyard is a circle, 60 feet in diameter, which acts as a unifying element for the complex and as a symbol of unity for the United States. It also helps to resolve the conflicting

8.17 (see also C.14). Elevation of the public square in front of the consulate. Grady J. Dagenais.

angles of street and park. Circulation takes place on the periphery in a 12-foot-deep covered walk. The Doric order is selected for the courtyard because of its serious character. The problem was thus reduced to the design of a circular outdoor room around which offices would fill up the odd spaces behind the regular facade.

DRAWING REQUIREMENTS
Ground floor plan and section at 1/16 inch scale.

WEEKS 3 AND 4: FORECOURT:
A SQUARE OUTDOOR ROOM
The consulate will be arranged on three sides of a forecourt. The forecourt will be separated from the street by a columniated screen. At least five steps will take visitors up to the centerpiece, a formal vestibule of ample proportions. As in the missions, and for the same reason, the chosen order is the Doric. A covered ramp will make direct vehicular access possible from the street to the basement.

DRAWING REQUIREMENTS
Ground floor plan; north-south section through the forecourt showing the vestibule facade; east-west section including the circular courtyard of the missions, all at 1/16 inch scale.

WEEK 5: PUBLIC SQUARE:
A THREE-SIDED OUTDOOR ROOM
To serve as a foil to the consulate, the public square should be designed in conjunction with the forecourt. The two spaces will form an urban ensemble in which the street and the screen are included. A semicircular shape will be given to the public square in deference to the forecourt. The buildings forming the square and the adjacent street will contain apartments, town houses, or professional offices; they will be three stories high, in scale with the consulate. The design will be sober, relying more on good proportions than on ornament. Particular care will be given to the corner buildings where street and square meet. A row of trees will be placed on each sidewalk.

DRAWING REQUIREMENTS
Ground floor plan and east-west section of the sequence public square-forecourt-circular courtyard; elevation of the public square showing part of the street (fig. 8.17); elevation of the consulate with the screen indicated in dotted lines.

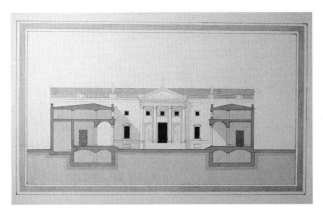

8.18 (see also C.15). Section through the forecourt showing the public facade of the consulate. The vehicular ramp to the basement is shown on the extreme left. Scott Delorme.

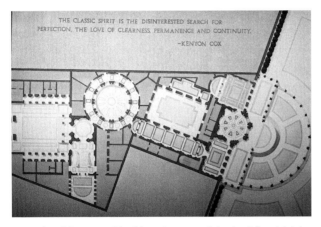

8.19. Plan of the piano nobile of the entire compound showing (left to right) the forecourt of the consulate, the circular courtyard of the missions and the embassy proper with the terrace overlooking the public park. Gregory Malette.

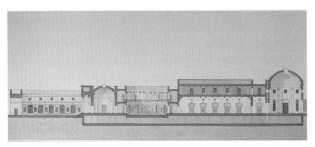

8.20 (see also C.16). Section through the embassy compound. Rick Colson.

WEEK 6: THE SCREEN IN CONTEXT: TRANSPARENCY

The function of the columniated screen is to separate two entities, but also to link them. The screen is critical as the boundary between the city (public realm) and the embassy (private realm), and its design should be compatible with both. It should protect the compound from potential disturbances and also allow passers-by to glimpse the consulate. Finally, the design should express the classical–western–democratic culture and, as a gateway, it should function smoothly for pedestrians and official motorcades as well.

DRAWING REQUIREMENTS

Street elevation of the consulate showing the screen in context. The building in the back of the courtyard will be delineated in pencil. The drawings prepared in the preceding week should be included in the presentation, corrected if necessary. All drawings at 1/16 inch scale.

WEEK 6: UNITY OF THE PARTS AND SURFACE ARTICULATION

Assemble the individual drawings to see, evaluate, and improve the design of the complete sequence as a whole. Use the Nolli technique of contrasting the sequence of major spaces in white by using light shading on the other, less important parts of the ensemble. Finalize the facades of the consulate that overlook the forecourt and the sections through the wings.

DRAWING REQUIREMENTS

Ground floor plan of the sequence, elevation of the facade overlooking the forecourt at 1/16 inch scale (fig. 8.18).

WEEK 7: SEQUENTIAL SPACE

Use the Nolli technique for the sections in order to refine the sequence of major spaces.

DRAWING REQUIREMENTS

Section at 1/16 inch scale.

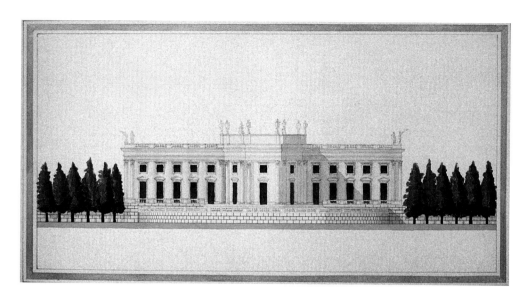

8.21 (see also C.17).
Facade of the embassy
overlooking the park.
Gregory Malette.

WEEK 8: PLANNING THE EMBASSY

There are five parts to the embassy proper,
which must be organized hierarchically: public
rooms, family quarters, guest suite, service, and
residence of the chief of missions. Complete the
processional access that originates in the forecourt. Work out the transition from a concen-
tric/radiating plan geometry in the missions
courtyard to a second orthogonal grid in the
embassy. Public rooms should take advantage of
the view over the park on the east side. A courtyard and/or one or two light wells may be useful in giving natural light and ventilation to
secondary rooms.

DRAWING REQUIREMENTS

Plan of the piano nobile at 1/16 inch scale,
plan of the second floor at 1/16 inch or 1/32
inch scale, east-west section at 1/16 inch scale
(figs. 8.19, 8.20).

WEEK 9: EMBASSY AND PUBLIC PARK

Since the architect was asked to propose a
design for the park, we took the opportunity
to make the area near the embassy a handsome foil for its facade and, conversely, design

the facade to be a visual treat for the users of
the park. A terrace or raised garden is necessary for several reasons. It will serve as an
extension of the reception rooms and as a
place from which to enjoy the view. It will
provide a podium for the facade, raise the
windows for privacy, and provide an additional measure of security.

DRAWING REQUIREMENTS

North-south section through the major
spaces of the embassy, facade overlooking the
park, both at 1/16 inch scale (fig. 8.21).

WEEK 10: INTEGRATION

Required drawings: Ground floor plan and
section through the entire compound between
the public square and the public park. 1/16 inch
scale.

WEEKS 11 AND 12: COMPLETION

Refine the design; coordinate the drawings;
prepare the final presentation. No matter how
carefully a designer works on every phase of the
process, there is always a range of tasks at the end
that requires a surprising amount of time.

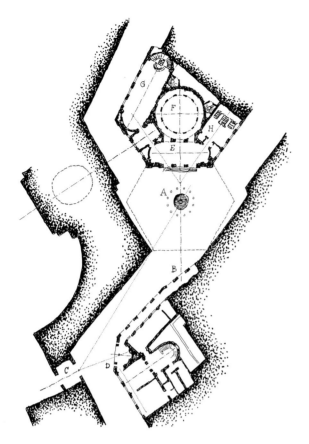

8.22. Plan diagram of the proposal for the American Center for Architecture with the underlying geometry of the concept and main sightlines. Gregory Malette.

8.23. The square linking the two buildings, with the monument between them. The exedra announcing the center to visitors can be seen on the right. Gregory Malette.

AN AMERICAN CENTER FOR ARCHITECTURE IN PARIS

This problem was posed for the 81st Paris Prize competition, organized in 1994 by the National Institute for Architectural Education. The first competition in the series was organized in 1903 by the Society of Beaux-Arts Architects, whose founders had all studied at the Ecole des Beaux-Arts. Their goal was to give an outstanding American student the same educational advantage they had received. This program was, fittingly, the design of living and working facilities for twelve American architecture students.

Briefly outlined, the main program requirements included four major public spaces consisting of an exhibition gallery (1,600 sf), a 50-seat lecture room, a library, and a quiet outdoor space where sculpture and architectural fragments would be displayed. Working and living spaces for the fellows include a design studio (1,600 sf), a refectory, twelve bedrooms, and two guest rooms. Additional spaces include a director's apartment (1,000 sf) with direct access to the street, administration offices and archives, kitchen, porter's lodgings, storage and service rooms as required.

The location is on the edge of the Latin Quarter, in a vital neighborhood replete with art galleries, antique shops, and bookstores. With the Ecole des Beaux-Arts a block away to the east and one of the great classical buildings in Paris, the Palais de l'Institut, casting its shadow on the site, the location for the new center could not be better.

The site itself, however, presented a challenge. Usually an urban or an otherwise restricted site has the advantage of limiting the options, but too many restrictions can complicate the design process. Here the main difficulty was to accommodate a single program in two sites, separated by a street intersection.

DESIGN SOLUTION
The designer first created an urban square as a link between the two buildings (fig. 8.22). A

monument, placed in the middle of the square, became the focal point of the concept. The hexagonal shape of the square was suggested by the angle between the existing streets. The monument suggested itself: a statue of Thomas Jefferson, who had lived in Paris and whose architectural designs reflect French influences (A on the plan). The statue would stand on a plinth in the middle of a fountain.

The facade of the larger building was placed on axis with the monument, facing the existing, three-bay arcade attached to the smaller building (B). The arcade was extended towards a new exedra (D) that can be seen from the existing pedestrian passageway opened through the west wing of the Palais de l'Institut (C). The passage becomes the monumental gateway to the complex from the river. The function of the exedra is threefold: to signal the presence of an important structure with a major frontispiece; to inform visitors of the nature of that structure; and to invite them to enter one of two doors. The one on the right gives access to the library, the refectory, and the stairs leading up to the offices, the director's apartment, and guest suites. The doorway on the left leads into the arcade, which directs pedestrians towards the second building. As they leave the arcade to cross the square, they will be able to read Jefferson's well-known words carved on the base of the statue: "Architecture is my delight and putting up and pulling down one of my favorite amusements."

Visitors to the second building are welcomed by three arches to an open vestibule (E on the plan). Beyond is the core of the building, a court open to the sky with a circular arcade around it (F). This is where the sculptures and architectural fragments are on display. From the open vestibule (E), visitors may choose to go left towards the exhibition gallery (G) or right towards the stairs (H) and the design studios on the second and third floors. The lecture room is under the courtyard. The living quarters are on the fourth floor.

8.24 (see also C.18). Section through the main building, showing the circular court open to the sky. Gregory Malette.

The section through the square shows the Jefferson statue between the two buildings (fig. 8.23). On the extreme right is the monumental frontispiece of the complex with the exedra. The main building with the open court is partially visible on the left. In the complete section of the main building (fig. 8.24), the open vestibule is on the right, with the design studios above. The double-height gallery with connecting stairs is on the left with the lecture hall below grade.

By incorporating the streets in the design, this proposal turned the awkward site conditions into an asset. Although not premiated, the project was recognized by the jury as a remarkable achievement.

CHAPTER 9

SMALL THINGS

Do not neglect small things, for that is where perfection is found; and perfection is no small thing.
— MICHELANGELO

Details give identity to classical designs and pleasure to the onlooker. They may be ornamental, functional, or both. They may be grand or modest, ranging from the monumental, commemorating a hero or a great event, to the almost insignificant, such as the humble doorknob or the nose of a step.

ORNAMENT

Since classical architecture is a celebration of mankind, the representation of the human figure is at the top of the list of ornaments. The plastic interpretation of the human figure is as rich and complex as the human being itself. From charming nudes to austere warriors, single or in groups, there have been portraits and allegories celebrating virtues or representing symbols such as the sun, the seasons, the arts, the parts of the world, and so on. It is interesting that, in antiquity, no particular value was attached to the originality of a sculpture; vast numbers of copies of the favored ones were made. During the Renaissance, several dozen masterpieces were recognized as the very best, and multiple copies were made. The intrinsic beauty of a piece was prized, rather than its uniqueness.

Most representations of human beings are imbued with dignity, and they are placed in such a way that we must look up to see them. With the exception of figures in fountains, looking down on a statue seems like an impropriety. Human figures must either be placed on pedestals or in positions of prestige, that is, above eye level (figs. 9.1, 9.2).

Next in the hierarchy of ornament is the column. Since columns do not have an intrinsic scale, they can be small enough to decorate a small clock or a candle holder or very large. Placed at the center of an urban square or at the end of a perspective, a freestanding column gains further importance from the space around it (figs. 9.3, 9.4). The relationship of its height with the size of the space in which it stands is critical: it must be neither overwhelming nor overwhelmed. There is no limit to the size of an obelisk either, but, more frequently than freestanding columns, obelisks are paired off or used in sets of four to define a space (figs. 9.5, 9.6).

Water enlivens public spaces and private gardens. While columns and obelisks are erect and appear dynamic, water tends to spread horizontally; it suggests repose and has a calming effect. Fountains are the exception; the sight and sound of splashing water is a perennial delight (fig. 9.7).

Among the other ornaments of the well-designed environment are topiary, terms, trees in boxes, urns, and benches, to list but a few. The humble bench is important for several reasons.

9.1, 9.2. Two elegant statues in the Tuileries gardens, in Paris. They are given exalted status from being elevated on pedestals.

9.3. The Jubilee column erected in Stuttgart in 1841. The enormous square required a monument of equivalent scale.

9.4. In the Piazza del Popolo, Ravenna, the column is in perfect accord with the surrounding buildings. An entablature sits on the capital and makes the order complete.

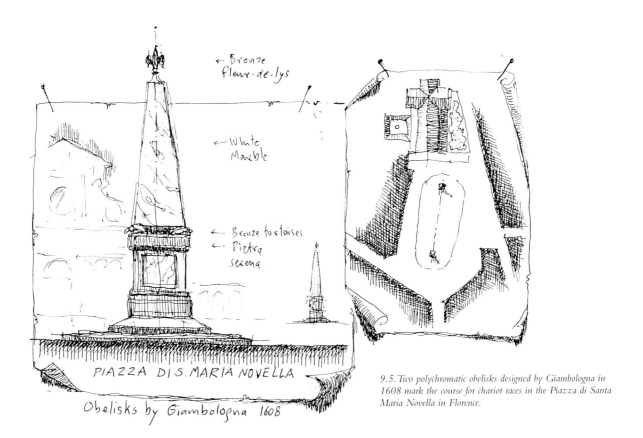

Bronze
fleur-de-lys

White
Marble

Bronze tortoises
Pietra
serena

PIAZZA DI S. MARIA NOVELLA

Obelisks by Giambologna 1608

9.5. Two polychromatic obelisks designed by Giambologna in 1608 mark the course for chariot races in the Piazza di Santa Maria Novella in Florence.

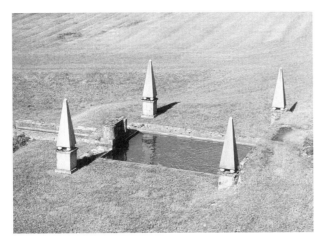

9.6. The pool at the chateau of Bussy-Rabutin in Burgundy is marked by four obelisks. Seen in the distance, it is difficult to estimate their true size in the absence of an element of comparison.

Useful as a place to rest, even a glimpse of a bench suggests hospitality and triggers relaxation. Benches are best when they have a back and face a view (fig. 9.8). The back need not be attached to the seat; it is perhaps more useful as a psychological protection than as a back support. A pair of facing benches creates a convivial setup, too often ruined when they face each other across a path. A single curved bench goes a step further towards conviviality (fig. 9.9).

Among small things, the doorknob is near the bottom of the hierarchy. A detail that has been designed in thousands of variations, it can become a poem in the hands of a gifted designer or worker who loves his or her craft. The appearance of a doorknob should suggest the character of the building and hint at the promise of a pleasant time beyond the door (figs. 9.10, 9.11).

GRASSE
Place aux Aires

9.7. A fountain in Grasse, a small town in Provence. In warm areas like this, shade trees and running water combine to provide a pleasant and much needed coolness.

9.9. A curved stone bench in Pompeii.

9.8. A wooden bench placed against a large tree trunk on the grounds of Carter's Grove, a plantation on the James River in Virginia. A small brick area on the ground adds to the sitters' comfort.

9.10. A doorknob that is also a door knocker at the royal chateau in St. Germain-en-Laye, near Paris. Probably from the seventeenth century.

9.11. A typical doorknob on a double door to a block of flats in Paris

9.12. A small window on Rue de Condé, a narrow street in Paris alongside the Theatre de l'Odéon.

9.13. Palazzo Iseppo Porto, Vicenza. Andrea Palladio. Detail of the street facade.

9.14. Villa Foscari, known as "Villa Malcontenta," near Venice, completed before 1560. Andrea Palladio. The central portion of the south facade.

A doorknob should not affect the shape of the door or its articulation. This is a fundamental rule of design that can be stated in simple terms: small things should be subservient to large things. Take stairs in the stair hall: the space that contains the stair is larger than the stair-object within, and therefore the stair should not be allowed to modify the space. Equally, the lower steps of a stair take precedence over the floor pattern. The pattern should give the impression that part of it is covered by the steps.

RUSTICATION

Rustication is the texture and pattern given to the surface of a stone wall by emphasizing the joints between the discrete elements of the wall. Instead of blending in the surface of a wall, the joints are underlined and often exaggerated. In fact, it is rare to see the actual joints; rustication seeks to idealize the wall structure.

The variety of patterns achieved with rustication is inexhaustible. All of them animate a facade and enhance the three-dimensional reality of a wall. Usually found on the ground floor, rustication may be contrasted with a smooth wall treatment on the upper stories. Emphasis is often placed on horizontal joints to express the crushing weight on the lower portion of the wall. The expressive power of rustication is epitomized in an extravagant keystone hanging over an otherwise insignificant window in Paris (fig. 9.12). A strong horizontal division of the facade occurs at the springing of the arch.

In a design by Palladio for the Palazzo Iseppo Porto (fig. 9.13), the rustication is confined to the ground floor with a pattern above derived from relieving arches. Rooms in Italy were vaulted to keep their occupants cool. Relieving arches are not structurally necessary; they are a device to animate what would otherwise be a blank area between the ground floor windows and the upper floor.

Villa Foscari (fig. 9.14), also by Palladio, is rusticated from the ground up. The south facade, dominated by a five-bay, three-story projection, is clearly organized by the fenestration. The presence of a huge, vaulted room in the middle is revealed by six openings gathered under one arch. The arch motif is echoed by relieving arches over five windows. Fenestration and rustication work in concert toward the visual interest of the facade. Sir William Chambers, on the other hand, relied on contrast for effect. In a design published in the *Treatise on the Decorative Part of Civil Architecture*, he juxtaposed the brute power of rustication with the refinement of a finely tuned Ionic order (fig. 9.15).

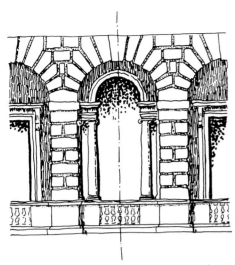

9.15. *Design based on William Chambers,* Treatise on the Decorative Part of Civil Architecture, *London, 1791.*

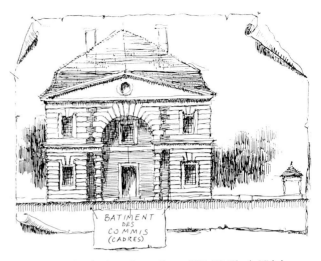

9.17. *Royal Saltworks, Arc-et-Senans, France, 1775–79. Claude Nicholas Ledoux. Facade of one of the two buildings housing the foremen.*

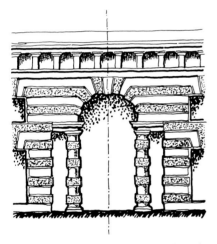

9.16. *A monumental gate designed by Claude Nicholas Ledoux.*

9.18. *An allegory of Abundance in a niche of the garden of the Palazzo Capponi in Florence.*

Ledoux sometimes added color and texture to rustication. Layers of stone with a smooth finish alternate with rough layers in a design for a monumental gate (fig. 9.16). A similar treatment is applied to the columns where drums alternate with square blocks; the blocks are textured while the cylindrical parts remain smooth. The simplified entablature over the Tuscan columns is abruptly replaced with a course of textured stone, which gives the impression that the rectangular openings on either side of the arch are nearly independent gates.

At the Royal Saltworks (fig. 9.17), Ledoux introduced color in a pair of matching buildings housing the foremen. Bricks of a soft orange reinforce the division of the stone facades in three parts.

The structural logic of masonry expressed on an arch does suggest a sunburst when it is centered on the head of a sculpted figure. Can there be a better way to enhance the representation of a young woman? This one, laden with baskets of fruit, celebrates abundance in a lush garden (fig. 9.18).

9.19. Darwin D. Martin house, 1904–8, Buffalo, New York. Frank Lloyd Wright.

9.20. Martin house. Raked joints.

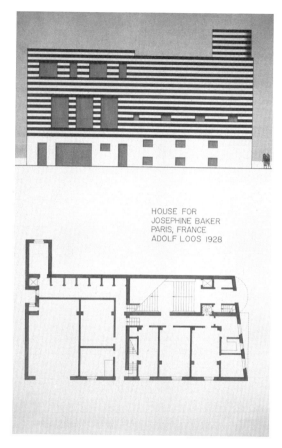

9.21. Project for a house for Josephine Baker, Paris, 1928. Adolf Loos. Drawing by Bruce Barkoff.

Even in a period when it was considered outdated, rustication found a new expression in the work of modern architects. During his prairie-style period, Frank Lloyd Wright asserted the dominance of horizontal lines in several ways. Ceilings were low, roofs were cantilevered out to the limit, and Wright even used light and color to achieve his aim. Roman bricks, longer and slimmer, took the place of traditional ones, and horizontal joints were raked to obtain sharp shadow lines. To ensure the absolute continuity of line, Wright eliminated the interruptions of vertical joints, which were flush with the bricks and painted to match them (figs. 9.19, 9.20).

Adolf Loos designed a house for Josephine Baker with striking black and white stripes on the facades (fig. 9.21). This is clearly a modern interpretation of rustication. The ground floor, devoted to service spaces, received a plain treatment contrasting with the piano nobile. Tradition would have suggested a more pronounced rustication at the lower level, but Loos reversed the convention.

BOLLARDS

In the hierarchy of small things, the humble bollard is at the very bottom. Sometimes called a post, it is a stumpy form usually made of stone whose original purpose was to keep carriages away from pedestrians and from exposed parts of buildings. Bollards played the part of today's

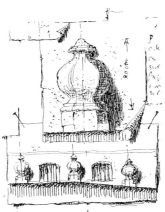

9.22. A row of bollards in the old part of the city of Basel.

9.24. Three of seventeen bollards attached to the wall of a town house.

9.25. Bollards in a row protect pedestrians and frame one of the fountains for which Aix-en-Provence is famous.

9.23. A bollard of unusual design protects the corner of a building in Semur-en-Auxois, a picturesque town in Burgundy.

9.26. Place de l'Odéon, Paris, c. 1782. Peyre and de Wailly. A row of bollards reinforces the semicircular shape of the urban square. Their shape and the stone of which they are made echo the colonnade in the background.

sidewalks, and they played it better. In recent decades, they have been reinvented, with the expanded role of keeping automobiles off the sidewalks in Paris and many other cities. In too many cases, unfortunately, slender metal poles have taken the place of traditional stone bollards.

Transcending their eminently utilitarian nature, bollards vary in form from plain chunks of stone to elaborate urban ornaments. Simplicity in the design of a repeated motif may be a virtue rather than a defect, as plain, tapered stones capped with subtly rounded forms attest in Basel (fig. 9.22). Some bollards seem to tell a story or present a riddle. At first glance, three superposed stone spheres of decreasing diameter (fig. 9.23) seem to be the invention of a whimsical imagi-

nation; on reflection, the structure may be the product of a geometer's systematic mind.

Bollards are never used individually. Seventeen bollards of intricate design line up along the facade of a town house in Montbard, in Burgundy. They play an important part in the decorative scheme of the building, which was the home of the eighteenth-century naturalist Buffon (fig. 9.24).

Whether their design is plain or elaborate, a row of freestanding bollards has the ability to define and enhance urban spaces. They may be small, but they are effective in public parks and city squares. Whether or not they are connected by a chain, they control pedestrians and vehicular traffic more surely, and more discreetly, than barricades (figs. 9.25, 9.26).

CHAPTER 10

EDGES AND TRANSITIONS

Architecture has developed from man's need to order the world in space and time,
which is a precondition to its being accessible to our understanding.

—SIR RICHARD ROGERS

All classical spaces are well defined; their form, their size, and their materials all contribute to making their function and character clear. The nature of the edges plays a crucial role in defining the space within. Edges come in many forms. We have just seen that a row of bollards can be a powerful edge, even though a bollard is an insignificant object by itself. Nevertheless, it is unusual for a space to be defined only by bollards. More often than not, a figural outdoor space is bound by several different types of enclosures, which together make the edge itself attractive and meaningful. Iteration is especially important for a sequence of interconnected spaces because those edges must also function as a transition between one space and the next.

WALLS

The wall is one of the most common types of boundaries. Four walls that surround a space open to the sky form a courtyard, where the most critical aspect is the height of the enclosure in relation to the length and width of the space within. This determines the amount of natural light it receives: the higher the walls, the more confining the space is. In the Royal Palace of Stockholm (fig. 10.1), the courtyard is formal

and austere, as befits its ceremonial function. The ground is paved, and there is no planting; the wall openings are governed by a tight grid. Activity is limited to elaborate rituals performed on a rigid schedule.

Fredensborg Castle, the royal summer residence of Denmark (fig. 10.2), also presents a dignified and orderly front, but, since it is in the country, the building spreads out. The facade it presents to the world closes only one side of a vast forecourt. The other two sides are formed by rows of trees. The emptiness of the paved space is awesome precisely because it is clearly designed for parades and ceremonies involving large crowds.

Hôtel de Biron in Paris (fig. 10.3), now the Rodin Museum, is a typical eighteenth-century residence built for a rich and powerful family. Like Fredensborg Castle, the building forms one side of an outdoor space, but in this case, it is a garden, planned more for pleasure than ceremony. The facade is animated in plan as well as in elevation. Round-headed windows, a large balcony on the upper floor, and broad steps on the ground floor encourage interaction between the inside and the outside. The garden, surrounded on one side by the house and on the others by dense foliage, is organized in two parts. At the back, a circular lawn with a pool in the middle and, between the pool and the house, a

10.1. *Royal Palace of Sweden, Stockholm. The courtyard.*

10.3. *Hôtel de Biron, Paris, 1731. Jean Aubert. Garden side.*

10.2. *Fredensborg Castle in Denmark. The parade grounds in front of the royal summer residence.*

10.4. *The central portion of the orangery at Versailles, 1684. J. H. Mansart.*

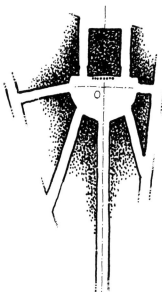

10.5. Park Crescent, a portion
of the celebrated Regent Street
sequence in London, 1811–26.
John Nash.

10.6. Place de l'Odéon.
Schematic plan. The center of
the circular enclosure is marked
"O" in front of the colonnade.

10.7. Place de l'Odéon.
Relationship between the
exedra and the colonnade
of the theater.

long rectangular formal lawn, or *tapis vert*. The ground is flat, and sanded allées invite leisurely walks. Nothing could be simpler, yet nothing seems to be missing, and restfulness emanates from the whole.

Let us see how a wall can be softened and accented at the same time. Like everything else in Versailles, the orangery (fig. 10.4) is conceived on a vast scale. Cliff-like retaining walls shelter the outdoor area on three sides, leaving the south one open to the sun. Cavernous spaces are found behind these walls, and visitors in the upper garden are unaware that they are walking on the roof of the orangery. Trees and other plants in boxes are lined up in front of the middle wall in order of size, with the largest ones close to the wall, where they can benefit from its radiant heat. There may be as many as ten rows of varied plants. The lowest layer is adjacent to a wide border of flowers, which makes the final connection with the lawn. The sensitive gradation of the plants provides a smooth transition where the intersection of bare wall and flat ground would have been abrupt. Far from weakening the effect of the boundary, it comforts and glorifies it.

The effect of an exedra is different from that of a straight wall. Even at a grand scale, a semicircular wall wrapped around a portion of outdoor space gives a comfortable sensation: we feel as if we were cradled. In typical British fashion, the Royal Crescent in Bath and Park Crescent in London (fig. 10.5) face park land. Place de l'Odéon in Paris (fig. 10.6) is an exedra facing a civic building, a theater. The urban ensemble was entrusted to the architects Peyre and de Wailly, who made the exedra into a sort of frame for the theater. Here the focus is not the colonnade but the void of the urban square. The grandeur of the colonnade is in sharp contrast with the restrained design of the other buildings, but a common height unifies the enclosures. The plan shows that the shape of the exedra is slightly more closed than a semicircle, indicating that the architects intended to accentuate the sense of enclosure (fig. 10.7). The buildings are tall in relation to the space they enclose, and the street openings between them are narrow, so that the total effect is almost that of a forecourt.

In the country, planting can replace masonry. In an exedra designed by William Kent for the gardens at Kew Palace (fig. 10.8), the enclosure is a series of concentric hedges with terms punctuating the circular form. Their color makes them stand out in a context of greens with gold accents; the fact that they bear the heads of philosophers adds intellectual substance to these slender objects.

10.8. Exedra at Kew Palace, near London. Attributed to William Kent.

The form of the exedra lends itself to a multiplicity of uses and circumstances. A profusion of water and some Roman ruins were at the origin of the gardens of La Fontaine in Nîmes (fig. 10.9), among the very first built for public use in France. The exedra is formed by high retaining walls embracing a pool. Mature trees on the terraces above provide shaded areas from which to contemplate the play of water. The walls frame a waterway and the corners framing the junction are doubled up, creating four observation points that overlook the pool and the waterway.

Tall, opaque, and continuous hedges can replace stone walls to advantage. The open-air theatre of Villa Marlia (fig. 10.10), near Lucca in northern Italy, is enclosed on all sides by green walls of ilex. Terra cotta statues occupy the stage except during performances.

10.9. Exedra in the gardens of La Fontaine, Nîmes, 1740–60.

RAMPS AND STEPS

Architecture should always enhance the natural environment. This goal is more easily achieved when interventions respect the site, that is, when the designer works with the landscape rather than against it. To organize, to create a sense of order, to formalize, to introduce a modicum of geometry should not require uprooting trees or substantial earthworks.

10.10. Open air theater at Villa Marlia, near Lucca, probably late seventeenth century.

10.11. *Open air theater in Denmark. The grass-covered tiers are edged in stone.*

10.12. *Stone stairs connecting two levels around the "Confessional" in the gardens at Vaux-le-Vicomte, begun in 1661. André Le Nôtre, Louis Le Vau, and Charles Le Brun.*

10.13. *Villa Medici in Poggio a Caiano, near Florence, 1480–85. Giuliano da Sangallo. Entrance on the main facade.*

Stairs or ramps are necessary on natural and artifical slopes. One of the most satisfying architectural interventions of this nature is an outdoor theater in Denmark that seems to be in total harmony with the site (fig. 10.11). The use of natural materials, such as stone, obviously contributes to a better integration with the site. With age, stones lose their sharp contours and acquire mosses and lichens, which give them an attractive mellowness. Similar effects can be obtained with climbing vines or hedges. In a sculptural stair at Vaux-le-Vicomte, a yew hedge screens the retaining wall and shade trees on the upper level promise shade and cool (fig. 10.12).

A change of level can be created by raising reception rooms on an upper floor. Villa Medici in Poggio a Caiano (fig. 10.13), was begun in 1480 as a stronghold. Later, when the Medici family had secured power over Florence, twin curvilinear stairs were added, reaching down toward guests in a gesture of welcome evoking outstretched arms. At the same time, a wide loggia was built at the top to receive the guests in comfort.

Stairs can be enhanced by the addition of a water element. At Sceaux, near Paris, the gardens were designed by André Le Nôtre, a master at exploiting the resources of a site. He had a large pool dug in a shallow valley on the east side of the chateau and opened up a vista toward the opposite side of the valley, until it seems to stretch to infinity. The upper half of the slope near the chateau is a tapis vert. Below is a series of terraces designed around small pools that cascade into each other all the way down to the large pool at the bottom. In spite of its magnificence, this perspective is secondary to the major one in the gardens (fig. 10.14). Pleached trees define the space that contains the Escalier d'Eau, or water stairs. Each pool is framed by two platforms, each with its own lawn. Openings in a low hedge invite strollers to follow the water in the middle; if they seek shade or privacy, they can find both under the trees.

In warm countries, the sound of running

water has a cooling effect. Used sparingly in Spain and in a more flamboyant way in Italy, examples abound of ingenious designs. The well-known garden of Villa Lante, north of Rome, is designed around a set of inspired variations on the water element and involves all the senses including touch. At Caprarola, near Viterbo, the stairs leading up from the main villa to the casino are set between two walls to direct attention to the bubbly water chain dividing the stairs (fig. 10. 15). The lateral walls appear to be of a piece with the facade of the casino and reinforce the sense of enclosure. The triple arcade of the second floor loggia can be seen from below, but the ground floor is hidden by the giant river gods and the mouth of the vase between them from which the water gushes.

MOATS, RETAINING WALLS, AND TOWERS

The word "moat" evokes a bygone world of knights, jousting, and fair maidens. Originally made to protect a settlement or a stronghold from assailants or wild animals, moats outlasted their function. A number of them survived, probably by accident, and architects and patrons then realized that moats had the power to give a special identity to the space they isolated from the undifferentiated context (fig. 10.16). Existing moats were then reconfigured to satisfy design requirements or new ones dug.

A channel or a river calls for a bridge, which, in turn, suggests a separate realm. At Cormatin in Burgundy, the chateau and gardens are built on several artifical islands connected by bridges (fig. 10.17).

Some moats are designed to be invisible from a distance. Known as "ha-has" in Britain, they are used instead of fences to keep cattle or unwanted animals at bay. The contrast between visual connection across a moat and physical separation between the two sides increases the

10.14. Escalier d'Eau in Sceaux, 1675. André Le Nôtre.

10.15. Stairs leading to the casino at the Villa Farnese, Caprarola, 1584–86.

10.16. Bodiam Castle, Sussex, late fourteenth century.

10.17. Cormatin, Burgundy. Partial view of the gardens from the chateau.

10.18. *The sixteenth-century garden of Diane de Poitiers at Chenonceau seen from the raised walk that surrounds it.*

10.19. *Garden of Diane de Poitiers. The retaining wall seen from the outside.*

10.20. *Hôtel de la Monnaie, Paris, 1775. Jacques-Denis Antoine. Retaining wall on the riverbank.*

sense of drama. In the Loire valley, at one of the gardens of Chenonceau, the situation is modified. A peripheral elevated walk gives the impression that the parterre in the middle is sunken (fig. 10.18). From the raised walk, visitors can both enjoy the beauty of the parterre and see the countryside across the moat. From the outside, however, the walk shields the garden from public view (fig. 10.19).

Retaining walls can play an important role, and they can be visual assets. A civic building standing on a riverbank will appear to be on a pedestal. Somerset House in London is one of these. The Collège des Quatre Nations is another, as is La Monnaie. The retaining wall of the latter (fig. 10.20) is stretched out to give the 400-foot building a strong base and to connect the building to the water. The wall projects in several places to form a terrace, to allow for stairs to the water level, and to create corners that match the articulation of the facade. The axis of symmetry of the composition as a whole is marked by a substantial arch in the retaining wall. Large-scale rustication with textures and patterns contrasts with the smooth, urbane surface of the building.

Once the defensive function of moats was abandoned, only the part in front of a principal facade remained popular, mainly because of the opportunity for a bridge or a causeway. Water was retained when possible, but if it was not available, a dry moat was deemed sufficient. The space-making potential of a moat at the hands of a great designer is demonstrated at the Meudon chateau, now demolished (fig. 10.21). At first, the curves and twists of the wall seem fussy, but, on closer inspection, they reveal themselves as the outcome of thoughtful design. All the shapes, the angles, and their relationships are governed by reason; at the same time, they seem to have arranged themselves spontaneously. The wings of the building are extended by the negative form of the moat. The quarter-circles right and left reflect the swelling of the facade center and allow carriages to maneuver (A). The polygonal forms to the right and left of the moat create two inviting spots along the balustrade from which to observe the activities in the forecourt (B). The fussy funnel shape at the entrance of the bridge expresses the emotion the balustrade itself should feel at the approach of important visitors. And so on; the analysis of the rest of the moat's outline reflects the extraordinary finesse of the architect. Like walls, moats present an obstacle to motion, but they do not block the view.

Paradoxically, towers present some similarities with moats: the view is better, but participation is limited. The size of a viewing platform restricts the number of spectators. Classical towers are not as common as those of Gothic design. James Gibbs was the first architect to solve the difficult problem of integrating a tower with a temple form, and he apparently did it with masterful ease. His 1721 design for St. Martin-in-the-Fields in London has been the model and inspiration for countless churches in the western world. In secular buildings, classical towers (fig. 10.22) usually are modest places where small groups gather to enjoy a view or a refreshing breeze in the summer. The top story takes the form of an elegant open pavilion. Partly because of their small size, they are often used in pairs.

A lantern or a pinnacle, either round or square, always terminates a classical dome. Many lanterns are only accessible for maintenance purposes or they may simply house a skylight or a bell. But in country houses, they were observatories from which the hunt, among other sights, could be followed by those who did not participate in the sport (fig. 10.23).

SCREENS

More subtle barriers than walls and moats can be used to define the edge of outdoor spaces. In

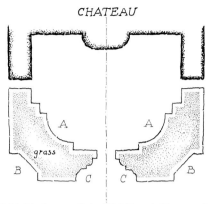

10.21. Meudon, near Paris, 1706. François Mansart or Louis Le Vau. The moat defining a forecourt is no longer extant.

10.22. Villa Medici, Rome, 1564. Annibale Lippi. One of the twin observation towers.

10.23. Chateau at Cheverny, completed 1634, with twin observatories.

10.24. Louisburg Square on Beacon Hill, Boston.

10.25. Place Royale, part of an urban ensemble erected in Nancy, 1752–55. Emmanuel Heré.

10.26. The park seen through a trellised arch at Oatlands, in Virginia.

Louisburg Square in Boston, Gramercy Park in New York, and many squares in London, the park is open only to the residents of the surrounding houses. In Boston, there are six different layers of separation between the street and the park. The first screen is a row of parked cars, followed by the curb, a row of trees, a row of lamp posts, the sidewalk, and finally the fence. None is a solid barrier, but in combination they form an effective buffer between the traffic and the pedestrian zone (fig. 10.24).

The enclosure of the Place Royale in Nancy (fig. 10.25) is practically continuous. Buildings of varying height but of homogenous design enclose all four sides. The transparency of wrought-iron grilles provides relief in the corners. The grilles frame spectacular fountains or serve as honorific gates to the piazza. A comparable effect can be obtained at a much more intimate scale. In the tea house at Oatlands in Virginia (fig. 10.26), a wooden trellis softens the view to the garden.

The design of Villa Giulia in Rome is unusual. This small but intricate complex erected on a perfectly flat piece of land is made totally private by the wall encircling it. Within the enclosure, outdoor spaces are more elaborate than interior rooms. Their regular—or figural—shapes are molded by the complex, sometimes ambiguous forms of the buildings wrapped around them. There are four levels, two of them below grade and holding a pool of water. The sequence of highly individualized spaces is held together by an enfilade on axis from the front door to the back wall. The vista extends through seven wall openings, some in the form of colonnades or "transparent walls" (fig. 10.27).

Awareness of location intensifies when the outside and the inside of the enclosure can be seen simultaneously, when a wing of the building is seen through a window of the main block, for example. The Salle de Bal at Versailles (fig. 10.28) is a circular arcade of great delicacy. You pass under one arch to enter, and you are instantly surrounded by thirty-one others.

In a general way, foreground objects enhance distant views by clarifying the relationship of foreground, middle ground, and background. When the object in the foreground is also worth looking at, it adds the finishing touch on the experience, even at the cost of obscuring the view. A detail of Stourhead in Wiltshire, one of the most celebrated English gardens of the eighteenth century, illustrates this point (fig. 10.29). In the foreground is one of the four columns of the small Pantheon designed by Henry Flitcroft and built in 1756. The background consists of dense woods. Between the two is a glimpse of the lawn and a portion of the lake.

This sort of visual teasing has been in use in architecture for centuries, consciously or not. There is no doubt, for instance, that the charm of countless farms, cottages, and country houses in Great Britain is in great part due to a certain secrecy. Steep roofs and tall chimneys suggestive of coziness and privacy emerge from behind walls, hedges, and borders (fig. 10.30).

The loss in the visual field is more than made up by the heightening of anticipation. Le Corbusier went to an extreme in his design for the monastery of La Tourette. The view from the roof was beautiful but, so his reasoning went, it would become even more beautiful if it could not be seen. This is how the decision was made to raise the height of the parapet above the eye level.

CROSSING THE EDGE

In ranking the classical elements of design in order of importance, gates and doorways would certainly be towards the top of the list. Entering a special place is an event that demands celebrating, regardless of program or size. The nature of the place is announced by the design of the gate, and the celebration honors three elements: the visitor, the host, and the place being entered.

10.27. Villa Giulia, Rome, 1550–55. Vignola, Vasari, Bartolommeo Ammanati. The shaft of space on the main axis, looking back toward the front door.

10.28. Salle de Bal in the gardens of Versailles, c. 1685. J. H. Mansart. Three hundred years of sun exposure have bleached the color of the 32-column screen.

10.29. Stourhead, Wiltshire. The view from the Pantheon towards the lake.

10.30. Loseley, near Guildford, Surrey. Farm buildings.

10.31. Main gate to the royal palace at Versailles.

10.32. An old farm in the Champagne area of France. The street entrance.

10.33. View from the stable yard to the seventeenth-century gate at Cheverny.

The gate to the gigantic court of honor at Versailles is remarkable for the elegance of its restrained design, its orientation, and the fact that it opens out rather than in. The first attribute requires no explanation but the other two do. The gate faces east, where the sun rises, and the emblem of the absolute monarch Louis XIV was the sun. The fact that Paris also lies to the east is secondary. As a gesture of courtesy towards honored guests, a gate or a door usually opens towards the place being entered, but not at Versailles, where no one was deemed worthy of more honor than the king. Therefore, the gate opens out (fig. 10.31).

When it is necessary to separate vehicular traffic from pedestrians, two openings are provided. On a farm, for instance, where animals must be kept in or out, it is easier to control the narrow opening than the larger one, which is usually kept closed (fig. 10.32).

Two unequal openings, dictated by practical and economic pressures, generate a design that is visually unbalanced. Symmetry can be reestablished by introducing two small doorways, one on each side of the vehicular access. A pyramidal composition emerges, suggestive of hierarchy, which presents the designer with a perennial problem that may be solved in multiple ways (fig. 10.33).

An archway spanning the gap between piers begins to suggest a triumphal arch, an allusion reinforced at Cheverny with a segmental pediment over the middle opening. The sharp spire in the distance imbues the composition with drama. The proximity, not to say confrontation, of two such sharply contrasted design elements like these was deliberately used by perceptive architects, Shaw and Lutyens among others.

A gateway frames the view beyond, and its design should be in harmony with the picture within. Formal similarity between the gateway and the background is one way to give unity to the space between them. For instance, an arcade seen from an arch of identical proportions (fig.

10.34) suggests that the four walls around the courtyard probably carry the same arcaded framework. The paving pattern connecting the front and the back across the courtyard is physical evidence of the relationship between the two arcades.

All that remains of an early seventeenth-century garden in a remote part of Burgundy is a haunting series of stone enclosures and portals (fig. 10.35). Since there is no record of the design of the gardens themselves, one is free to imagine the cornucopia of fountains, bowers, aviaries, espaliers and the feasts of color, pattern, fragrance, and flavors that graced the gardens of the period between the Middle Ages and the Renaissance. The portals that remain seem to welcome you cheerfully.

There is no sense of mystery in the gardens of Villa di Castello in Florence. The setting is unusual because the villa was built at the bottom of a hill. The garden climbs the hillside, the last part of it closed by a retaining wall seen against a background of mature trees (fig. 10.36). The axis terminates in a grotto within the retaining wall. The portal to the uppermost garden and the grotto motif appear to be the same height and width. Taking advantage of the slope, wide steps give the grotto the needed substantial base.

A constant in classical design is the principle of limiting the number of elements and exploiting each one to the maximum, which creates both variety to sustain interest and simplicity to foster repose and avoid confusion. Once adopted, a good idea like framing will not be discarded if it can be reinterpreted. A mansion set back from the street will be announced by a pair of pavilions guarding the access to a long straight drive shaded by symmetrical rows of trees at the end of which the house can be glimpsed (fig. 10.37). The end of the drive will be framed again by two sculptural objects carried on pedestals marking the edge of the forecourt. Finally, the simple door to the house in the middle of a substantial facade will constitute

10.34. Courtyard at 1 Borgo Croce, Florence, seen from the street.

10.35. Two of the surviving portals at the Jardins Coeurderoy, Burgundy.

10.36. Villa Castello, Florence, 1537–50, Niccolò Tribolo, Bartolomeo Ammannati, and Bernardo Buontalenti. The terrace at the top of the gardens.

10.37, 10.38. The entrance sequence to a beautiful estate in a residential area north of Chicago.

10.39. Eighteenth-century gate to a hôtel in Dijon.

10.40. One of the two elegant piers that mark the entrance to the grounds of the Church of Our Saviour, Copenhagen.

the ultimate passage into the privacy of the house (fig. 10.38).

In cities, where space is scarce, a more restrained form of double frame can be devised in the shallow setback required for a carriage to turn at a right angle. Two urns add a touch of refinement to the outer piers of a portal in Dijon (fig. 10.39).

Each pier of a set is, and should be, asymmetrical because of different side conditions: the void of the gate on one side of a pier and the interrupted enclosure on the other (fig. 10.40). Seen together, however, piers present a mirror image of each other. Symmetry improves the appearance of any set. The top of a typical pier is a simplified entablature on which stands an ornamental sculpture. Rustication is common, and a bracket with a volute negotiates the difference in height between the pier and the lower wall.

The degree of refinement in piers is much less critical than the framing itself. The view of a Georgian house is slowly revealed to visitors as they move closer and closer (fig. 10.41). Here the idea of framing is skillfully associated with the idea of screening.

Gates need not be monumental to produce a good effect. A small gap in a picket face will enhance the spaces on either sides by giving them both a more definite character (fig. 10.42).

In architecture, the frame can be more beautiful or more significant than the picture inside it. A uniform facade built around an urban square constitutes a frame that may be the only interesting thing in the square. Wherever the uniform facade is interrupted to let a street into the square, there is a gap enframed by the symmetry of the buildings on either side. Piazza Beccaria in Florence is one of those unappreciated urban squares that suffer from the proximity of more famous ones (fig. 10.43). At the center stands Porta alla Croce, the ruin of a fortified gate to the city, an ungainly but historically significant object. The facade by the architect G.

10.41. *A gate framed with plain piers at Rosehill, Angus, Scotland.*

Rosehill, Brechin
J.F.G. 2002

10.42. *Garden of a Georgian house, University of Georgia, Athens, Georgia.*

10.43. *Piazza Beccaria, Florence, 1880. G. Pozzi. Porta alla Croce is partly visible on the left.*

*10.44. Piazza Beccaria.
Entrance to Borgo La Croce.*

*10.45. Looking out on the
Place des Vosges from the
piano nobile of the Hôtel
de Chaulnes.*

*10.46. Palladian bridge at
Stourhead, Wiltshire, 1750.
Henry Flitcroft.*

Pozzi surrounding the square includes a dignified Corinthian colonnade resting on a high rusticated base.

Among the seven "gates" that open into the Beccaria enclosure, the most successful is the one from Borgo La Croce, a narrow street of great historical interest (fig. 10.44). To adapt the grand scale of his square to the narrow medieval street, the architect worked out a double corner that makes a smooth transition. The simplification of the architectural treatment of the reentrant corners is worthy of attentive study.

A final transitional element is the "french door," which is both a door and a window. Although usually a feature of the ground floor, the french door is even more attractive on an upper story, where it creates a feeling of greater freedom and lightness (fig. 10.45). Since the lower part of the wall under the window has been removed, the view is significantly enlarged. Even without a balcony to walk on, one can lean on the guard rail and stand practically outside. If the guardrail is a delicate wrought-iron screen, so much the better.

Although nothing could be more different than a gate and a bridge, their basic function is identical; a bridge, like a gate, is a means to cut through an otherwise impassable barrier. The difference is that going through a gate is often like crossing a line, while a bridge always has width and length, which make it a place in which one could stand and linger. What makes a bridge special is that it seems to hover in space. Observe people strolling onto a bridge: almost invariably they will lean over the guardrail as if to confirm a suspicion that they are walking on air.

Personal indulgence created two delightful bridges built in England in the 1750s. The one at Stourhead, set in a beautifully designed landscape, has five arches and is covered with inviting turf (fig. 10.46). The other, inspired by Palladio, as was the one at Stourhead, is a covered bridge of a design replicated in several locations. James Gibbs built the first one at Stowe in 1738.

10.47. Palladian bridge at Prior Park.

10.48. Hertford Bridge, Oxford, 1913. Thomas Jackson.

Another, at Prior Park, near Bath, (fig. 10.47) is a large open pavilion built over water and accessible by stairs at both ends.

In the last decades, pedestrian bridges connecting buildings on opposite sides of streets have proliferated. A street is a link between two points in a city; but it is also an edge, a separation that may need to be bridged over. Hertford Bridge, over College Lane in Oxford (fig. 10.48), seems exemplary in the self-contained energy it projects; it has some of the playful exuberance of the best baroque as well as classical discipline. Like the bridge of Prior Park, it is more than a passageway; a post of observation is revealed by the elaborate venetian window at midpoint.

CHAPTER 11

STUDENT PROJECTS
FOR OPEN SITES

*The more extensive your acquaintance is with the works of those
who have excelled, the more extensive will be your powers of invention.*

—SIR JOSHUA REYNOLDS

In this, the third and last series of student projects, the common factor is an open site. "Open sites" are situations where the pressures from the physical context are few, or minor. These are likely to occur more often in the open country but they are occasionally found in urban contexts as well. Such is the case in the first three programs.

In his seminal book *A Pattern Language*, Christopher Alexander has summarized the principles that should guide the designer of public spaces in urban contexts:

A town needs public squares; they are the largest, most public rooms that the town has. There are two fundamentally different kinds of outdoor spaces: negative and positive space. Outdoor space is negative when it is shapeless, the residue left behind when buildings—which are generally viewed as positive—are placed on the land. Negative spaces are so poorly defined that you cannot really tell where their boundaries are. Outdoor spaces which are merely "left over" between buildings will in general not be used. An outdoor space is positive when it has a distinct and definite shape, as definite as the shape of a room, and when its shape is as important as the shapes of the buildings which surround it.

Make all the outdoor spaces which surround and lie between your buildings positive. Give each one some degree of enclosure; surround each space with wings of buildings, trees, hedges, fences, arcades, and trellised walks, until it becomes an entity with a positive quality and does not spill out indefinitely around corners.

A SMALL URBAN SQUARE

An indifferent urban context almost requires that all possible means of asserting the presence of an urban oasis be used. Instead of being subjected to compressive action from the existing environment, the architectural intervention takes control. This site is a leftover space in a chaotic area of the city. The surrounding nineteenth-century buildings now house a variety of thriving businesses. The program is to design a 160- x 90-foot rectangular park to fit between four streets.

For the safety of children, there will only be two points of entry into the park. The ground will be raised along the periphery and a continuous parapet built around the edge to minimize the impact of traffic noise. The raised area will be planted with two rows of trees to provide shade. The center of the park will be a sunken lawn surrounded with benches along the edges. To give presence to the park, pavilions measuring 20 x 20 feet will be built in the four corners to accommodate a variety of possible functions: shelter, meeting place, refreshment stand, ticket sales, storage, and restrooms.

DRAWING REQUIREMENTS

Plan of the square in context at 1/32 inch scale. Changes of level will be expressed with shading. Plan, section, and elevation of one pavilion at 1/16 inch scale.

DESIGN SOLUTIONS

The plan indicates points of entry on the narrow sides, and wide stairs occupy the entire space between the corner pavilions. The sunken area is entered in the middle of the long sides (fig. 11.1). In another proposal, Palladian openings and ornamental balls at the corner endow the pavilions with a cheerful character (fig. 11.2).

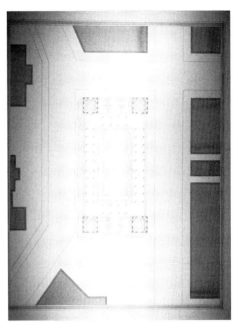

11.1. Plan of the square in context. Christopher Pizzi.

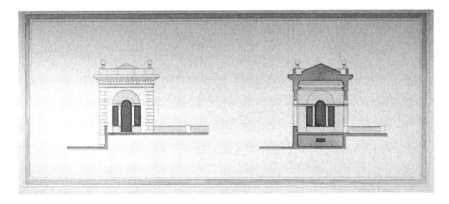

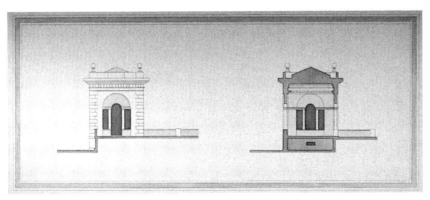

11.2 (see also C.19). Plan, sections, and elevations of a corner pavilion. Matthew Manuel.

11.3. Axonometric view of a portion of the arcaded street. There is a slight error in the drawing of the roofs. Glen Dabaghian.

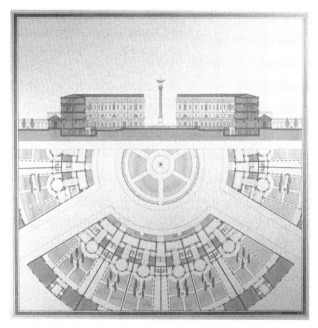

11.4 (see also C.20). A circular residential square. Elevation/section and half-plan. The opening to the arcaded street is beyond the freestanding column in the middle. Services spaces are shown in pale red. Jim Bouffard.

AN ARCADED STREET

This was the introduction to an ambitious, semester-long urban design problem where an arcaded street connects two large urban squares, each with a character of its own. The spatial sequence is a new urban development; the site is therefore non-specific. Three-story buildings line the street, which could be closed to vehicles at both ends during part of the day. A covered sidewalk on both sides protects strollers and shoppers from the weather; its depth is twelve feet. Upper stories could accommodate offices, storage, or apartments.

The island in the middle carries two rows of open market halls, but their width is double that of the covered sidewalks. To give unity to the street, the design of the market halls replicates that of the arcades under the lateral buildings.

Since this was a one-week problem, presentation requirements were limited to line drawings. This proposal (fig. 11.3) shows a portion of the street in axonometric form. To improve legibility, the building closer to the viewer was indicated by its foundation only.

TWO URBAN ROOMS

The arcaded street just discussed connects two squares. The circular form at the south is solely residential, while the larger square at the north end is more complex.

The circular plan is divided in equal sections by three streets converging on the center, which is occupied by an island with a freestanding column symbolizing the unity of the community. The space is enclosed by a circular row of identical two-family town houses. One residence is a triplex apartment that includes an "English" basement and a garden at the back. Above is a duplex apartment. Garages and workshops or storerooms at the rear of the property are accessible to both tenants from a shared covered passageway. Vehicular traffic in the square is restricted.

Some regulations to observe:

• Sidewalks must be at least five feet wide. Curb radius must be at least five feet. Curb height is six inches.

• Walk-ups are not allowed above the third floor. However, duplexes are allowed on third and fourth floors.

• Firewalls with a specific fire rating must separate all dwellings. Town houses must have fire exits. Fire exits must be enclosed and situated as far from one another as possible. "English" or dry moats must be accessible directly from the sidewalk.

• Light and air shafts, if any, must be at least 16 percent of the entire footprint of the buildings.

DRAWING REQUIREMENTS

Half-plan of the square, including at least one typical private garden, at 1/32 inch scale.

Cross section of the square looking north and including the town houses and the monumental column.

DESIGN SOLUTION

The central island is developed into a public garden with a row of benches that turn their back on the traffic. The opening to the arcaded street on the north can be seen behind the monumental column (fig. 11.4).

The north square measures 300 x 300 feet. It is open only on the south side, where the arcaded street intersects another going east-west. A civic center doubling as a community building dominates the square as well as the urban enfilade from one square to the other.

The center of the square is a paved island protected by a row of bollards. Four obelisks or columns mark the corners of the island. Limited traffic is permitted around the perimeter.

Identical four-story town houses surround the square. Each contains a residential duplex above two stories of professional offices. All are accessible from the front through a ceremonial entrance and from the back for vehicular access. Whenever possible, a back garden separates the garage from the town house and a covered walk connects the two.

The square is conceived as an *agora*, a Greek term that means invitation or welcome. Community ceremonies and celebrations take place there, with crowds gathered around or sitting on the ample steps of the community center to watch. The steps can also serve as a stage for choirs and political addresses. The numerous windows of the town houses reinforce the concept of the square as a metaphorical amphitheater.

The width of the civic building is at least 60 feet. Its facade should express community pride. A gathering place for the community, the building provides a venue for such functions as adult education, library, senior club, dog training, fitness, acting and ballet classes, weddings, dances, parties, youth club, and more. On the raised piano nobile is a suite of well-proportioned and well-appointed public rooms opening onto one another and easily accessible from the wide outdoor stairs. Office and service spaces are accommodated above and below the piano nobile.

An outdoor area at the back of the building can serve as overflow space for the building or as forecourt for access from the back. A public building must be completely accessible to the handicapped with grade level entrance or ramp. Elevators must provide access to every floor.

The regulations that govern the south square also apply to this square.

DRAWING REQUIREMENTS

General plan of the entire square with a few bays of the arcaded street at 1/32 inch scale or an enlarged plan of a corner of the square showing the varied dwelling plans at 1/16 inch or 1/32 inch scale.

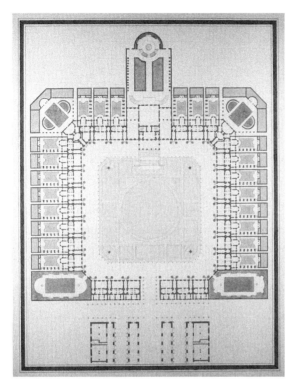

11.5 (see also C.21). A square urban room. General plan at the piano nobile level. The beginning of the arcaded street is shown at the bottom of the drawing. Sue Robbins.

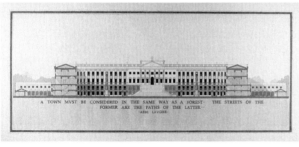

11.6 (see also C.22). Cross section of the square, facing north. Sue Robbins.

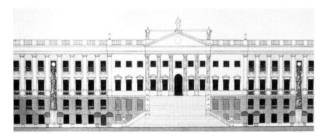

11.7. Partial elevation of the north side, with the civic building and attached town houses. Sue Robbins.

Cross section of the square, facing north and including the facade of the civic building and the private gardens with the garages at 1/16 inch scale. Alternatively, the plan and cross section may be combined on one board, with the section/elevation drawn across the plan, at the same scale or smaller.

Longitudinal section, including the garden beyond the civic building and three bays of the arcaded street at 1/16 inch scale.

DESIGN SOLUTION

The plan and cross section reveal that the steps in front of the civic building reach out to the island, creating a protected entrance underneath for the handicapped (figs. 11.5, 11.6, 11.7).

The problems presented by the corners of the square were solved in ingenious ways. Town houses with a special plan and a larger garden occupy the corners on the north side. Three bays at a 45-degree angle in each corner give privacy to adjacent units.

As a general strategy for the design of the facade, a colonnade corresponding to the residential upper tiers runs around the entire square. The two lower stories, occupied by professional offices, are treated more soberly as a base. Balconies on three floors demonstrate a vital relationship between public and private domains by encouraging active participation in civic events and celebrations (figs. 11.8, 11.9). The south corners consist of two secluded gardens accessible only from the square. There, the colonnade wrapped around the square becomes a screen (fig. 11.10).

A HOSPICE BY THE OCEAN

Every two years the Royal Oak Foundation, an affiliate of the National Trust of England, Wales, and Northern Ireland, sponsors a competition intended to foster a sympathetic collaboration between architecture, interior design, and landscape architecture. This program for a hospice is based on that written for the 1995 competition by the landscape architect and planner Laurie D. Olin.

A hospice provides a dignified and compassionate environment for the terminally ill. This location benefits from a gentle, soothing climate in California. The site is a strip of land between a narrow beach on the west and a two-lane road on the east. The average distance between the beach and the road is 300 feet; the length of the site is approximately 550 feet. A wooded area on the north covers about half of the land. There is a 10-foot drop in the terrain from the road to the water.

The individual rooms, where the residents spend most of their time, are the most important part of the program, and, like the rest of the facilities, they must be designed for people in wheelchairs. There is a second bed in every room for a companion, usually a close relative. All rooms have direct access to the outdoors. There is a large common room, a kitchen, a reception room, staff quarters, and a medical suite. Parking is provided for staff and visitors.

The landscape is designed as carefully as the buildings because it plays a crucial role in the emotional condition of the residents. A variety of spaces is essential, large and small, sunny or shaded, exposed or protected, with a view or secluded, including gardens that the residents can work in if they wish.

DESIGN SOLUTIONS

Proposal A: Residents' rooms are arranged in a semicircle and open on a flower garden that expands into a large terrace. Two open pavilions are built over the water. Visitors enter through a pergola on the left. They can see the common room straight ahead, across the flower garden. Nursing care is provided from a special corridor behind the rooms (fig. 11.11).

Proposal B: Residents' rooms form two sides of a colonnaded courtyard, with the main entrance on the third side. Each room has a pri-

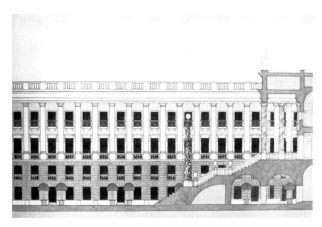

11.8. Section through the stairs connecting the civic building to the island, showing the covered drive underneath. Sue Robbins.

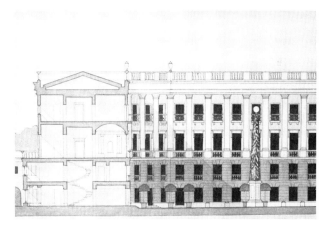

11.9. Section through a town house, showing one of the north side corners. Sue Robbins.

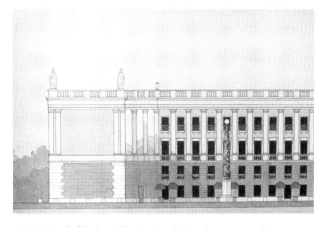

11.10. Detail of the longitudinal section, showing the entrance to the square and the southwest corner of the square. The colonnade in the corner is treated as a screen between the square and the secluded garden. Sue Robbins.

11.11 (see also C.23). Plan of the hospice. Robert Laterza.

11.12. Axonometric view of the hospice. Peter Rust.

vate outdoor patio and garden facing away from the center. The common room is a large breezeway between the ocean and the courtyard; two smaller, enclosed rooms frame the breezeway (fig. 11.12, 11.13).

A PALLADIAN VILLA

The late William Pearson, who ran an art gallery on Moreton Street in London, considered building a Palladian house on a four-acre site near Pillow Mound in Ashdown Forest, East Sussex, close to coastal resorts Brighton and Eastbourne. Situated on raised ground, some 700 feet above sea level, the property commands extensive views in several directions. The area is home to deer and other wildlife.

Before starting their design, students looked at plans, elevations, sections, and photographs of villas designed by Palladio. They made diagrams and formulated a list of the features that are common in his country houses. The objective of the design process was not to ape Palladio but to arrive at a personal interpretation of his design objectives.

PROGRAM
• Drawing room on the main axis, possibly with a loggia overlooking a formal garden.
• Four to six bedrooms with private baths.
• Garages required but not allowed to interfere with the view.
• Allée of cypress trees to enhance the visual impact of the first impression
• Fountain in the forecourt.
• Raised terrace overlooking a formal garden with a summer house near the swimming pool.

DESIGN SOLUTIONS
To keep out the deer, the gardens are enclosed with walls or fences. In the design proposals illustrated here (figs. 11.14, 11.15), there are two small garages instead of a single large one to minimize their visual impact. In one

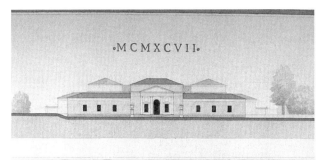

11.13 (see also C.24). From the top down, entrance facade, view from the ocean, cross-section on the main axis, with the entrance on the right and the ocean on the left. Peter Rust.

case, covered passages connect the garages to the villa.

The massing of the two house designs is very different. One drawing room is at the back, with a long living room on one side and the dining room on the other. Dining room and kitchen are adjacent to an herb garden, while the living room opens onto a flower garden. In both designs, the raised terrace in the back of the house is extended by a walk that circles the main garden and leads to the swimming pool on the opposite side. In the second case, the summer house is

11.14 (see also C.25). Axonometric drawing of the villa and its enclosed garden. The forecourt with the two garages is at the bottom. Trevor Lavoie.

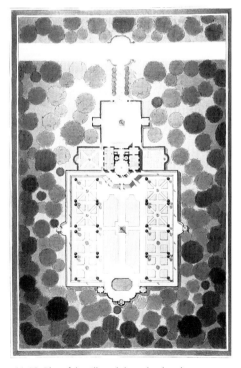

11.15. Plan of the villa and the enclosed garden. The forecourt is at the top. Joaquin Bonifaz.

11.16. Floor plans of the villa. The main floor is at the bottom. The drawing room is a two-story octagonal space. Dining room and kitchen are on the right, living room on the left. The second floor plan, at the top, shows the master suite on the left and three guestrooms on the right. Joaquin Bonifaz.

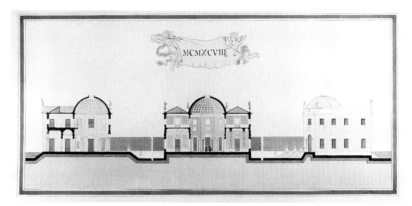

11.17. Center: *cross section of the villa through the drawing room, with the living room on the right and the dining room on the left.* Left: *cross section on the main axis showing the entry sequence to the drawing room.* Right: *the lateral elevation showing that the dining room and kitchen windows open onto the kitchen garden. Joaquin Bonifaz.*

11.18. The entry facade at the top with a garage on either side. The garden facade is shown below, with a cross section through the main garden. A raised walk surrounds the garden. Joaquin Bonifaz.

reinterpreted as a pair of small pavilions framing the swimming pool. The drawing room is octagonal and projects towards the garden. In the first design the drawing room is square and opens towards the main garden through a loggia. Both drawing rooms are two stories high. Instead of a grand staircase, there are two small enclosed stairs, similar to those Jefferson designed for Monticello. Like Palladio, Jefferson did not favor monumental stairs. In his view, "great staircases are avoided, which are expensive and occupy a space which would make a good room in every story" (fig. 11.16). Openings on the second floor make a visual connection to the octagonal drawing room. The owner's suite is on the left, and three guestrooms occupy the right side.

The second design is further illustrated with facades and section drawings (figs. 11.17, 11.18).

A VILLA FOR A PRIVATE ART DEALER

Sir Bannister Chip-Bolton specializes in classical works of art, including superb statuary, paintings, mosaics, books, and other objets d'art. As a private art dealer, he sees clients by appointment. They might make repeated and extended visits to debate fine points of aesthetics, history, and provenance and stay for lunch to discuss financial arrangements.

The site is a shallow valley oriented east-west in a forested area. Access to the site is from the east. The climate is temperate, with mild winters.

Sir Bannister requires a varied setting for his outstanding collection of works of art. The centerpiece is a day villa standing in a formal garden at the intersection of two perpendicular axes. The owner's residence is nearby, next to his secure warehouse. Both the day villa and garden provide appropriate settings for the display of works of art and rooms for connoisseurs to meet in comfort, share ideas, and exchange opinions. A substantial library is to be included in the villa.

Visitors will leave their cars in a forecourt on the east side and proceed to the villa on foot. Several structures will surround the villa to organize the estate in a coherent ensemble. They will form the boundaries of the garden and provide a variety of backgrounds for statuary and architectural fragments. A summer house facing south is planned on the north side and a *nymphaeum* for the south side, facing north. The summer house is modeled on an orangery while the nymphaeum is inspired by the grotto, or *sala fresca* of Italian villas of the Renaissance. Closing the gardens on the west will be another landmark whose form is still to be determined.

DESIGN PROCESS

This complex assignment was broken up into a sequence of short problems, increasing in difficulty as the students became familiar with the classical language. Forming an ensemble of discrete buildings offers an opportunity for the all-important design of the connecting spaces (fig. 11.19).

The Forecourt: A walled-in, 100-foot-square clear space with ten arcaded stalls for cars; possibly a pair of one-room pavilions to control access and containing restrooms and a lounge for

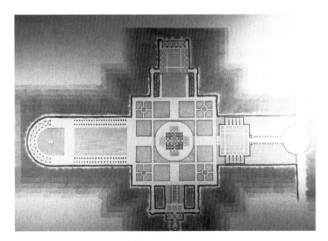

11.19. Plan of the estate with the entrance on the left. The villa stands at the center. Shawn Kirk.

11.20. Elevation of the nymphaeum. Robert Parise.

11.21 (see also C.26). Plan and elevation of the summer house. Robert Parise.

drivers. Rely on sober design means such as good proportions and rustication and refrain from using columns here.

DRAWING REQUIREMENTS
Plan, east elevation, north–south cross section at 1/16 inch scale.

The Nymphaeum: The structure should be conceived as an excavated space. It will be tucked into the hillside and covered by cross vaulting or a barrel vault. Since it is built over a spring, water will run through small channels and pools. The facade will not exceed 60 feet and will be composed of three or five bays. The architecture will be suitably massive, with the surface treatment rough and heavily textured. Sculpture will be installed in apses and niches (fig. 11.20).

DRAWING REQUIREMENTS
Plan, north elevation, two cross-sections at 1/16 inch scale.

The Summer House: The summer house will be on axis with the nymphaeum, and the two buildings will face one another across the valley. In contrast to the shadowy nymphaeum, the summer house should be light and open. It will serve as a backdrop to the activities taking place in front of it. The client's model is an orangery. What he has in mind is a room measuring 80 x 20 feet to be used for summer entertainments combining business with charities and occasionally masked balls on summer nights. The terrace in front will be used as overflow space for parties.

The roof will rest on wooden trusses spanning the 20-foot depth of the building. From the outside, the roof will be screened off by a balustrade supporting urns or sculptures. To emphasize the festive character of the place, there will be a substantial reflecting pool in front of the terrace (fig. 11.21). In one of the designs, the end arches are set in a heavier structure. In another, the five arches are identical and include engaged columns (fig. 11.22).

DRAWING REQUIREMENTS

Plan of the building with its terrace, southern elevation, and two perpendicular cross-sections at 1/16 inch scale.

An Architectural Garden: The three structures are beginning to define the space between them. They face a common point on the site where the main building will be erected; their axes intersect on this point. A fourth structure of your own choice is intended to terminate the long axis on the west side. On this basis, it is possible to begin to give architectural form to the context. Classical gardens make the transition between buildings—expressions of civilized life—and untamed nature. In general they are formal, geometric gardens.

When completed, the five buildings will be the origins and destinations for walks or promenades. The objective of such walks is not to create the shortest route from point to point but to provide an enjoyable experience along the way. Great classical gardens succeed in this with the simplest means: sand allées, lawns, pools, fountains, subtle changes of levels, vistas, perhaps some flowers, rows of trees, and stone benches.

In determining the distance between buildings, consider the general rule that the best distance to see a thing well is about three times the largest dimension of that thing. The articulation of a facade is too timid if it cannot be perceived at that distance. Finer details add to the enjoyment of strollers moving closer and closer to the building.

Finally, there are some similarities between the principles of urban design and those of garden design. As Leon Krier noted in his essay entitled *Washington, D.C.*, "Public buildings, national memorials, squares and gardens form the focal points in the city. They occupy dominant geographical and topographical positions. The lines of vision and avenues (orthogonal and diagonal) link near and distant focal points amongst each other." Attempts to find literal analogies between

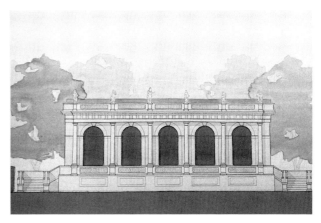

11.22 (see also C.27). Elevation of the summer house. The structure is raised on a podium. Cory Berg.

the parts of a garden and the parts of a city would be futile, but there are some interesting correlations:

forecourt	harbor, railroad station
entrance pavilions	food market, hotel
day villa	palace, city hall, government building
summer house	theater, library
nymphaeum	therma, pool
architectural garden	agora, arena

DRAWING REQUIREMENTS

Plan and two cross-sections of the entire estate at 1/64 inch scale. For the sake of clarity, adopt a simple color code. Water, grass, and trees should each have their own color. Reserve the white of the paper for walking surfaces.

The Day Villa: The design of the four structures that will form the boundaries of the ensemble and the distance from each of these to the future villa create a sufficient context to design the day villa. The forecourt, the summer house, the nymphaeum, and the west structure all coincide with one of the cardinal points, and each one of them provides a focus for one of the facades of the villa. Since these structures are dis-

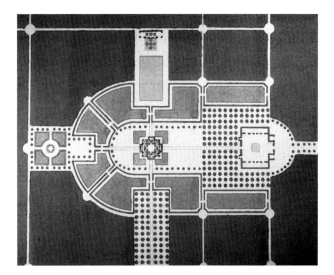

11.23. Plan of the gardens with the villa on center, the forecourt on the right, and the summer house at the top. Here the fifth structure takes the shape of a circular temple standing in its own garden. The nymphaeum is just out of the picture at the bottom. Clipped hedges and regular tree planting define the main walks and the principal spaces. Robert Parise.

tinctive enough to prevent boredom or confusion but of equal interest, it is possible for the four facades of the villa to be identical (fig. 11.23).

There will be a minimum of four and a maximum of nine rooms on the piano nobile. The central space, if there is one, will be 30 feet across and be twice as high. There might be a partial upper story where a large collection of books and prints will be kept. Plan stairs accordingly. The basement will be vaulted. Services and mechanical spaces will be housed there: kitchen with direct access to the outside, restrooms, safe, storage, and possibly staff quarters.

The footprint of the villa may be square, circular, cruciform, or octagonal. Two or more of these figures may be artfully combined.

DRAWING REQUIREMENTS

Plan of piano nobile, cross section, and elevation at 1/16 inch scale for the preliminary studies; 3/32 inch scale for final. Plan and section including the context at 1/64 inch scale.

DESIGN SOLUTIONS

Proposal A: Although the consensus among the students was that a square building should carry four identical facades, they discovered that some variety may be introduced. For instance, if there is a colonnade, the wall behind it can be moved forward or backward, so that a loggia might appear on one facade and be replaced by an enclosed vestibule on another (fig. 11.24). Wide steps might be judged excessive where they lead to a narrow door but they offer a pleasant place to sit on a nice day. In this design the stairs to the upper rooms are located in two of the corner pavilions. Clerestory windows let light into the very high room in the middle (figs. 11.25, 11.26).

The villa in context shows how the designer chose to terminate the gardens on the west side: he introduced four small pavilions connected by a semicircular pergola wrapped around a pool of the same shape (fig. 11.27).

Proposal B: Another design shows no differences on the facades, but the vestibules are of two kinds, large and rectangular in two opposite sides and small and square in the others. The main room is octagonal, and circulation around it is interrupted only by the stairs. An oculus at the top of the dome lets light into the octagonal room (figs. 11.28, 11.29). The character of the elevation is that of a building erected for pure enjoyment, a true folly (fig. 11.30). The impression is confirmed by the design of the structure at the western end of the garden, which is a simple semicircular enclosure. Made of tall hedges, not masonry, the dark green is a perfect background for five statues on pedestals. Stone benches alternate with the sculptures (fig. 11.31).

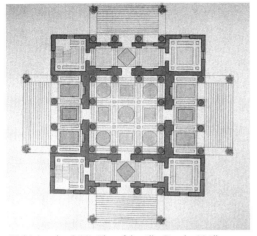

11.24 (see also C.28). Plan of the villa. Douglas Neidhart.

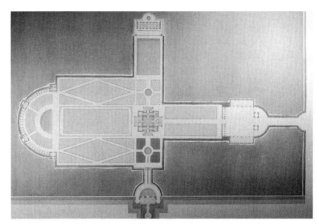

11.27 (see also C.30). General plan of the gardens. Douglas Neidhart.

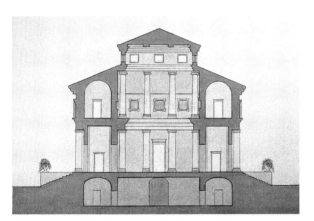

11.25 (see also C.29). Section of the villa. Douglas Neidhart.

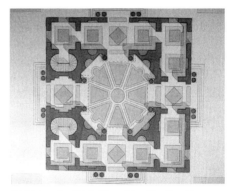

11.28 (see also C.31). Plan of the villa. Cory Berg.

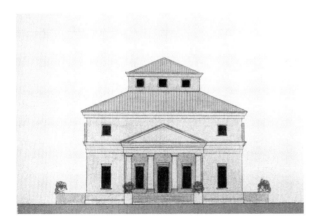

11.26. Section and elevation of the villa. Douglas Neidhart.

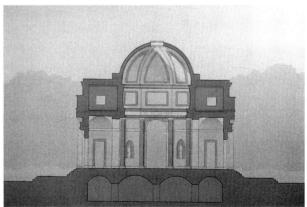

11.29 (see also C.32). Cross section of the villa. Cory Berg.

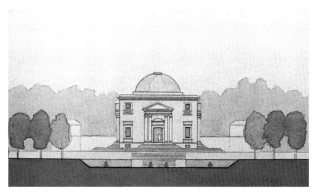

11.30. Elevation of the villa. Cory Berg.

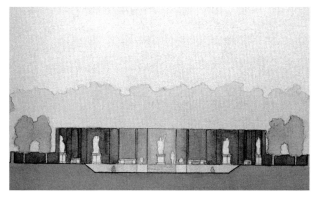

11.31 (see also C.33). An exedra facing the villa on the west side of the gardens. Cory Berg.

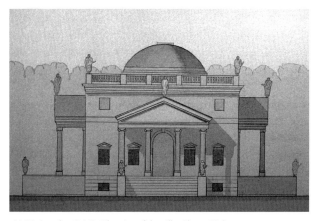

11.32 (see also C.34). Elevation of the villa. Shawn Kirk.

In contrast with the intimate charm of this design is a truly palatial interpretation of the same program. The impressive building stands at the core of a fittingly grand garden setting (fig. 11.32).

AN AMERICAN ACADEMY IN PROVENCE

The academy will be a compound where about twenty-five promising American artists, architects, and scholars will be able to develop their talent by studying the best classical works, from Roman ruins and neoclassical buildings to sculpture and painting. It will be designed according to classical canons, especially those formulated by Vitruvius: commodity, solidity, and visual delight.

The site is an 800- x 400-foot rectangle oriented north-south. Two existing roads, each 30 feet wide and running east-west, form the north and south boundaries. Two private service roads, 15 feet wide, will be added along the eastern and western edges of the property. The compound itself will occupy a 600- x 300-foot rectangle within the property lines. The land is completely flat. The climate is usually warm and dry, but underground springs provide an abundant supply of water.

THE PROGRAM

Forecourt: Entered through a gateway in the form of a sober triumphal arch, a court of honor will be located on the north side, with service buildings and garages for twenty cars.

Main Building: The building will be planned around a courtyard measuring 60 feet square, including a portico 12 to 15 feet wide on at least three sides. There will be a fountain in the middle of the courtyard, which may be open to the outside on the north or south side. One or two large and elegant rooms connect to the courtyard. Other spaces include a spacious refectory with kitchen; library; administrative offices; painting studios (six, each 15 x 15 feet); architecture studios (six, each 10 x 15 feet); writing studios (six, each 10 x 10 feet); workshops and photo studios (1,200 sf total); suites with private bathrooms for thirty residents and guests; director's apartment.

Gardens: The property is enclosed by an 8-foot masonry wall. The wall may be interrupted as many times as necessary for deliveries, maintenance, and vistas, but the corners must be solid. Include five or six freestanding sculpture studios (each 18 x 18 feet) and a swimming-cum-reflecting pool with a summer house or two for social gatherings. To define the space, consider changes of level, moats, steps, balustrades, allées of shade trees, *bosquets* (clearings within dense plantings). Choose among traditional elements such as tapis vert, pergolas, stone benches, fountains, statuary, obelisks, and so on.

DESIGN PROCESS

In the studio, the project was sequenced as weekly assignments:

WEEK 1

General layout: identify the pieces of the puzzle, their size, their shape; locate them on the site to satisfy functional relationships.

WEEK 2

The main building: plan, section, and elevation in relation to the land and the other elements of the complex.

WEEK 3

The courtyard as the nucleus of the overall composition: plan, section, elevation; relationship with the other rooms; relationship with the outdoors.

WEEK 4

Sculpture studios: one design for all; consider vehicular access and the role of the buildings in the definition of the gardens.

WEEK 5

Overall design, coordination and development: does it function organically?

WEEK 6

Review of revised design.

WEEK 7

Pool and summer house(s) in context. How do they relate to the whole? View from the main building is critical.

WEEK 8

Court of honor with service buildings: does it make the right impression on residents and visitors?

WEEK 9

Interior architecture.

WEEK 10

Overall enclosure.

WEEK 11

Surrounding landscape (*entourage*): focus on transitions between buildings and gardens.

WEEKS 12 AND 13

Overall design: development, coordination, finishing touches.

WEEK 14

Final review and evaluation.

DESIGN SOLUTIONS

Proposal A: A lake was added along the south side. The court of honor is circular, the summer house overlooks a reflecting pool on one side and a swimming pool on the other, and the sculpture studios form a semicircle at the back of the site (fig. 11.33). The section and half-plan

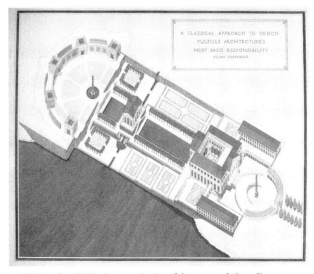

11.33 (see also C.35). Axonometric view of the compound. Steve Fernaays.

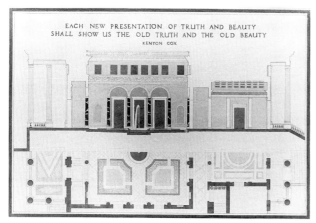

11.34. Half-plan and section through the main building. Steve Fernaays.

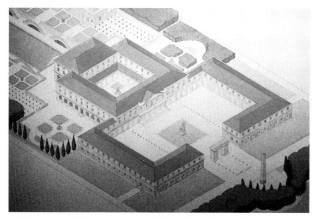

11.35 (see also C.36). Axonometric of the main building and the court of honor. Marcell Graef.

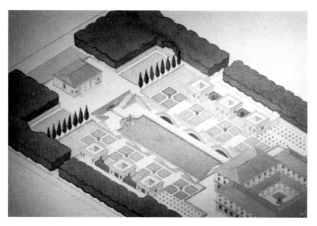

11.36. Second part of the axonometric. The main building and the rest of the gardens. Marcell Graef.

through the courtyard of the main building show the spatial sequence from right to left: a vaulted vestibule preceded by a portico, the courtyard in the middle, and a large loggia overlooking the reflecting pool on the left (fig. 11.34).

Proposal B: This design accommodates some of the studios on the upper floor of the buildings framing the court of honor. There is a freestanding monumental gate on the right (fig. 11.35). The summer house is placed at the back of the property and the sculpture studios are lined up on either side of the pool (fig. 11.36).

Proposal C: In a somewhat similar general parti, the summer house seen from the back of the main building is reflected in the pool. The sculpture studios frame the view (fig. 11.37).

Proposal D: The view towards the main building from the summer house is just as important. Here the main house is stretched out horizontally and the pool is treated as a narrow canal in the middle of a sunken garden (fig. 11.38).

Proposal E: The summer house is raised to match the upper story of the main building. The impression of a sunken canal is created by tall hedges that screen the sculpture studios (fig. 11.39).

Proposal F: The courtyard, entered from the left, uses a giant order; the effect is monumental and the scale is in keeping with that of the main room overlooking the garden (fig. 11.40).

A RESIDENTIAL COMMUNITY IN FRANCE

A developer has acquired a property on the outskirts of Dijon, which he intends to turn into a residential community of 42 four- or five-bedroom houses, each with a footprint of approximately 2,400 square feet. The site comprises forty hilly acres of brush and timber with a number of underground caves—hence the name "Bois des Grottes." Some fifty years ago, the previous owner built a house for his family of eight

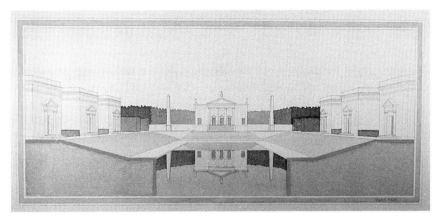

11.37 (see also C.37). The view from the loggia of the main building focuses on the summer houses and includes the sculpture studios. Adam Kehr.

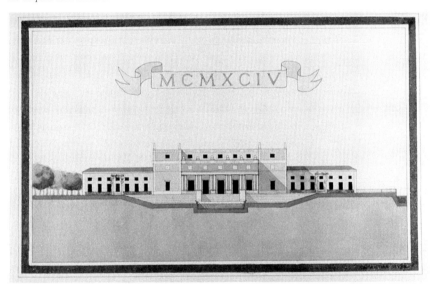

11.38 (see also C.38). The main house seen from the summer house. Samantha Divak Eio

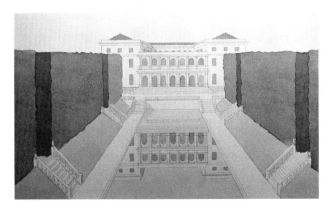

11.39 (see also C.39). The main house seen from the summer house. Mark Degnan.

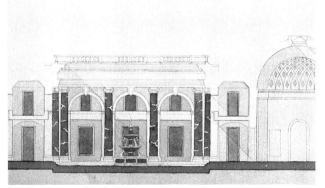

11.40 (see also C.40). Section through the main building. The large room overlooking the gardens is on the right. Christian Bolliger.

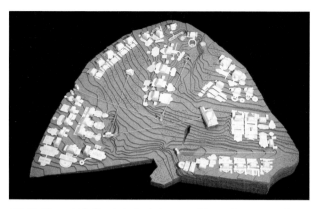

11.41. Site model built early in the design process. The gatehouses are on the east (left); the obelisk approximately in the middle; the original house right of center, above the cleft leading into the abandoned quarry; the fishing pavilion just below the cleft; the pond at the bottom; the colonnaded resting place near the top, slightly to the right. The houses are shown with private gardens. Major visual connections are shown with straight white lines.

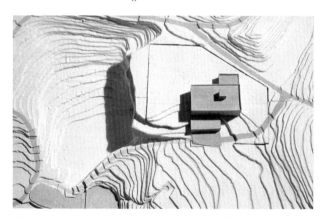

11.42. Model of the existing house in context. The box-like mechanical penthouse in the middle of the roof marks the location of the elevator shaft. The entrance to the quarry below is at the bottom of the cliff on the left; the end of the pond can be seen in the bottom left corner.

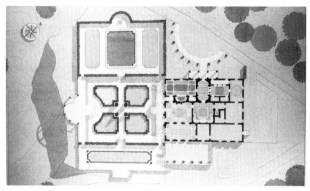

11.43. The existing house adapted to its new function as a clubhouse. Plan of the ground floor. The elevator to the swimming pool is just off the entrance on the south side. Colin Lowry.

children. At that time, the largest cave, which the Romans had used as a quarry, was transformed into a recreation space that includes a year-round swimming pool. The family house was built right above the cave, with a 100-foot elevator shaft connecting the two.

The new development plan was our starting point in the studio. We built a model of the site and, using the planned road system as our guide, we tried to arrange the houses in rows or clusters to achieve a sense of community. We left as much as possible of the existing woods in its natural state. To give some order to the wilderness, we established visual relationships across the land. This required clearing trees off in a few straight corridors and placing landmarks at the ends of these. Their sightlines were determined by the landform and their function by the way that the residents, their children, and guests might use them. A pair of small pavilions would frame the main entrance, situated in the middle of the western edge, at left on the model (fig. 11.41). We observed that an obelisk would be visible from the entrance if it was erected on a rise near the center of the property. From there, visitors would see the original house, which we retained as the social center of the community. Midway between the gate and the obelisk two other structures would face one another across the entry drive: on the left, a tiny green theater in the hill for the children, and on the right, a Palladian bridge spanning a sheer ravine.

From the obelisk, three other landmarks are visible: a fishing pavilion overlooking an existing pond, a colonnaded resting place near the top of the land, and the Palladian bridge. One more folly would be located at the far end of the pond, a place from which to contemplate the reflection of the fishing pavilion. Finally, the entrance to the quarry would be formalized and endowed with the rich symbolism of a grotto.

The Roman quarry is the most unusual feature on the site. Its large size and its swimming pool are assets to the developing community.

11.44 (see also C.41). The garden facade with the cliff on the right. Underneath, a half-scale drawing of the entrance side. Colin Lowry.

Since the existing house is already connected to the quarry, both can be easily integrated into the new social center. The quarry has often been the setting for social events involving several hundred guests. In addition, large rooms in the club-house above are needed for banquets, dances, chamber music concerts, and lectures; they should be extended by terraces and a formal garden. A kitchen for the preparation of catered food, storage, and restrooms should be included.

Other amenities include a quiet room with fire-place, a card room, an office or two, a conference room for twenty, babysitting or day care room(s) with a protected outdoor area. The apartment on the lower level of the house, near the garages, should be retained for a guard or administrator.

DESIGN SOLUTIONS

The existing main house is a boxy building of the 1950s (fig. 11.42). Transforming it into a classical building more in keeping with its new context was one of our goals. One design shows an enlarged building with symmetrical facades on the street and on the terraces and gardens. These overlook the cleft and the pond (fig. 11.43). Three major rooms open directly on the garden. The entry facade has seven bays: a colon-naded portico provides shelter over the front door (fig. 11.44). The mansard roof was sug-gested by the profusion of such roofs in the region. Here, it has the advantage of emphasizing the horizontal lines of the facade. The building shown on the site model was enlarged to make the facade overlooking the garden wide and the view over the top of the cliff more accessible.

Much of the rugged natural terrain is retained, and individual gardens are architectural in form and adapted to the topography of each individual building site. We avoided the effect of aloof individual houses ignoring their neighbors. Houses appear friendly when they become parts of larger compositions. Three houses might share a forecourt and form a U-shaped ensemble without losing their individual character. Attached garages and service rooms link the houses together, giving the owners the possibil-

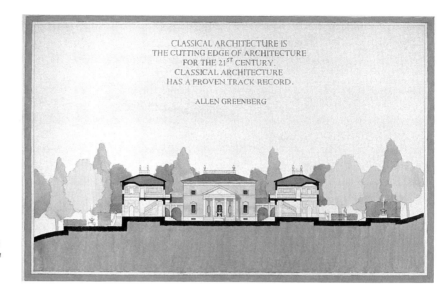

CLASSICAL ARCHITECTURE IS
THE CUTTING EDGE OF ARCHITECTURE
FOR THE 21ST CENTURY.
CLASSICAL ARCHITECTURE
HAS A PROVEN TRACK RECORD.

ALLEN GREENBERG

11.45 (see also C.42). Three houses wrapped around a common forecourt. The cross section through the side houses shows the facade of the house in the middle. Each house has a private garden at the back. Timothy Houde.

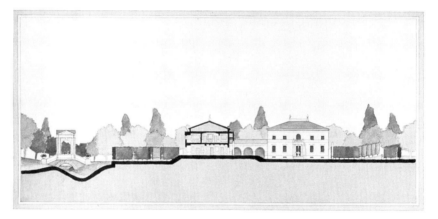

11.46. The cross section through the house in the middle shows the facade of one of the lateral houses. The Palladian bridge is seen on the left. Timothy Houde.

ity of occupying more or less space according to their needs (fig. 11.45). A pedimented porch is added to the center house because a unique feature is expected to be there. Other than that, only the interiors differ. A comparison of the cross sections reveals a double-height room on the garden side of the lateral houses. This emphasizes the importance of the private garden in the life of the home. The private gardens in the back are enclosed by hedges rather than walls (fig. 11.46).

A more adventurous geometry organizes a cluster of five houses on a triangular site.

Complex symmetries are involved here. The houses in the corners are cylindrical and taller than the other two, rectangular ones (fig. 11.47). The space in the middle is a shared garden. A challenging approach like this deserves further studies (fig. 11.48).

The private gardens were understood as outdoor extensions of the houses, made of one or several outdoor rooms (fig. 11.49). A mansard roof, like the raised basement, allows for a perfectly habitable story; it also evokes safe and comfortable shelter (fig. 11.50). Both slate and clay tiles are used for mansard roofs in the

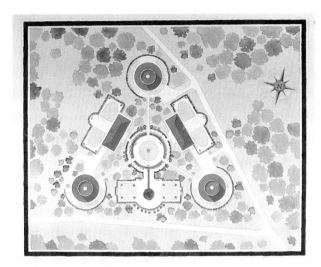

11.47 (see also C.43). A cluster of five houses. Blake Guyer.

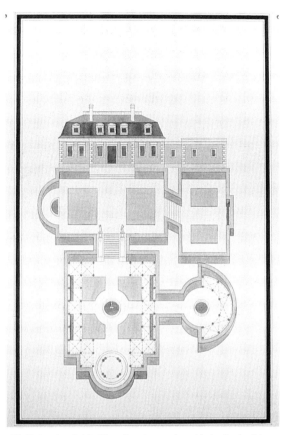

11.49 (see also C.45). Plan of a private garden with the facade of the house. An herb garden occupies the rectangular space on the right. The context must be imagined filled with dense vegetation. Rachana Ky.

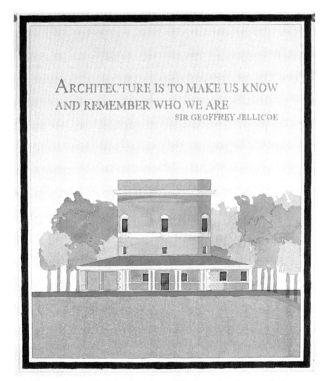

11.48 (see also C.44). Elevation of one of the houses based on a cylinder. Blake Guyer.

11.50 (see also C.46). Garden facade of one of the houses. Eric Godin.

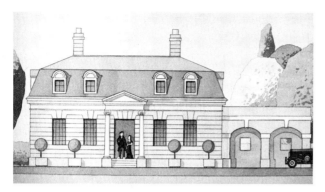

11.51. Public facade of a house. Maher Sweid.

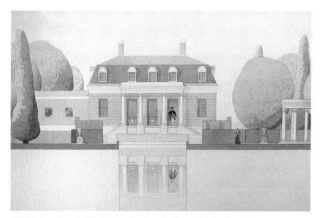

11.52 (see also C.47). Private facades of a house. Maher Sweid.

11.53 (see also C.48). Half-plan of one of the outdoor rooms with elevation of a summer house. Maher Sweid.

region. An elegant pediment marks the front door of the next house. Taking advantage of a change in grade gives the portico a dominating position and a better view of the garden (figs. 11.51, 11.52). A reflecting pool and temple-like pavilion give this design a theatrical character (fig. 11.53).

A MUSEUM OF THE TWENTIETH CENTURY

This program, adapted from the 1999 Royal Oak Foundation competition, assumed that a private donor has provided sufficient funding for the creation of a museum in a midsize American city. The benefactor wished to create a place for display and interpretation of the artistic and technological developments of the twentieth century: films and videos, paintings, sculptures, furniture, textiles, literary and musical manuscripts, as well as representative objects of the technology that enabled or assisted these works: lighting devices, computers, tape recorders, televisions, cameras, and so on.

The goal was to propose a design concept that would enable a visitor to understand some of the complex relationships of art and technology throughout the century. The layout and type of galleries were left to the designer to determine; they may be for temporary or permanent exhibitions or both.

The gardens were to be considered in similar terms. Considerable design flexibility was allowed in the exterior. No specific design vocabulary was suggested; on the contrary, a wide range of interpretation was invited.

The museum will occupy a derelict area on the bank of a major river separating the city center from the industrial zone. There are superb views of the city across the river. Longer views include a group of nineteenth-century steel mills and factories. Low and undistinguished industrial buildings surrounding the site will be replaced by a municipal park. Public transportation and parking for the museum will be nearby.

The available area for the museum complex is approximately 220 x 300 feet with a river front easement of 200 feet and three side easements of roughly 150 feet each. No permanent structure may be erected on the easements, but a landscape scheme may be developed.

PROGRAM REQUIREMENTS

• Vehicle drop-off point at the entry of the museum.

• Main lobby for display and receptions; small gift shop; restrooms (3,000 sf).

• Exhibition galleries (10,000 sf).

• Lecture, film and video theater seating 75.

• Library for printed and multimedia material (1,000 sf).

• Offices for director, curator, and support staff; conference room (1,000 sf).

• Laboratory, a multi-use room for diagnostic work and video editing (1,000 sf).

• Collection storage: most of the collection holdings are stored in an off-site facility. This area is for the preparation of exhibitions, conservation, and minor repairs.

• Loading dock with controlled access for the transfer of collection material; temporary secure storage (800 sf).

• Mechanical room (1,200 sf).

• General storage (500 sf).

DRAWING REQUIREMENTS
FOR THE COMPETITION

The project is to be presented on two 30- x 40-inch boards and the drawings must be black and white. Scale and composition are at the competitor's discretion but the following information is required:

Site plan including the surrounding landscape, preferably at 1/16 or 1/8 inch scale.

Floor plans. First floor may be included on site plan if legible at same scale.

Site section through garden and representative gallery space.

One or two large scale detail drawing(s) of gallery sequence or individual gallery.

One or two large scale detail drawing(s) of garden.

Any additional drawing helpful or necessary to explain the design.

A brief written description of design concept, integrated into board layout.

DESIGN STRATEGY

The brief specifies that the museum will be a small building—21,500 square feet—to be erected in a midsize city. The artistic evolution of the twentieth century is substantial, but the technological developments of that period are staggering. A person born in the first years of the century could have witnessed the first airplane flights and observe the beginnings of interstellar exploration fifty years later. Telephone, radio, television, fax machines, and electronic mail appeared one after another to revolutionize communications. These developments have had immeasurable effects on the way we conduct business, politics, and personal relationships.

The main challenge for the designers of this museum is to fit a theme of gigantic proportions in a small container. To achieve a reasonably comprehensive presentation of the major artistic and technological achievements of the twentieth century would require a vast space, something in the order of Disney World. To attempt it in a small museum requires a rigorous selection and a thoughtful design strategy.

In fact, the program indicates that the nucleus of the exhibition is a rather small collection. The following are ways to streamline the themes and narrow the focus of the museum:

• Select only American achievements.

• Organize the exhibitions around individuals who have contributed to the arts of civilization rather than to purely scientific and technical fields.

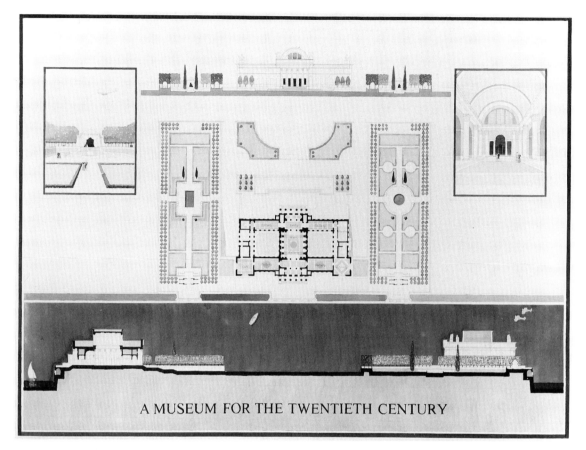

A MUSEUM FOR THE TWENTIETH CENTURY

11.54. General plan and sections of the museum and grounds. Circulation is organized around two courtyards. The lateral gardens are framed by raised walks. The entrance facade is shown at the top with a view of one of the pavilions from the sunken garden on the left. A perspective view of the main hall is shown at the right. The drawing at the bottom shows sections through the main hall on the left and through a sunken garden on the right. Brendan Stratton. Ferguson Shamamian & Rattner Architecture Prize, 1999.

• Focus on the outstanding individuals whose work has facilitated international understanding and cooperation.

• Limit the exhibits to a few representative fields. Communications, for example, which encompass literature, film, advertising, cartoons, and television, could illustrate the interaction between artistic thought and technology.

• Focus on the major architectural movements and the outstanding architects of the twentieth century, illustrated in scale models of iconic buildings, original drawings, photographs, films, and interviews on video.

Once the direction of the exhibits is established, the next challenge is to select an appropriate style for the building. Is there a twentieth-century style of architecture? Is it Art Nouveau? Art Deco? Constructivism? Futurism? International Style? Brutalism? High-tech? Postmodern? All of them have enriched our architectural heritage, but none is representative of the entire century.

Since museum visitors will live in the twenty-first century, a futuristic building might be considered, but who can predict the architecture of the future? Since the museum must

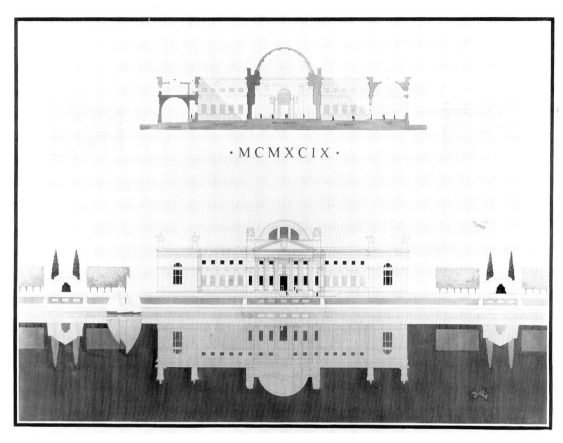

11.55. River side facade of the museum and, above, cross section through the main hall and the courtyards. Brendan Stratton.

above all fit into the time continuum, the sensible choice is the classical, which is more representative of western culture than any other style.

DESIGN SOLUTION

The general massing consists of three rectangles forming a U in plan (fig. 11.54). The rectangle in the middle is the museum building. The others are self-contained gardens. The main building is pulled back from the road to create a large forecourt. Wide steps connect the drop-off area and the main lobby. Placed close to the river, the museum building will look spectacular from the town center on the other bank. Its bold and simple massing, enhanced by its reflection in the water, will be clearly legible from a distance, and so will the fenestration, at night in particular (fig. 11.55).

The main hall in the building is right on center. The other galleries lead in and out of it; the corners of the building house the lecture hall, a library, a café, and the main stairs.

Elevated walks with double rows of pleached trees give a strong definition to the gardens, which function as outdoor exhibition spaces. A promenade with spectacular views connects two tent-like pavilions for educational demonstrations on the river side.

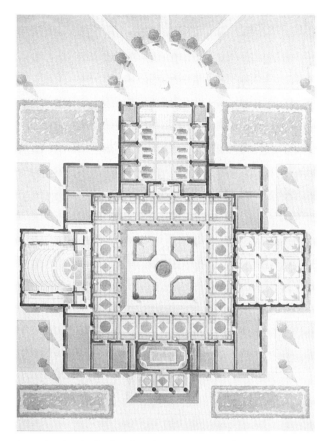

11.56 (see also C.49). Plan of an athenaeum. Enrique Vela. Ferguson, Shamamian & Rattner Architectural Prize, 2002.

11.57 (see also C.50). Entrance facade. Enrique Vela.

A section across the forecourt and the gardens shows the entrance facade. Two additional cross sections perpendicular to the river show the space sequence through the main lobby and the great hall (left) and one of the gardens (right).

There is also a large-scale cross section through the main hall and the two courtyards. The virtual section plane is shifted forward to include the café on the left and the library on the right.

AN ATHENAEUM

An athenaeum is a private cultural institution whose facilities include a library, art galleries, and an auditorium for lectures, film screenings, and chamber music concerts. In this case, the site is in a public park bordering on a major street on the north side. It was agreed that the landscaping adjacent to the building would be designed to accommodate the building, not the other way around.

DESIGN SOLUTION

The building is organized around a square atrium with parterres and a fountain in the middle (figs. 11.56, 11.57). A single entrance on the south controls access to the building; it is celebrated by a portico crowned by allegories of the four major arts. The vestibule opens directly into the atrium, around which everything revolves. An ample peripheral colonnade serves both as circulation space and as a sculpture gallery. The atrium is also the social center of the athenaeum: animated on certain occasions by large groups, it is an oasis of peace and quiet for members on summer days.

The other major functions are divided between the auditorium on the left (west) side of the atrium, the painting gallery on the right (east), and the reading room on the north, directly across from the vestibule. These three functions carry approximately equal weight and occupy somewhat similar, double-height volumes admitting natural light from clerestory windows. Perhaps the library dominates slightly over the others by virtue of its place on the main axis. The south corners of the building house administrative offices, the committee room, cloakrooms, and an apartment for the caretaker. Library offices and conservation workshops are found in the north corners. The basement contains mechanical spaces, storage, and other ancillary functions

The qualities of this project can be observed in the plan. It has a logical layout, appropriately inward-looking and organized hierarchically: every component of the program seems to be logically placed. Perfectly clear and fluid, this design would make a practical, inviting, and congenial building. The formal unity of the design results from the predominance of squares in the plan. The way squares relate to one another through varied devices such as concentricity, axis-sharing, or modularity prevent monotony.

· · · ·

The formal organization of these last designs is dictated by their internal needs. They are self-contained, self-reliant organisms. What is their design strategy? What holds them together and how is the specific character of each determined?

The small urban square needed strong edges and solid corners to assert its presence in a shapeless void between powerful building blocks.

The large urban squares at the ends of the arcaded street are contrasted by their distinctive shapes. Buildings of continuous design form the enclosures, which are only rarely interrupted. The focus is an empty stage for public events in the first and a quiet garden in the other.

Buildings are also wrapped around outdoor spaces in the hospice and the athenaeum, both of which require a peaceful atmosphere. A self-sufficient intellectual community, the athenaeum is completely introverted, but the hospice is partially open towards the woods and the ocean for

the healing effect they may have on the residents.

The Palladian villa is a compact building on one side of a large garden. The practical purpose of the enclosure is protection from deer and other animals. All parts of the garden can be enjoyed from multiple paths and alcoves for rest and contemplation. In this program and the next, the principal organizer of the composition is the main axis of symmetry.

At the American academy, planned for a mild climate, the functions are dispersed among various buildings. Each sculpture studio is an independent structure for acoustical separation. Some of the resident scholars and artists seek solitude in the gardens for reflection or relaxation.

The villa for an art dealer stands in the middle of a garden that stretches out in four directions. Strategically placed structures offer venues for tranquil communion with artwork. As they stroll from one to another, visitors can enjoy the effect of diverse settings along the way.

While the dense vegetation of Bois des Grottes ensures the privacy of the individual houses, the topography prevents a clear and geometric organization of the site. Instead, residents and visitors find their way by visual connections established between distinctive architectural landmarks.

A bold outline makes the Museum of the Twentieth Century clearly visible from the city on the other side of the river. Its dignified and elegant silhouette would make it an object of pride in the community.

The projects discussed here are the work of beginners demonstrating applications of the fundamental rules and principles of classical architecture. However simple, these principles remain true at the most sophisticated level. It is the designers, not the principles, who change over time. As designers become more mature and more experienced, they are able to put the same principles to work in richer, more significant, and more beautiful ways.

CHAPTER 12

A PORTFOLIO OF
RECENT CLASSICAL BUILDINGS

Order is a desire of the mind; and order is found in classical architecture.
—GEOFFREY SCOTT

Many firms are known for their classical work in the United States and Europe. Some were committed to classicism from the beginning; others became disenchanted with modernism and evolved towards classicism. In making this selection of projects, the difficulty was not in finding enough material but rather in choosing among hundreds of worthwhile realizations.

Eleven firms were invited to contribute graphic documents along with a short text describing a recent project that the architects considered classical. The criteria used in the selection were diversity in treatment, building type, climate and cultural context, and size. The projects come from the United Kingdom, France, Italy, and the United States. There are domestic, institutional, civic, and commercial functions. Some are large and complex; others are modest in size or budget. The sites may be densely urban or deeply rural. The size of offices varies from one-person operations to firms employing more than one hundred architects.

There is a divergence of opinion about what makes a classical building today. It is probably too early for definitive judgment, but we can certainly celebrate the vitality of the movement.

A FINANCIAL CENTER

John Blatteau Associates, Philadelphia, Pennsylvania

This is the headquarters of the Paul Cushman III International Financial Center in the 1500 block of Connecticut Avenue in Washington, D.C. (fig. 12.1). The work included a new corner pavilion and renovation of the existing bank building and seven town houses, which created a 44,000-square-foot office area for eighty members of the International Banking Division of the Riggs Bank (fig. 12.2).

On Connecticut Avenue, the facades of the town houses were renovated to maintain their original commercial character. The bay-window storefronts, which had been previously removed, were returned to their original appearance. The stamped metal frieze and decoration, as well as the marble base, were built to carefully match original materials.

Even though the town houses were renovated to meet contemporary programmatic needs, their interiors still maintain much of the character of the original buildings (fig. 12.3). Wherever feasible, fireplaces with original man-

12.1. Connecticut Avenue facade. John Blatteau Associates.

12.2. New corner pavilion.

12.3. Rear view of the corner pavilion.

tels and wall sconces were reused. Refurbished skylights allow natural light to penetrate the interior spaces and many rooms maintain their English-style beamed ceilings with stuccoed walls.

At the northern end of the complex, near the Metro entrance, a new pavilion was added to provide a new entry lobby and conference space

12.4. Main lobby of the corner pavilion. © Tom Crane 1999.

12.5. Section of the new pavilion. John Blatteau Associates.

(figs. 12.4, 12.5, 12.6). The classical nature of the design enhances the image of the block and adds a new, elegant ending to the complex. It provides a sense of dignity, stability, and permanence appropriate to the context of the neighborhood and provides the plaza facing the Metro entrance with the flair of a European square. The limestone and granite facade with pedimented windows contains marble inlays and decorative ironwork. The arched windows on the street level frame the space of the main lobby, while the Palladian windows above denote a conference room.

Pairs of bronze doors lead into an elegant entry lobby delineated with ornamental plaster moldings, bracketed cornices, paired pilasters, and marble base. The rich natural finish of the hardwood parquet floor and subtly painted colors lends a grand domestic scale to this prominent public space. The lobby design interprets the classical eighteenth-century style of architecture and thought that formed much of the physical and political nature of Washington, D.C.

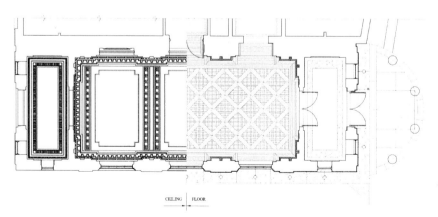

12.6. Reflected ceiling plan/floor plan. John Blatteau Associates.

12.7. Bird's-eye view of the villa with the attached winery on center and the workers' quarters on the far left. Most of the vineyards are to the right and not shown. Studio Bontempi.

12.9. Facade overlooking the front garden. Studio Bontempi.

12.8. Front view of the villa. Photo Mauro Davoli.

12.10. Facade overlooking the vineyards. Studio Bontempi.

A VILLA IN THE VINEYARDS

Studio Bontempi di Pier Carlo Bontempi, Gaiano di Collecchio, Italy

Situated on the hills south of Parma, Signor Borelli's villa is attached to his winery and to the dwellings of the workers (figs. 12.7–12.10).

The formal parts are treated with a mix of crushed limestone while the capitals and moldings are made of Venetian stone. Local rough-hewn stone and brick are used for the rest of the complex. The roofs are covered with terra cotta pantiles and the chimneys are capped with a "little house for the smoke."

Both gates open into a medieval pilgrim's path to Rome, which also give access to the adjacent vineyards.

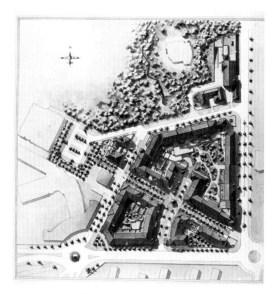

12.11. General plan. Atelier Breitman.

12.13. Street side. © F. Achdou/Urba Images.

12.12. Street entrance. © F. Achdou/Urba Images.

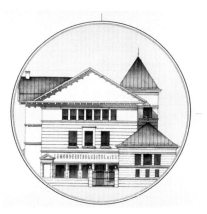

12.14. Detail of the project. © Breitman.

AN URBAN DEVELOPMENT

Atelier Breitman, Paris

Le Bois des Vallées is a recently developed area of Plessis-Robinson, on the outskirts of Paris. The urban context was a large, drab, and repetitive community devoid of amenities and mainly occupied by low-income families. The new development consists of 600 dwellings, a high school, and a home for the disabled (fig. 12.11).

The street highlighted here is typical (figs. 12.12, 12.13). It is a true street that includes multiple functions. The buildings present an uninterrupted front on both sides. There are sidewalks, trees, and parked cars along the curb. The quality of materials, attention to detail, and public spaces with a human scale together create a timeless environment. The variety of buildings is such that each can be described by the residents because of some unique feature—the design of a doorway, the color of a facade, the

12.15. Facade overlooking the lake. © Fairfax & Sammons.

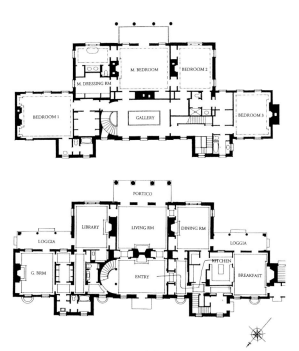

12.16. Ground floor (bottom) and second floor plans. © Fairfax & Sammons.

profile of a loggia, the shape of a pediment, even the position of the building in context. The rich formal vocabulary is held together by the application of classical principles (fig. 12.14).

The studied homogeneity of the design makes visitors unable to distinguish between coop buildings and low-income housing. The township residents have given Bois des Vallées the highest rating for its quality of life. It has become a model for urban designers, thanks to the courage of developers willing to invest in an innovative urban concept. Here urban life regains its rights, its vitality, and its architecture.

A COUNTRY HOUSE

Fairfax & Sammons, New York

Farmlands is a 600-acre estate on the shore of Lake Otsego, celebrated as Glimmerglass by James Fenimore Cooper (figs. 12.15–12.18). The house replaced an earlier wood-frame building. It is built with substantial, load-bearing walls of local stone and heavy roof slates, materials chosen for their durability to serve future generations of the family without the burden of constant maintenance.

12.17. Facade overlooking the lake seen from the side. © Fairfax & Sammons.

12.18. Lakefront facade in context. © Fairfax & Sammons.

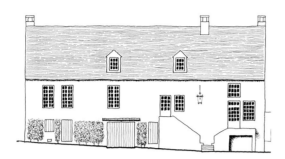

12.19. Public facade. © J.F. Gabriel.

12.22. Interior view. © J.F. Gabriel.

12.20. Garden facade. © J.F. Gabriel.

12.23. Street front. © J.F. Gabriel.

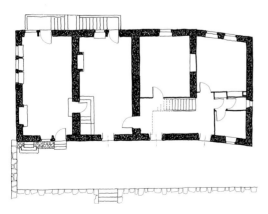

12.21. Main-floor plan. © J.F. Gabriel.

12.24. Garden side. © J.F. Gabriel.

Care was taken in the design to reflect the image of the old house, and the new house incorporates original elements, including the entry door and its surrounds.

The house is oriented to take advantage of the stunning views and of mature planting.

Inside, paneled rooms were carefully detailed with fine millwork throughout. The principal rooms all face the lake, and each has a fireplace—a welcome feature in the chill winters of upstate New York.

A SMALL MANOR HOUSE

J. François Gabriel, Syracuse, New York,
and Villotte St. Seine, France

Located two hundred miles southeast of Paris, nestled among hills and woods, this family house was built with traditional methods. Rough-hewn beams span the intervals between load-bearing walls and clay tiles clad the simple roof. The owner wanted a house that would blend into the rural context and suggest the refined taste of an old manor house (figs. 12.19–12.24).

Taking advantage of an abrupt change in grade, there is a walk-in basement accessible only from the public side. In local farms, this is where animals and farm implements would be kept. Here, it accommodates the garage, mechanical space, utilities, and storage. The main story is just above, with a view of the gardens of the seventeenth-century chateau across the public lane.

There are two large rooms, a study, and one bedroom on the main floor, level with a gravel terrace and a large field on the garden side. Three more bedrooms and a double-height studio are found in the attic story. The floor of the main story is finished with flagstones and terra cotta tiles. Parquet floors are used in the attic story.

The slight bend in the plan acknowledges a stringent alignment regulation in relation to the public lane enacted about two hundred years ago.

12.25. *Gable wall.* © *Leon Krier.*

12.26. *Lateral wall.* © *Leon Krier.*

A VILLAGE HALL

Leon Krier, Claviers, France
Associate Architects for construction:
Merrill & Pastor, Vero Beach, Florida

Occupying the focal point of major vistas and avenues and flanking a public square, the village hall is both a meeting hall and a symbol for the new community of Windsor, in Florida—at once its profane and sacred heart (figs. 12.25–12.30).

Raised on a podium, thirty white pillars carry the steep roof well above the horizontal lines of

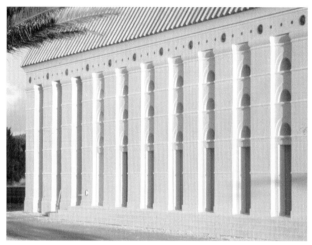

12.27. Lateral wall, seen at an angle. © Leon Krier.

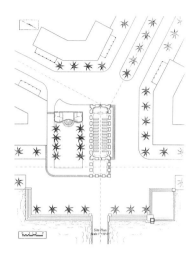

12.29 Plan in context. © Leon Krier.

12.28. Side wall with fountain. © Merrill & Pastor.

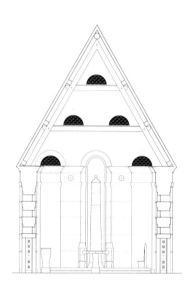

12.30. Section. © Leon Krier.

town center, houses and walled gardens, making a highly visible architectural and urban magnet. Rather than disrupting the skyline, the building becomes an essential component.

The simplicity of the internal and external volumes differs from the articulate plasticity of the houses. Its elevated porch, the multitude of doors and arched windows, its very openness contrasting with the protective enclosures of the private residences further enhance the public character of this unique structure. The monumentality of its scale, the unfamiliar size and sheer repetition of its elements at once establish and proclaim the exceptional, the uniquely civic status of the hall as shelter for and symbol of the community.

A TOWN CENTER

Merrill & Pastor, Vero Beach, Florida

The site of the Vero Beach Town Center is at the entrance to a neighborhood of about three hundred houses, at the convergence of five roads. There are four prominent exposures, and nowhere to hide services. The site is the hinge between the rural countryside and the informal urbanism of the streets. The Town Center buildings form the perimeter of a block and provide means for pedestrians to move into the interior gardens. There are two apartment buildings, a small store, a small post office, a fitness club, a clock and observation tower and three gardens, one for civic use, one for the store, and one divided among the ground floor apartments. The buildings are based on classical plan types. They are sited to capture views upon approach, to mark entrances to the interior gardens, and to make movement through the site interesting and enjoyable (figs. 12.31–12.33).

A MONUMENT

Liam O'Connor, London

The Memorial Gates on Constitution Hill in London honor the contribution the 4.7 million Commonwealth volunteers who fought alongside Britain in the two World Wars. As it is fitting that the purpose of a monument is to immortalize great deeds, it is also fitting that a simple, noble, and universal architectural language be used to express the significance of those deeds (figs. 12.34–12.38).

The site, at the heart of London's historic core, required that a monument fit well in the context of important civic buildings. Four sculpted stone piers, surmounted by bronze urns, form at once a cenotaph and a public space, a precinct, set apart from the space around

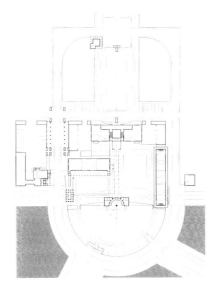

12.31 General plan.
© Merrill & Pastor.

12.32. Perspective drawing. © Merrill & Pastor.

12.33. Vero Beach Town Center. Photo © Merrill & Pastor.

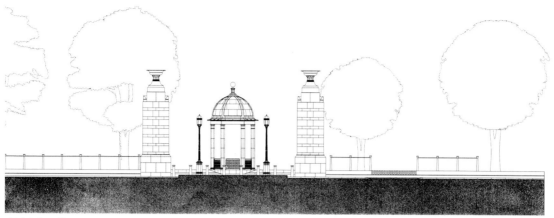

12.34. Overall view. Design © Liam O'Connor.

12.35. The pavilion. Design © Liam O'Connor. Photo © The Nick Carter Photographic Studio.

12.36. Pavilion with piers. Design © Liam O'Connor. Photo © The Nick Carter Photographic Studio.

12.37. Urn atop pier. Design © Liam O'Connor. Photo © The Nick Carter Photographic Studio.

12.38. Night view. Design © Liam O'Connor. Photo © The Nick Carter Photographic Studio.

it. The space between the piers is a perfect square, a mandala, framing views towards Decimus Burton's neoclassical Wellington Arch to the west and a domed pavilion to the north. The pavilion forms the heart of the composition; a belvedere in the park flanked by two plinths, each a monolith carved with a list of campaigns from the two World Wars. Cast bronze railings with a peacock theme form balconies from which the four main piers may be viewed across a bridle path.

The simple moldings of the pavilion columns owe much to Mughal architecture, yet they consciously refer to classical Hellenic paradigms. The piers and pavilion together suggest a union between eastern and western architectural traditions. The red granite paving is from India while the superstructure is in Portland limestone, the traditional material for the monuments and public buildings of London. Similarly, the details reflect both Mughal and European traditions.

Twelve fluted bronze bollards are raised to close Constitution Hill to traffic on Sundays. Their design matches the fixed bollards located between the piers.

A RESIDENTIAL DEVELOPMENT

Ferguson Shamamian & Rattner
Donald M. Rattner, Partner-in-Charge, New York

McAllister Point is a residential enclave created within The Ford Plantation, an 1,800-acre development in Savannah, Georgia (figs. 12.39–12.41). The new neighborhood draws on two main traditions of Southern urbanism and architecture. From Savannah comes the distinctive green at the center of the property, its scale and shape evoking the public squares that punctuate the city's street pattern. Compositionally, the center green organizes the houses around it and gives the neighborhood an identity and

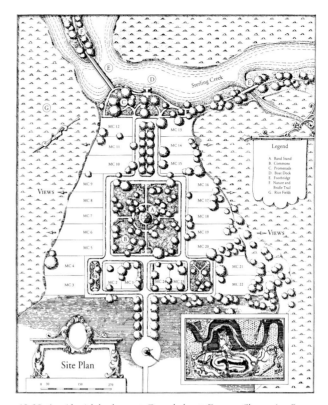

12.39. A residential development. General plan. © Ferguson Shamamian & Rattner, Architects.

12.40. Watercolor perspective with band stand. © Ferguson Shamamian & Rattner, Architects.

12.41. One of the houses. © Ferguson Shamamian & Rattner, Architects.

sense of place. For the configuration of the individual lots and neighborhood architecture, the Charleston sideyard provides the model. In this urban paradigm, the house sits to one side of a rectangular plot, its narrow elevation toward the street. Overlooking the side garden are stacked porches, called piazzas. A false doorway on the street gives the house a face, but the entrance is on the porch.

Ranging from 2,500 to 5,000 square feet, the six prototype houses are based on a module that maintains a consistent footprint and arrangement of openings and allows a variety of interior plans and exterior treatments. Clients can customize their homes by choosing from a palette of exterior materials, door and window configurations, porch and roof types, and ornamental details. The "kit-of-parts" approach balances unity and diversity and facilitates an economy of architectural production and construction.

While strongly influenced by traditional form, the McAllister houses are subtly adapted to the patterns of contemporary life. Unlike their antecedents, for example, plans are oriented to the

rear of the house to take advantage of the natural vistas. The piazzas similarly make superb platforms for satisfying the modern taste for embracing views. In merging the architectural and urban achievements of the past with contemporary life styles, McAllister Point is a convincing argument for the viability of the classical tradition.

AN INSTITUTIONAL BUILDING COMPLEX

Robert A. M. Stern Architects, New York
Associate Architects: Ayers Saint Gross,
Baltimore, Maryland

The new Darden campus at the University of Virginia is set, acropolis-like, atop the natural crest of a twenty-acre site. Anchored by a central commons building and flanked by matching ranges of academic pavilions to the south and by a library and auditorium with executive dining rooms to the north, the new Darden campus mirrors the village-like scale and character of the university. Like Jefferson's "academical village," the buildings are at once separate yet interlocked for convenience, efficiency, and sense of community (figs. 12.42–12.46).

Approached from Massie Road to the east, a sixty-room addition to the Sponsors Hall Executive Residence acts as a gatehouse and directs the eye up the hill to the commons building. A broad, tree-lined boulevard leads up the hill to a motor court that divides a 180-car parking lot to the south from the service drive and after-hours parking to the north.

In architectural expression, the new Darden School reflects the buildings of Jefferson, which so much define Virginia's architectural persona: sand-struck Virginia red brick walls with clean detailing of white painted wood and limestone rise to red painted metal roofs.

Saunders Hall, the cruciform commons building, contains a suite of generously propor-

12.44. The south court. © Robert A. M. Stern Architects.

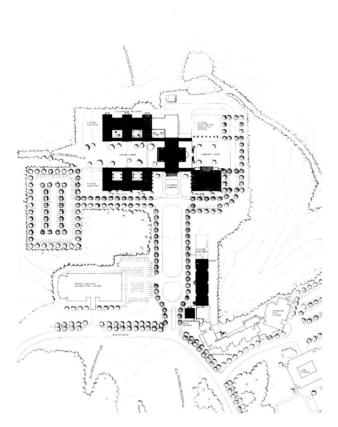

12.42. General plan. © Robert A. M. Stern Architects.

12.45. Courtyard garden on the southwest corner of Saunders Hall.
© Robert A. M. Stern Architects.

12.43. View from the west. © Peter Aaron/ESTO.

12.46. Interior of Saunders Hall.
© Peter Aaron/ESTO

12.47. Entrance with the service wing on the right and the bedroom wing on the left. Courtesy Mara Cooper.

12.48. View of the living room from the dining room. Courtesy Mara Cooper.

tioned reception rooms on the main level. These provide for informal student and faculty gatherings as well as formal meetings and receptions; they also satisfy the requirements of a student café and the traditional daily Darden "coffee hour." To the south, Saunders Hall is connected by covered arcades to a two-story faculty office wing and classroom wing with clustered group study rooms. Together, the three elements define a large academic quadrangle, which rises gently towards an open, southern view. To the north is the library quadrangle, to be framed by the three-story library to the east and the future auditorium and executive dining building to the west.

A PALLADIAN VILLA

Ken Tate, Madisonville, Louisiana

Based on the Villa Emo, this residence (figs. 12.47–12.50) uses stucco and clay-tile roofing along with a palette of terra cottas, ochres, and umbers to evoke the resonance, tactile qualities, and aroma of a Palladian villa. Louisiana's bayou country heightens the effect by suffusing the structure with a soft light reminiscent of the Veneto.

Although the surrounding landscape seems wild, the neighborhood is semi-urban. Since the site would not accept the expanse of Villa Emo's wings, the architect pulled them closer to the center block to create a forecourt. The entrance loggia, inset at Emo, is pushed forward here and enhanced with arcaded stucco sidewalls. This treatment sets the house apart from the traditional southern Greek revival. The building supplies its own reciprocal views: the wings can be seen through the arches, and the loggia can be seen from the wings.

Beyond the walnut entrance doors, a sequence of carefully proportioned interior spaces unfolds. Like Palladio, the architect used

12.49. Back view with the loggia open-air living room. Courtesy Mara Cooper.

Vitruvian ratios as a starting point, verified or modified by the eye, aided by a series of elevation studies and interior perspectives.

Following the grand public spaces, the kitchen could have been anticlimactic, but its details are bold and fully articulated. The rear loggia is an open-air living room. In contrast to the double-height entrance, columns and arches are down scaled for a more relaxed and intimate atmosphere.

To maintain symmetry, a purely decorative chimney was placed on the roof, opposite the functional one, an example of the "morality of the eye," which carries the obligation to make the building beautiful and supersedes the obligation to make it "honest." Similarly, blank windows at the upper level of both loggias maintain the regularity and symmetry of the facades. That the placement of the garage and bedroom wings should express their functions is secondary to the fact that this arrangement is pleasing to the eye.

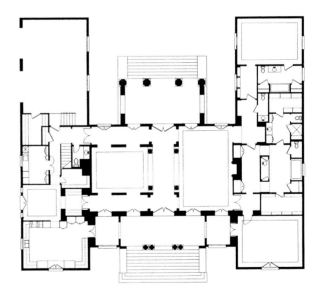

12.50. Ground-floor plan. Courtesy Ken Tate.

AFTERWORD

Many leading classical architects currently practicing are self-taught. Fighting against many odds to reach their goals, they were not motivated by nostalgia but by the desire to keep alive some of our best traditions. They do not copy the past. They seek inspiration from it. As their number increases so does the need for a classical culture in architecture schools.

Freehand drawing, descriptive geometry, the study of the classical form-language and its use in the design studio are the essential components of a classical curriculum. Descriptive geometry is the best possible foundation for the ability to visualize three-dimensional forms. An architect requires serious training in freehand drawing to confidently produce accurate representations of designs that exist only in the mind. The eye becomes finely tuned in the process, giving the architect the ability to compare design sketches and select the best one. Students must also understand that a good idea is only the germ of a design. What matters most is the development of the idea, and 90 percent of the designer's time should be spent on development.

Architecture students must be trained to read and process a coherent problem statement, and to generate a reasonable concept, a parti, in a few hours. The Beaux-Arts system, which was responsible for the American Renaissance, revolved around the esquisse, or diagrammatic design. Each student was given a printed program and required to turn in an esquisse by the end of the day. Four to six weeks later, the completed project was compared with the original diagram, and if the two did not match in their essential lines, the student received no credit for the project. The experience taught the students to think fast and to concentrate on developing the original idea. Design reviews were blind. It was the students' responsibility to include in their drawings all the information necessary for the judges to understand and evaluate the projects.

Such high expectations may appear excessive today, but the satisfaction experienced by the successful students was their reward, and the fact is that the level of visual literacy among Beaux-Arts-trained architects and their clients was very high indeed.

Should these features be reintroduced in architecture schools, we might hope for another American Renaissance. In the meantime, aspiring classical architects will, I hope, find in this book the encouragement and the assistance they need.

ACKNOWLEDGMENTS

The author wishes to thank the following individuals:

John Blatteau, Marc and Nada Breitman, Richard W. Cameron, Bernd Dams, Anne Fairfax, Alvin Holm, Leon Krier, Paul Malo, Michel Marot, Thomas V. Noble, Donald M. Rattner, Witold Rybczynski, Richard F. Sammons, Steven Semes, Seth J. Weine, and Andrew Zega for having traveled long distances to Syracuse, New York, or Florence, Italy, to review the design projects of the author's students.

The many students with whom it has been a pleasure to work, among whom are:

Cory Berg Kallfelz, Christian Bolliger, Joaquin Bonifaz, James R. Bouffard, Chris Campbell, Thomas Chin, Richard K. Colson, Jessika Creedon, Glen B. Dabaghian, Grady J. Dagenais, Mark Degnan, Scott Delorme, Samantha Divak Eio, Steven D. Fernaays, Eric Godin, Marcell Graef, Blake Guyer, Katherine Mercedes Hogan, Timothy R. Houde, Adam Kehr, Shawn Kirk, Joel Kline, Rachana Ky, Robert Laterza, Trevor Lavoie, Colin T. Lowry, Gregory Malette, Matthew Manuel, Ariadne Milligan, Douglas Neidhart, Ben Nicholson, Robert Parise, Christopher M. Pizzi, Christopher Reed, Sue Robbins, Peter Rust, Brendan Stratton, Maher Sweid, Enrique Vela, and James R. Wisniewski.

The architectural firms whose work appears in this book: John Blatteau Associates, Studio Bontempi, Atelier Breitman, Fairfax & Sammons, Leon Krier, Merrill & Pastor, Liam O'Connor, Ferguson Shamamian & Rattner, Robert A. M. Stern Architects, and Ken Tate; and Nancy Green, for being the first to think of this book.

BIBLIOGRAPHY

Ackerman, J. S. 1966. *Palladio*. New York: Penguin Books.

Alexander, C., et al. 1977. *A Pattern Language*. New York: Oxford University Press.

Alphand, A. [1873] 1984. *Les Promenades de Paris*. New York: Princeton Architectural Press.

Anon. Catalogue. 1968. *Bauhaus 1919–1969*. Würtembergischer Kuntsverein.

____. 1980. *Viollet-le-Duc*. Paris: Editions de la Réunion des Musées Nationaux.

Aslet, C. 1986. *Quinlan Terry*. New York: Viking.

Aslin, E. 1969. *The Aesthetic Movement*. New York: Frederick A. Praeger.

Bacon, E. N. 1974. *Design of Cities*. New York: Viking.

Baker, P. R. 1980. *Richard Morris Hunt*. Cambridge, MA: MIT Press.

Ballon, H. 1999. *Louis Le Vau*. Princeton, NJ: Princeton University Press.

Bastlund, K. 1967. *José Luis Sert*. Zurich: Les Editions d'Architecture Zurich.

Bedford, S. M. 1998. *John Russell Pope: Architect of Empire*. New York: Rizzoli.

Benjamin, A. 1839. *Practice of Architecture*. Boston: B. B. Mussey.

____. 1845. *The Architect, or Complete Builder's Guide*. Boston: B.B. Mussey.

Bétourné, R. 1931. *René Sargent, Architecte*. Privately printed.

Bill, M. 1949. *Robert Maillart*. Berlin: Verlag für Architektur AG.

Billington, D. P. 1979. *Robert Maillart's Bridges: The Art of Engineering*. Princeton, NJ: Princeton University Press.

Blazer, W. 1965. *Mies van der Rohe*. New York: Frederick A. Praeger.

Bonta, E. 1925. *The Small House Primer*. Boston: Little, Brown and Co.

Boudon, P. [1977] 1985. *Pessac de Le Corbusier*. Paris: Editions Dunod.

Borsi, F., Godoli, E. Mark Vokaer, ed. 1977. *Paris 1900*. New York: Rizzoli.

Braham, A. 1989. *The Architecture of the French Enlightenment*. London: Thames and Hudson, Ltd.

Breitman, N., and M. Breitman. 1995. *Bruay-la-Bussière*. Belgium: Pierre Mardaga.

____. 2000. *Le Plessis-Robinson*. Belgium: Pierre Mardaga.

Brion-Guerry, L. 1960. *Philibert de l'Orme, 1510–1570*. New York: Universe Books.

Brooks, H. A. 1972. *The Prairie School*. New York: W. W. Norton & Company.

Brown, J. 1989. *The Art and Architecture of English Gardens*. New York: Rizzoli.

Burckhardt, J. [1867] 1985. *The Architecture of the Italian Renaissance*. Chicago: The University of Chicago Press.

Burckhardt, L., ed. 1977. *The Werkbund: History and Ideology 1907–1933*. New York: Barron's.

Cardwell, K. H. 1977. *Bernard Maybeck: Artisan, Architect, Artist*. Layton, UT: Peregrine Smith, Inc.

Chambers, J. 1985. *The English House*. W. W. Norton & Company.

Chambers, W. [1791] 1968. *A Treatise on the Decorative Part of Civil Architecture*. Benjamin Bloom, Inc.

Champigneulle, B. 1972. *L'Art Nouveau*. Paris: Somogy.

Chevallier, P. 1977. *Le Panthéon*. Paris: Caisse Nationale des Monuments et des Sites.

Choisy, A. 1873. *L'Art de Bâtir chez les Romains*. Librairie Générale de l'Architecture et des Travaux Publics.

Choisy, A. 1954. *Histoire de l'Architecture*. Paris: Vincent Fréal.

Cipriani, G. B. [1837] 1986. *Architecture of Rome*. New York: Rizzoli.

Clark, R. J., ed. 1992. *The Arts and Crafts Movement in America, 1876–1916*. Princeton, NJ: Princeton University Press.

Cole, W. A. J., and H. H. Reed, eds. 1997. *The Library of Congress*. W. W. Norton & Company.

Condit, C. W. 1964. *The Chicago School of Architecture*. Chicago: The Chicago University Press.

Constant, C. 1985. *The Palladio Guide*. New York: Princeton Architectural Press.

Cordingley, R. A. [1819] 1951. *Normand's Parallel of the Orders of Architecture*. London: Alec Tiranti Ltd.

Cullen, G. 1995. *The Concise Townscape*. New York: Elsevier.

Culot, M., Grenier, L. et al. 1976. *Henri Sauvage 1873–1962*. Paris: Archives d'Architecture Moderne.

Curl, J. S. *Classical Architecture: An Introduction to Its Vocabulary and Essentials, with a Select Glossary of Terms*. W. W. Norton & Company.

Current, W. R., Current, K. 1974. *Greene and Greene: Architects in the Residential Style*. Fort Worth, TX: Amon Carter Museum of Western Art.

Curtis, N. C. [1923] 1935. *Architectural Composition*. Cleveland, OH: J. H. Jansen.

Curtis, W. J. R. 1982. *Modern Architecture since 1900*. London: Phaidon Press, Ltd.

Dams, B. H., Zega, A. 1995. *Pleasure Pavilions and Follies: In the Gardens of the Ancient Régime*. New York: Flammarion.

____. 2002. *Palaces of the Sun King*. New York: Rizzoli.

Dennis, M. 1988. *Court and Garden*. Boston: MIT Press.

Dixon, R. Muthesius, S. 1978. *Victorian Architecture*. New York: Oxford University Press.

Dormoy, M. 1951. *L'Architecture Française*. Paris: Vincent Fréal.

Dowling, E. M. 1989. *American Classicist: The Architecture of Philip Trammell Shutze*. New York: Rizzoli.

Downes, K. 1969. *Hawksmoor*. London: Thames and Hudson Ltd.

Doyon, G., Hubrecht, R. 1957. *L'Architecture Rurale et Bourgeoise en France*. Paris: Vincent Fréal.

Drobecq, P. 1942. *La Cheminée dans l'Habitation*. Paris: Vicent Fréal.

Dunster, D., ed. 1979. *Edwin Lutyens*. London: Architectural Monographs and Academy Editions.

Durand, J. N. L. 1819. *Leçons d'Architecture, Partie Graphique*. Privately published.

Ecole Nationale Supérieure des Beaux-Arts. 1928–1929. *Les Concours d'Architecture de l'Année Scolaire*. Paris: Vincent Fréal.

Economakis, R., ed. 1993. *Building Classical*. London: Academy Editions.

Editors of the Classicist. 2002. *A Decade of Art and Architecture 1992–2002*. New York: Institute of Classical Architecture/Classical America.

Edwards, T. 1924. *Good and Bad Manners in Architecture, Second Edition*. London: Philip Allan & Co.

Egbert, D. D. 1980. *The Beaux-Arts Tradition in French Architecture*. Princeton, NJ: Princeton University Press.

Esher, L. 1991. *The Glory of the English House*. New York: Bulfinch Press.

Esquié, P. *Traité Elémentaire d'Architecture* (n.d.) Ch. Massin.

Evenson, N. 1969. *Le Corbusier: The Machine and the Grand Design*. New York: George Braziller.

Faber, C. 1963. *Candela: The Shell Builder*. New York: Reinhold Publishing Corp.

Fanelli, G. 1980. *Brunelleschi*. Florence: Scala Instituto Fotografico Editoriale.

Fels, Comte de. 1924. *Ange-Jacques Gabriel*. Paris: Editions Henri Laurens.

Ferriday, P., ed. 1964. *Victorian Architecture*. Philadelphia: J. B. Lippincott Co.

Frampton, K. 1980. *Modern Architecture*. New York: Oxford University Press.

Frank Lloyd Wright Foundation. 1968. *The Early Work of Frank Lloyd Wright*.

Friedman, T. 1984. *James Gibbs*. New Haven: Yale University Press.

Gabriel, J. F., ed. 1997. *Beyond the Cube: The Architecture of Space Frames and Polyhedra*. Hoboken, NJ: John Wiley & Sons, Inc.

Gallet, M. 1964. *Demeures Parisiennes, l'Epoque de Louis XVI*. Nantes: Les Editions du Temps.

Gallet, M. 1980. *Soufflot et Son Temps*. Paris: Editions CNMHS.

Gallet, M., Bottineau, Y., ed. 1982. *Les Gabriel*. Paris: Picard.

Garner, P. 1974. *The World of Edwardiana*. London: The Hamlyn Publishing Group, Ltd.

Gebhard, D. 1972. *Schindler*. New York: Viking.

____. 1975. *Charles F. A. Voysey, Architect*. Santa Monica, CA: Hennessey and Ingalls, Inc.

Geretsegger, H., and M. Peintner. 1970. *Otto Wagner: 1841–1918*. New York: Frederick A. Praeger.

Giedion, S. [1941] 1970. *Space, Time and Architecture*. Cambridge, MA: Harvard University Press.

Girouard, M. 1979. *The Victorian Country House*. New Haven: Yale University Press.

____. 1900. *The English Town: A History of Urban Life*. New Haven: Yale University Press.

Glück, F. 1931. *Adolf Loos*. Paris: Editions G. Grès et Cie.

Gravagnuolo, B. 1982. *Adolf Loos*. New York: Rizzoli.

Gresleri, G., ed. 1977. *Le Corbusier, 80 Drawings*. Bologna: Edizioni Ente Fiere di Bologna.

Gromort, G. 1910. *Plan de Grandes Compositions Exécutées*. Paris: A. Vincent.

____. 1922. *Italian Renaissance Architecture*. Paris: A. Vincent.

____. 1930. *L'Architecture de la Renaissance en France*. Paris: Vincent Fréal.

____. 1932. *Introduction à l'Etude du Tracé des Ombres*. Paris: Vincent Fréal.

____. 1933. *Jacques-Ange Gabriel*. Paris: A. Vincent.

____. 1950. *Lettres à Nicias*. Paris: Vincent Fréal.

____. 1953. *Introduction à l'Etude de la Perspective*. Paris: Vicent Fréal.

____. 1959. *Petit Recueil d'Eléments Décoratifs*. Paris: Vincent Fréal.

____. 1986. *Small Structures*. Paris: Vicent Fréal.

____. 2001. *The Elements of Classical Architecture*. New York: W. W. Norton & Company

____. *L'Art des Jardins*. n.d. Ch. Massin.

____. *Essai sur la Théorie de l'Architecture*. n.d. Ch. Massin.

Gwilt, J. [1842] 1982. *The Encyclopedia of Architecture*. New York: Crown Publishers.

Hamlin, T. 1944. *Greek Revival Architecture in America*. New York: Oxford University Press.

Haselberger, L. 1985. "The Construction Plans for the Temple of Apollo at Didyma." *Scientific American* 256:6.

Hatje, G. 1964. *Encyclopedia of Modern Architecture*. New York: Harry N. Abrams.

Hegemann, W., and E. Peets. [1922] 1988. *Civic Art*. Princeton, NJ: Princeton Architectural Press.

Hewitt, M. A. 1991. *The Architecture of Mott Schmidt*. New York: Rizzoli.

Hilberseimer, L. 1956. *Mies van der Rohe*. Chicago: Paul Theobald and Co.

Hillier, B. 1968. *Art Deco*. London: Studio Vista, Ltd.

Hitchcock, H. R. [1936] 1966. *The Architecture of H. H. Richardson and His Times*. Cambridge, MA: MIT Press.

Hitchcock, H. R., Johnson, P. [1932] 1966. *The International Style*. W. W. Norton & Company.

Hogan, R. 1991. *The Lawn: A Guide to Jefferson's University*. Charlottesville, VA: The University Press of Virginia.

Honour, H. 1991. *Neo-Classicism*. New York: Penguin.

Hughes, R. 1980. *The Shock of the New*. New York: Alfred A. Knopf, Inc.

Huxtable, A. L. 1960. *Pier Luigi Nervi*. New York: George Braziller, Inc.

Irish, S. 1999. *Cass Gilbert, Architect: Modern Traditionalist*. New York: Monacelli.

Irwin, D. 1997. *Neoclassicism*. London: Phaidon Press Ltd.

Jacques, A., and R. Miyake. 1987. *Les Dessins d'Architecture de l'Ecole des Beaux-Arts*. Paris: Arthaud.

Jeanneau, H., Deshoulières, D. 1980. *Rob Mallet-Stevens Architecte*. Archives d'Architecture Moderne.

Jeannel, B. 1985. *Le Nôtre*. Paris: Fernand Hazan.

Jenrette, H. J. 2000. *Adventures with Old Houses*. Charleston, SC: Wyrick and Co.

Jestaz, B. 1996. *Architecture of the Renaissance: From Brunelleschi to Palladio*. London: Thames and Hudson, Ltd.

Jordy, W. H. 1972. *American Buildings and Their Architects: Progressive and Academic Ideals at the Turn of the Century*. New York: Anchor Books.

_____. 1976. *American Buildings and Their Architects: The Impact of European Modernism in the Mid-Twentieth Century*. New York: Anchor Books.

Joudion, G. 2001. *La Folie de M. de Sainte James*. Neuilly-sur-Seine: Spiralinthe.

Ketcham, D. 1997. *Le Désert de Retz*. Cambridge, MA: MIT Press.

Kidney, W. C. 1974. *The Architecture of Choice: Eclecticism in America 1880–1930*. New York: George Braziller.

Kilham, W. H., Jr. 1973. *Raymond Hood, Architect*. New York: Architectural Book Publishing Co., Inc.

Kornwolf, J. D. 1972. *M. H. Baillie Scott and the Arts and Crafts Movement*. Baltimore, MD: Johns Hopkins University Press.

Kostof, S. 1999. *The City Assembled: The Elements of Urban Form through History*. New York: Bulfinch Press.

Krier, L. 1988. *Atlantis*. Brussels: Archives d'architecture moderne.

Krier, L. 1998. *Architecture: Choice or Fate*. London: Andreas Papadakis.

Kunstler, J. H. 1993. *Geography of Nowhere: The Rise and Decline of America's Man-made Landscape*. New York: Simon & Schuster.

Kunstler, J. H. 1996. *Home from Nowhere: Remaking Our Everyday World for the Twenty-First Century*. New York: Simon & Schuster.

_____. 2002. *The City in Mind: Meditations on the Urban Condition*. New York: Simon & Schuster.

Lablaude, P. A. 1995. *Les Jardins de Versailles*. Paris: Scala.

Lambourne, L. 1980. *Utopian Craftsmen*. Layton, UT: Peregrine-Smith.

Latham, I. 1980. *New Free Style: Arts and Crafts, Art Nouveau, Secession*. Architectural Design Profile.

Lavedan, P. 1944. *L'Architecture Française*. Paris: Larousse.

Lazzaro, C. 1990. *The Italian Renaissance Garden*. New Haven, CT: Yale University Press.

Le Corbusier 1958. *Le Modulor*. Paris: Editions de l'Architecture d'Aujourd'hui.

_____. 1958. *Le Livre de Ronchamp*. Paris: Les Cahiers Forces Vives/Editec.

_____. [1946] 1963. *Manière de Penser l'Urbanisme*. Paris: Editions Gonthier.

_____. [1927] 1960. *Towards a New Architecture*. New York: Architectural Press Praeger Publishers, Inc.

Ledoux, C. N. [1847] 1983. *L'Architecture*. Princeton Architectural Press.

Lemoine, B. 1986. *L'Architecture du Fer, France XIXe Siècle*. Seyssel: Champ Vallon.

Letarouilly, P. [1860] 1982. *Edifices de Rome Moderne*. New York: Princeton Architectural Press.

Lowndes, W. S. 1930. *Rendering Architectural Drawings*. Scranton, PA: International Textbook Company.

Loth, C., and J. T. Sadler Jr. 1975. *The Only Proper Style*. Norwalk, CT: New York Graphic Society.

Loyrette, F. 1985. *Gustave Eiffel*. Rizzoli.

Maass, J. 1972. *The Victorian Home in America*. New York: Hawthorn Books.

Mabille, G., L. Benech, and S. Casteluccio, 1988. *Views of the Gardens at Marly, Louis XIV Royal Gardener*. Paris: Alain de Gourcuff.

MacDonald, W. L. 1976. *The Pantheon*. Cambridge, MA: Harvard University Press.

Macleod, R. 1968. *Charles Rennie Mackintosh*. London: The Hamlyn Publishing Group, Ltd.

Mansbridge, M. 1991. *John Nash, A Complete Catalogue*. New York: Rizzoli.

Madsen, S. T. 1956. *Sources of Art Nouveau*. Cambridge, MA: Da Capo Press.

Marrey, B. 1990. *Les Ponts Modernes, 18e–19e Siècles*. Paris: Picard Editeur.

McCoy, E. 1960. *Richard Neutra*. New York: Georges Braziller.

McGoodwin, H. [1926] 1989. *Architectural Shades and Shadows*. Washington, D.C.: The American Institute of Architects Press.

McHale, J. 1962. *R. Buckminster Fuller*. New York: Georges Braziller.

McKim, Mead, White [1915] 1973. *A Monograph*. New York: Benjamin Blom.

Metcalf, P. C., ed. 1988. *Ogden Codman and the Decoration of Houses*. Boston, MA: David R. Godine.

Middleton, R., Watkin, D. 1980. *Neoclassical and 19th Century Architecture*. New York: Electa/Rizzoli.

Moholy-Nagy, S. 1969. *Matrix of Man, An Illustrated History of Urban Environment*. New York: Frederick A. Praeger.

Moore, C., G. Allen, and D. Lyndon. 1979. *The Place of Houses*. New York: Holt, Rinehart and Winston.

Moore, C., W. J. Mitchell, and W. Turnbull Jr. 2000. *The Poetics of Gardens*. Cambridge, MA: MIT Press.

Moreux, J. C. 1954. *Carnet de Voyage*. Paris: Presses Universitaires de France.

____. 1999. *Histoire de l'Architecture*. Paris: Editions Gallimard.

Morgan, K. N. 1995. *Shaping an American Landscape, The Art and Architecture of Charles A. Platt*. Lebanon, NH: University Press of New England.

Mosser, M., Teyssot, G., eds. 1991. *The Architecture of Western Gardens*. Cambridge, MA: MIT Press.

Moussinac, L. 1931. *Mallet-Stevens*. Paris: Editions G. Grès et Cie.

Murat, L. 1995. *The Splendor of France*. New York: Rizzoli.

Naylor, G. 1980. *The Arts and Crafts Movement*. London: Studio Vista.

Newman, J. 1990. *Somerset House*. London: Scala Books.

Norberg-Schulz, C. 1983. *Meaning in Western Architecture*. New York: Rizzoli.

____. *Baroque Architecture*. Harry N. Abrams, Inc.

Normand, C. [1819] 1951. *Nouveau Parallèle des Ordres*. London: Alec Tiranti Ltd.

____. 1821. *Le Vignole des Ouvriers*. Privately published.

O'Gorman, J. 1973. *The Architecture of Frank Furness*. Philadelphia: Philadelphia Museum of Art.

Orsenna, E. 2000. *Portrait d'Un Homme Heureux: André Le Nôtre, 1613–1700*. Paris: Fayard.

Overy, P. 1969. *De Stijl*. London: Studio Vista Ltd.

Palladio, A. [1570] 1965. *The Four Books of Architecture*. Mineola, New York: Dover Publications.

Papadakis, A. 1997. *Classical Modern Architecture*. Paris: Editions Pierre Terrail.

Percier et Fontaine. 1820. *Choix des Plus Célèbres Maisons de Plaisance de Rome et de Ses Environs*. Laplanquais-Chédeville.

Perrault, C. [1673] 1995. *Les Dix Livres d'Architecture de Vitruve*. Paris: Bibliothèque de l'Image.

Petit, J., ed. 1961. *Un Couvent de Le Corbusier*. Paris: Les Cahiers Forces Vives/Editec.

Pierrefeu, F. de. 1932. *Le Corbusier et P. Jeanneret*. Paris: Editions G. Grès et Cie.

Pevsner, A. 1943. *An Outline of European Architecture*. Pelican Books.

Pevsner, N. 1962. *The Sources of Modern Architecture and Design*. New York: McGraw-Hill.

Pevsner, N., and J. M. Richards, eds. 1973. *The Anti-Rationalists, Art Nouveau, Architecture and Design*. New York: Harper and Row.

Pierson, W. H. 1980. *American Buildings and Their Architects: Technology and the Picturesque, the Corporate and the Early Gothic Styles*. New York: Anchor Press/Doubleday.

Pierson, W. H., Jr. 1986. *American Buildings and Their Architects: Volume 1 The Colonial and Neoclassical Styles*. New York: Oxford University Press.

Pillet, J. J. 1900. *Cours de Lavis Théorique*. Paris: Librairie des Arts du Dessin.

Porphyrios, D. 1998. *Classical Architecture*. London: Andreas Papadakis.

Prak, N. L. 1968. *The Language of Architecture*. The Hague: Mouton & Co.

Prévost, J. 1948. *Philibert Delorme*. Paris: NRF Gallimard.

Prown, J. D. 1977. *The Architecture of the Yale Center for British Art*. New Haven: Yale University Press.

Raeburn, M., ed. 1980. *Architecture of the Western World*. New York: Rizzoli.

Rapoport, A. 1969. *House Form and Culture*. New York: Prentice-Hall.

Raval, M., and G. Cattaui. 1960. *Claude-Nicolas Ledoux 1736-1806*. Paris: Electra Editrice.

Raynaud, M., D Laroque, and S. Remy. 1983. *Michel Roux-Spitz Architecte 1888-1957*. Brussels: Pierre Mardaga.

Reagan, O., ed. [1927] 1997. *American Architectural Masterpieces*. New York: Princeton Architectural Press.

Reed, H. H. 1971. *The Golden City*. New York: W. W. Norton & Company.

Rice, P. 1987. *Man As Hero: The Human Figure in Western Art*. New York: W. W. Norton & Company.

Richardson, A. E. [1914] 2001. *Monumental Classic Architecture in Great Britain and Ireland*. Mineola, NY: Dover.

Rieder, W. 2000. *A Charmed Couple: The Art and Life of Walter and Matilda Gay*. New York: Harry N. Abrams.

Roland, C. 1970. *Frei Otto: Tension Structures*. New York: Frederick A. Praeger.

Rossi, A. 1994. *The Architecture of the City*. Cambridge, MA: M.I.T. Press.

Rybczynski. W. 2002. *The Perfect House: A Journey with the Renaissance Architect Andrea Palladio*. New York: Simon & Schuster.

Rykwert, J., and A. Rykwert. 1985. *Robert and James Adam*. New York: Rizzoli.

Saddy, P. 1977. *Henri Labrouste Architecte, 1801–1875*. Paris: CNMHS.

____. and C. Malécot. 1988. *Le Corbusier, le Passé à Réaction Poétique*. Paris: CNMHS.

Saint, A. 1976. *Richard Norman Shaw*. New Haven: Yale University Press.

Salny, S. M. 2001. *The Country Houses of David Adler*. W. W. Norton & Company.

Sansot, Pierre. 1995. *Jardins Publics*. Paris: Editions Payot & Rivages.

Schinz, M., and G. van Zuyten. 1991. *The Gardens of Russell Page*. New York: Stewart, Tabori & Chang.

Schultze, J. 1970. *Art of Nineteenth-Century Europe*. New York: Princeton Architectural Press.

Scobeltzine, A. 1998. *Narcisse ou la Fabrique du Regard*. Lausanne: Editions L'Age d'Homme.

Scott, G. [1914] 1974. *The Architecture of Humanism*. W. W. Norton & Company.

Scully, V. 1955. *The Shingle Style*. New Haven, CT: Yale University Press.

Sear, F. 1982. *Roman Architecture*. Ithaca, NY: Cornell University Press.

Semes, Steven W. 2004. *The Architecture of the Classical Interior*. New York: W. W. Norton & Company.

Serlio, S. 1996. *Serlio on Domestic Architecture 1537–1575*. Mineola, NY: Dover Publications.

Service, A. 1977. *Edwardian Architecture*. Oxford University Press.

Sharp, D. 1966. *Modern Architecture and Expressionism*. New York: George Braziller.

Shepherd, J. C., and G. A. Jellicoe. [1925] 1986. *Italian Gardens of the Renaissance*. New York: Princeton Architectural Press.

Shillaber, C. 1963. *Massachusetts Institute of Technology School of Architecture and Planning 1861–1961: A Hundred Year Chronicle*. Cambridge, MA: M.I.T. Press.

Simonin, P., Clement, R. 1966. *L'Ensemble Architectural de Stanislas*. Paris: Librairie des Arts.

Sitte C. [1889] 1996. *L'Art de Bâtir les Villes*. Paris: Editions du Seuil.

Smith, J. F. 1941. *White Pillars: The Architecture of the South*. New York: Bramhall House.

Smith, M. A. 1983. *Gustav Stickley, The Craftsman*. Syracuse, NY: Syracuse University Press.

Snodin, M. 1991. *Karl Friedrich Schinkel: A Universal Man*. New Haven, CT: Yale University Press.

Sommer, R. 1969. *Personal Space*. New York: Prentice-Hall.

Spencer, R. 1972. *The Aesthetic Movement*. London: Studio Vista.

Stamp, G. 1982. *The Great Perspectivists*. New York: Rizzoli.

Stanton, P. 1971. *Pugin*. London: Thames and Hudson, Ltd.

Stratton, A. [1925] 1987. *Elements of Form and Design in Classic Architecture*. Studio Editions.

Strong, R. 1992. *Royal Gardens*. London: BBC Books/Conran Octopus.

Summerson, J. [1969] 1986. *The Architecture of the Eighteenth Century*. London: Thames and Hudson.

____. 1986. *Architecture in Britain 1530-1830*. New York: Penguin Books.

____. [1963] 2001. *The Classical Language of Architecture*. London: Thames and Hudson Ltd.

____. [1945] 1988. *Georgian London*. London: Barrie and Jenkins.

Tagliaventi, G. and L. O'Connor. 1992. *A Vision of Europe*. Florence: Alinea Editrice.

Taillard, C. 1993. *Le Grand Théâtre de Bordeaux*. Paris: CNRS Editions.

Tavernor, R. 1991. *Palladio and Palladianism*. London: Thames and Hudson.

Thompson, D. W. [1917] 1969. *On Growth and Form*. Cambridge University Press 1969.

Torroja, E. 1958. *The Structures of Eduardo Torroja*. New York: F. W. Dodge Corporation.

Triggs, H. [1902] 1988. *Formal Gardens in England and Scotland*. Antiques Collector's Club.

Tzonis, A. and L. Lefaivre. 1986. *Classical Architecture: The Poetics of Order*. Cambridge, MA: M.I.T. Press.

Van der Ree, P. Smienk, and G. C. Steenbergen, 1992. *Italian Villas and Gardens*. Bussem, The Netherlands: Thoth Publishers.

Venturi, R. 1966. *Complexity and Contradiction in Architecture*. New York: The Museum of Modern Art.

Waddy, P. 1990. *Seventeenth Century Roman Palaces: Use and the Art of the Plan*. Cambridge, MA: M.I.T. Press.

Ware, W. R. [1903] 1994. *The American Vignola*. Mineola, NY: Dover.

Wharton, E. and O. Codman Jr. [1902] 1998. *The Decoration of Houses*. New York: W. W. Norton & Company.

Whiffen, M., Koeper, F. 1981. *American Architecture, vol. 1: 1607–1860*. Cambridge, MA: M.I.T. Press.

Windsor, A. 1981. *Peter Behrens, Architect and Designer: 1868–1940*. London: The Architectural Press, Ltd.

Wittkover, R. 1971. *Architectural Principles in the Age of Humanism*. W. W. Norton & Company.

Woodbridge, K. 1986. *Princely Gardens*. New York: Rizzoli.

____. 1989. *The Stourhead Landscape*. The National Trust.

Wundram, M., and T. Pape. 1993. *Andrea Palladio*. Köln, Germany: Benedikt Taschen Verlag GmbH.

INDEX